THE HEYDAY OF GWR
TRAIN SERVICES

Page 1: An archetypical GWR branch-line train at the end of the 1930s. Small Prairie tank No 5565 heads a two-coach, non-corridor 'B Set' on Witham-Yatton local in March 1936.

Passengers alight at Newton Abbot in June 1920, the station bearing little resemblance to what it was like after rebuilding later that decade. Note the high porter:passenger ratio and the one-colour coach livery of that time. The 'Saint' class 4-6-0 *Kirkland* on the left, was renamed *Charles J. Hambro* in 1935.

THE HEYDAY OF
GWR
TRAIN SERVICES

P. W. B. SEMMENS

MA, CChem, FRSC, MBCS, MCIT, FRSA

DAVID & CHARLES
Newton Abbot London

British Library Cataloguing in Publication Data
Semmens, P. W. B. (Peter William Brett), *1927*–
The heyday of GWR train services.
1. England. Railway services:
Great Western Railway, history
I. Title
385′.0942

ISBN 0–7153–9109–7

Photoset and printed in Great Britain
by Redwood Press Limited, Melksham, Wiltshire
for David & Charles Publishers plc
Brunel House   Newton Abbot   Devon

CONTENTS

In May 1936 streamlined railcar No 11 was photographed as it passed under the canal aqueduct near Limpley Stoke. This unit was only completed in February that year, and, in view of the lineside interest and its splendid exterior condition, may have been on an inaugural Bristol–Weymouth working.

ACKNOWLEDGEMENTS

My thanks are due to Phil Atkins and his staff in the Library at the National Railway Museum for their advice and the ready provision of the documents I needed for my research. I am also grateful to my old friend, the late Derek Barrie, for his graphic reminiscences of what it was like to travel to Cornwall on the Great Western Railway on summer week-ends in the 1930s. Finally I would like to acknowledge the help I received from John Edgington, who has kindly read my typescript and provided me with a number of valued comments and corrections.

P. W. B. Semmens,
York,
February 1990

Except where otherwise indicated, all illustrations are from the Locomotive and General Railway Photograph Collection.

INTRODUCTION

More than forty years have now passed since the last Great Western train puffed its way into the darkness of a December night, but there are still many who have vivid memories of travelling by that railway, while countless others have savoured it at second-hand through the printed word in the many books and articles that have been written about 'God's Wonderful Railway', both during and after its 113 years' existence. Much has appeared about the GWR locomotives, its rolling stock, stations and routes, but, surprisingly, no specific study has so far been written on the development of the train services themselves. It was to fill this gap that I was asked to prepare the present book, covering the period between the two World Wars, when the design and performance of the GWR's locomotives and their train scheduling reached its zenith.

In order to keep our study manageable, it is clearly necessary for us to be selective, since the GWR typically operated more than 30,000 passenger trains every week, or well over 5,000 every week-day. We are thus dealing with a grand total of well over 30,000,000 trains, with something like forty changes of timetable, while in 1920 the total train mileage for the year came to 44,000,000. To trace the fortunes of even one train among all these successive alterations would produce mental indigestion, and the last thing intended is to get involved in following through every change of a minute or two in timings, except when they are part of a continuing process of acceleration. Overall the aim is to try and convey a general impression of what facilities were offered to the travelling public during this period, and what it was like to 'Go Great Western'.

A railway company's operations are designed to meet the commercial demands from the public, but are constrained by the framework of its routes and the resources available from its motive power and rolling-stock departments. So, although this is primarily a study of the Great Western's train services, they cannot be looked at in isolation. We will thus inevitably be casting glances sideways to note the changes in the public's travelling habits, as well as the developments in locomotives and rolling stock that emerged from Swindon between the wars, together with the various changes to the company's lines that occurred during the same period. It is one thing to design a timetable, and another to operate it, so we will also be looking at the way in which performance on the tracks matched or surpassed that called for by the planners. Additionally to be considered is the changing economic and legislative framework under which the GWR operated, alongside the other three railway companies of the Grouping era, with whom it competed or co-operated.

Any large organisation has a built-in reluctance to make drastic alterations in its organisation or operations, the management of change still being one of the hardest tasks that face today's leaders of industry. This was particularly so in the case of a main-line railway company over half a century ago, whose lines and structures had been built to stand the test of time, while its motive power and rolling stock in the days of steam were typically expected to have a working life of at least thirty years. Even rails would be 'cascaded', to use modern

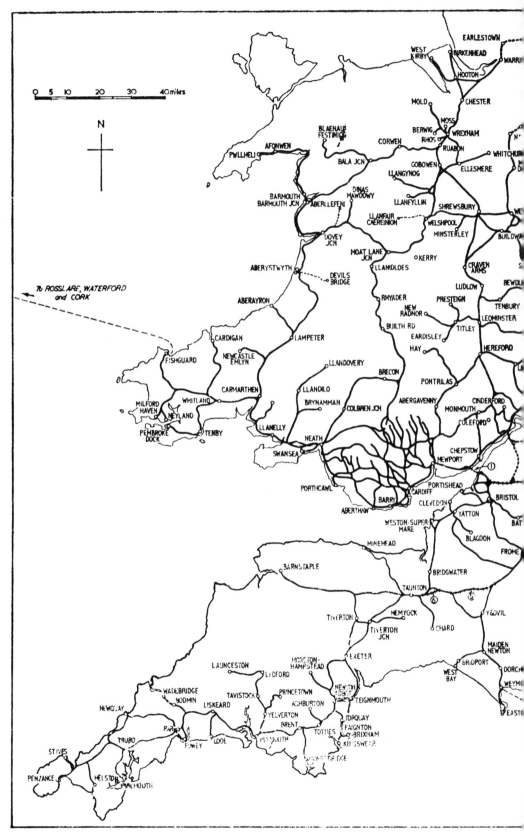

General map of the Great Western system at its maximum extent and showing the cut off lines built at various stages in the company's history to provide more direct routes.

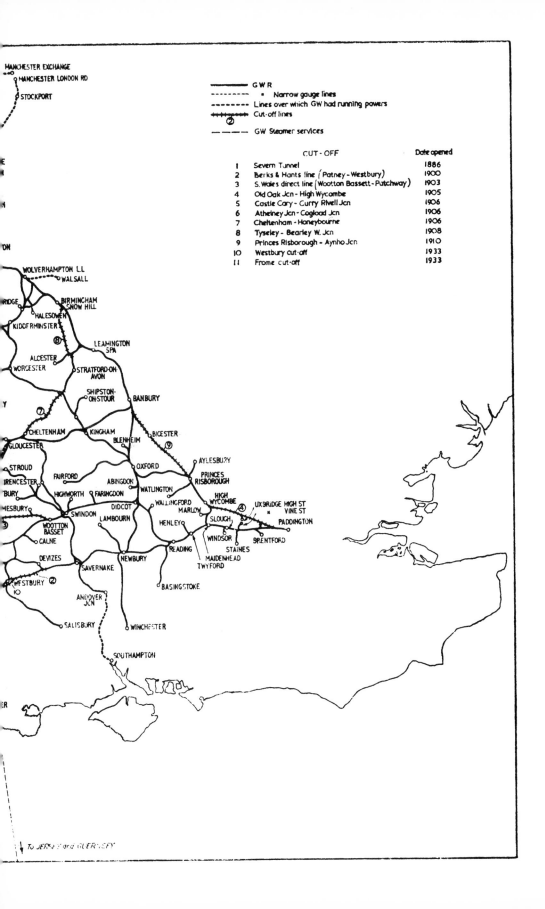

GWR

Narrow gauge lines

Lines over which GW had running powers

Cut-off lines

GW Steamer services

	CUT-OFF	Date opened
1	Severn Tunnel	1886
2	Berks & Hants line (Patney – Westbury)	1900
3	S. Wales direct line (Wootton Bassett – Patchway)	1903
4	Old Oak Jcn – High Wycombe	1905
5	Castle Cary – Curry Rivell Jcn	1906
6	Athelney Jcn – Cogload Jcn	1906
7	Cheltenham – Honeybourne	1906
8	Tyseley – Bearley W. Jcn	1908
9	Princes Risborough – Aynho Jcn	1910
10	Westbury cut-off	1933
11	Frome cut-off	1933

parlance, from main to branch lines, and the same applied to the locomotives and carriages. It is thus necessary to set the scene by looking at the way in which the Great Western Railway had developed up to the days after World War I, when our study starts in detail.

Even a branch-line station could appear quite busy when the daily freight called, as at Compton, between Didcot and Newbury in May 1919. Amongst the commodities being handled were tyres for road vehicles, straw and timber, while three wooden-wheeled horse-drawn railway vehicles were being moved by rail.

CHAPTER ONE

SETTING THE SCENE

For the calendar year 1920, the Great Western Railway's receipts of £35,768,692 put it in third place amongst the railways of this country, while, from a mileage point of view it ranked first, operating routes totalling 2999$\frac{1}{2}$ miles, although earlier in the century they had been just over the 3000-mile mark. It advertised itself as 'the line of 1000 stations', and had conveyed more than 116,000,000 passengers a year to or from them, exclusive of the journeys made by season-ticket holders. The GWR's total net revenue came to £6,400,000, which enabled the company to declare a total dividend for the year of 7$\frac{1}{2}$%. Minerals and merchandise that originated on its system exceeded 37,000,000 tons, although the coal strike that started at the end of the year was to cause all the railway companies in the country to lose revenue and find difficulty in continuing to operate their normal train services because of the shortage of fuel. By March 1921 the GWR had made cuts of about 7000 train-miles/day, mainly on the freight side.

It is, however, necessary for us to go back much earlier than this to touch on aspects of the Great Western's history that were to have an effect on their train services in the 1920s and 1930s. The railway started as a trunk route between London and Bristol, the latter at that time being a major maritime centre and the country's second city. Long before the opening of the Stockton & Darlington Railway there were suggestions for a line linking London and Bristol, but the first Act was not passed by Parliament until 1835, after much preliminary work by the separate Bristol and London Committees. In the spring of 1833 they appointed an engineer, Isambard Kingdom Brunel, then aged twenty-three, whose energy and drive were to dominate the years that followed. Not for him was the wagon-way gauge of 4 feet 8$\frac{1}{2}$ inches, or thereabouts, that had been adopted for railways in the north-east, and the GWR was built to the 'Broad Gauge' of 7 feet 0$\frac{1}{4}$ inches.

Thanks to the present-day practice of building replicas of historic locomotives to mark railway anniversaries, we are now able to gaze at the reproduction of Gooch's *Iron Duke* 4-2-2 in the National Railway Museum at York, and compare it with the contemporary standard-gauge *Columbine* on the next track. The capabilities of these broad-gauge locomotives were brought to people's notice in 1848, when, in the course of a discussion on train resistance at the Institution of Civil Engineers that occupied three separate evenings, Gooch made the remark, *en passant*, that '. . . the express [from Paddington] was in the constant practice of running the fifty-three miles to Didcot, without stopping, in forty-eight to fifty-nine minutes . . .'. This involved average speeds of up to 66 mph, while the instantaneous maximum attained by these locomotives was achieved when the original *Iron Duke* was new. Three engines were tested by Brunel and Gooch, being run flat out down the 1 in 100 of the Dauntsey Incline, west of Wootton Bassett, when the dynamometer car recorded a speed of no less than 78 mph, which was an absolute British speed record for many years. However all this excitement was not to lead to any sustained fast running on the GWR for the next fifty years. After speeds had fallen off during the previous decade, 1862 saw a schedule of fifty-seven minutes to Didcot re-introduced, once again making it the fastest train in the world, but two years later the Didcot stop was cut out, which lowered the average speed considerably. Then, following the financial difficulties of the late 1860s, the trains were slowed once more. Finally it was the turn of the forthcoming gauge conversion to overshadow the company for much of the remainder of the century, until, over a single week-end in 1892, the Broad Gauge passed into history, with the narrowing of 171 route miles west of Exeter by a specially assembled workforce of 4200.

In 1866 there was a national crisis in the railway industry, with the failure of several banks which had been financing the building of new lines by contractors, and the latter, as well as several established railway companies, got into great difficulties. Amongst these was the Great Western Railway, which only turned the corner by adopting a policy of the utmost economy, their 'Flying Dutchman' – the crack West of England express of the day – even being taken off for a period. The strict economy practised by the railway continued throughout the 1870s and 1880s, and led to it being known as the 'Sleepy Giant', but with the last of the Broad Gauge behind them, the company faced up with renewed vigour to the challenge of the new century, during the first decade of which our railways were to reach the zenith of their economic prosperity and influence.

In 1896 the GWR appointed Joseph Wilkinson to the post of general manager, and he was followed in 1903 by James Inglis, both of whom were to be knighted for their service to the company, and who accelerated its progress into the forefront of British railway practice. Back in 1892 the Great Western had introduced the first steam-heated, corridor train in the country, providing lavatory facilities for all three classes between London and Birkenhead. A dozen years later *City of Truro* achieved a speed of 100 mph descending Wellington Bank, between Exeter and Taunton, with an Ocean Mail special, and this was so far ahead of normal practice at the time that the company kept the details quiet until a further eighteen years had elapsed. In the same year a new seven-hour express was introduced between London and Penzance, which within the first twelve months helped create an increase of no less than 68% in passenger receipts at the western terminus.

By this time too, serious consideration was being given to the construction of major new lines to reduce the roundabout distances that had to be travelled, which hitherto had led many to suppose that the initials GWR stood for the Great Way Round. The process had actually started earlier with the boring of the Severn Tunnel, much of its length of just over four miles being beneath the waters of the estuary. After thirteen years of unremitting effort, the completion of the work in 1886 was said to be 'outmatched by no experience in the long account of human endeavour', and shortened the route between London and South Wales by twenty-five miles. In 1903 the opening of the South Wales & Bristol Direct Railway from Wootton Bassett to Patchway, via Badminton and the two and a half-mile Chipping Sodbury Tunnel, cut a further ten miles off the distance, and additionally provided a shorter, and faster, route to Bristol. The line also enabled the Great Western to compete via Fishguard with the London & North Western's Holyhead Irish traffic after the completion of the ten and a half mile connection from Clarbeston to Letterston in 1906. Later, in 1909, came the start of calls being made there by Trans-Atlantic liners *en route* to Liverpool, which lay off the GWR's new port to transfer their passengers ashore by tender to 'The Gateway of Europe'. From here they were whisked to London, only five hours away by 'Ocean Liner Express'. Through a subsidiary company the Great Western also operated shipping services from Fishguard to southern Ireland.

In 1900 the completion of fourteen miles of new line from Patney & Chirton, on the Berks & Hants Extension Railway, to Westbury provided a shortened route to Weymouth, the port from which the Great Western operated its own steamer service to the Channel Islands. Six years later, Castle Cary on this route became a junction when the new line to Cogload Junction on the Bristol–Taunton line was completed, utilising in part an existing branch line, suitably regraded for high speeds. This reduced the distance to the West of England by just over twenty miles compared with the original line via Bristol, and enabled the timing of the 'Cornish Riviera Express' to be cut to four hours seven minutes between Paddington and Plymouth, which gave a new boost to what was still the longest regular non-stop run in the world, even if the distance was now shorter.

Finally in 1910 came the new route to Birmingham, which gave the GWR another opportunity to compete with the London & North Western Railway, this time with Robert Stephenson's pioneering London & Birmingham line from Euston via Rugby. The Great Western's long detour via Oxford was eliminated in quite an elaborate fashion, with the assistance of the Great Central. Between Northolt Junction, south of Ruislip, and Ashendon Junction there was now a joint line, with direct GWR running from Paddington being possible by means of their 1903 line from Old Oak Common. Finally came the Great Western's own Ashendon–Aynho link in 1910, complete with flying junctions at each end to avoid even the slightest delay to the planned new services. In 1922 the GWR and LNWR were both running their fastest expresses between London and 'The City of a Thousand Trades' in a level two hours. GWR publicity made much of the fact that their route was now the shortest, carefully disguising the fact that their trains were actually slower in terms of average speed.

Back in the 1840s, the first serious meeting of the Broad and Standard Gauges had taken place at Gloucester, which became well known for the chaos that took place, or was deliberately induced, during the visit of the Gauge Commissioners. By utilising running powers from those days, the Great Western were able, sixty years later, to develop a new route which enabled them to compete with the Midland Railway for the West Midlands–West of England traffic. This was achieved by constructing two major new lines, from Tyseley to Bearley and from Honeybourne to Cheltenham, together with a new connection at Westerleigh between the Midland line and the South Wales & Bristol Direct. This line was not a cut-off in quite the same sense as the other railways described, being, in effect, a competitive new route, as no self-respecting traveller would have used the GWR's earlier one via Swindon and Oxford, in preference to the direct Midland alternative.

In 1902 George Jackson Churchward had taken over the post of Locomotive & Carriage Superintendent at Swindon, and immediately set about improving the Great Western's motive power out of all recognition, in the course of which he made an enormous step-change in the whole of British locomotive history. After a careful and thorough study of contemporary practice throughout the world, he drew up plans for a series of standard designs that were, at the time, streets ahead of anything else to be seen in this country. Even in appearance they were vastly different from the smaller double-framed express designs that had previously been associated with the GWR. These had parallel boilers, with all their cylinders and motion hidden away between the frames, except for the coupling rods on the 4-coupled locomotives. These characteristic features were replaced by tapered boilers with angular Belpair fireboxes, supported by single inside plate-frames, and set above a high running plate that exposed to view the outside cylinders, connecting and coupling rods, and most of the wheels. The valve gear was still located between the frames, where it took more than a passing glance from a station platform to determine the significance of what had been provided, although one only had to listen to the square-cut exhaust bark of the GWR locomotive starting from the station to realise something was different. Long-lap piston valves were driven by a very robust form of Stephenson's gear, and this was designed to be of the long-travel variety, which gave a far more efficient use of steam, as well as permitting high power outputs to be achieved when the train was running fast. Churchward's target was a locomotive that would produce a continuous drawbar pull of 2 tons at 70 mph which corresponded to the availability of approximately 850 horsepower to haul the train, and this was duly maintained.

For the fastest expresses, the 4-4-0s of the turn of the century were replaced by the

2-cylinder 'Saint' 4-6-0s, and they were very quickly joined on the heaviest passenger workings by the 4-cylinder 'Stars' with the same wheel arrangement. All the GWR 4-cylinder designs used Walschaert's valve gear, also mounted between the frames, with the valves for the outside cylinders being worked by rocking levers. Another hidden feature that was adopted by Churchward in 1906 was the superheater, a 'Saint' being the first locomotive in Britain to be fitted with one of the Schmidt fire-tube variety, while three years later a 'Star' was turned out with the first of Swindon's own standard design. Superheating increases the effective use of steam in the cylinders, and also cuts down on the water consumption, both factors having a marked effect on the locomotive's efficiency.

Churchward's 4-cylinder designs were restricted to the largest locomotives for express passenger work, but plans were sketched out to apply the basic 2-cylinder features to a complete new range of locomotives that spanned the whole of the railway's motive-power requirements. There was, however, no wholesale programme of scrap and replace, like there was on the London & North Western in the years that followed Webb's retirement and death in 1903, and one of the standard Swindon designs that was sketched out by Churchward was not actually built until 1951, three years after Nationalisation. Thus, during the first decade of the Twentieth Century, Churchward provided the Great Western Railway with motive power that was far ahead of the rest of this country, while, under the general managership of Sir James Inglis, the company was put into an excellent position to exploit the Edwardian boom to the full.

All this progress, however, was stifled by World War I, which saw the fortunes of the railways in Britain take a marked turn for the worse. Although this country suffered far less physical bombardment during that conflict than was to be the case in World War II, the effect on the nation and its services was probably more severe. More than 2400 of the GWR's staff were to die in the armed forces during the four years of hostilities, which represented nearly 10% of the 25,479 who joined the colours. Back at home, with no worthwhile road-transport system yet in existence, the railways had to handle all the extra traffic associated with the war effort, in addition to keeping the people fed. Civilian traffic also remained buoyant for much of the war, the 'Cornish Riviera' continuing to run in as many as three parts as late as the summer of 1916. In the following year, however, passenger services were cut quite drastically, with restaurant cars and slip coaches being discontinued 'for the duration'.

Although it was the Southern Group of companies that conveyed most of the movements of troops for the Western Front, up to the time of the Armistice in 1918, the GWR had handled 4564 troop trains for the British Forces and 1079 for the Americans. Although that traffic rapidly fell off, ambulance trains for the wounded continued, with 5895 of them passing over the GWR in just less than five years up to June 1919. Many Great Western locomotives and wagons were sent overseas too, but, in spite of this, that company was responsible for sending on its way the largest single new flow of freight traffic during the war, and one of the most important. This was the coal for the Grand Fleet, based at Scapa Flow and other ports round the coasts of our island. Ninety percent of the 6,000,000 tons shovelled into the warships' boilers during the four years came from the Rhondda and Aberdare districts, and was worked across to Pontypool. From here the Great Western hauled the procession of wagons by three routes to Warrington, or through the Severn Tunnel *en route* to naval bases in the south of England, handling more than 5,000,000 tons of Welsh steam coal in this way during the four years of the conflict.

Frank Potter had taken over from Sir James Inglis as General Manager in 1912, and in the Spring of 1919 he became ill and was advised to take a rest. The task of running the country's largest railway during the war proved too much for his health, however, and he died after journeying to the Great Western's Tregenna Castle Hotel at St. Ives to recuperate. His successor was Charles Aldington, who had similarly been involved in the stresses of running the railway during the war, and he resigned on health grounds in 1921. He was followed by perhaps the grestest of all those distinguished General Managers who left their mark on the Great Western, Felix J. C. Pole, energetic, thoroughly versed in the complex organisation of the company, and, above all, a splendid publicist. He had been editor of the pioneering *Great Western Railway Magazine* for many years, and, amongst other things, later played a large part in setting up what in time was to become the British Tourist Authority.

In the same year Churchward retired after twenty-nine years in charge of one of the largest work forces this side of the Atlantic, his position at Swindon being taken over by C. B. Collett, the succession there, as at Paddington, being 'kept in the family'. Coming events were, however, to cast their shadow before them when it came to the appointment of a new Chief Goods Manager in 1921, that post going to Edward Lowther, the General Manager of the Port Talbot Railway & Docks, one of the companies that were swept into the Great Western fold by post-war legislation.

During World War I, all the railways of this country came under the control of the government, and this was to continue until the middle of August 1921. For much of this time, even before the cessation of hostilities in 1918, there was considerable discussion about the companies' future, with nationalisation even being considered as a possibility. This was not, in the end, to be the preferred course of action, and the 120 or so separate railways were instead grouped into the 'Big Four' companies. With the receipt of the Royal Assent on 9 August 1921, the Railway Act became law, and it was under this legislation that the grouping of the railways in Britain took place. The four new organisations were still private companies, and thus ultimately responsible to their own shareholders, although they were still subject to all the regulatory legislation of the Victorian and Edwardian eras.

The railways could only change their fares and freight rates after approval by a public tribunal, which initially set rates that were intended to provide each group with an annual net revenue that was at least equal to that achieved by its separate companies in 1913. Receipts, unfortunately, were not to work out anything like this during the period in which we are interested, which was to prove a fruitful subject for debate between railways and legislators during the 1920s and 1930s.

Inflation had hit the country in a big way during and after the war, with the pound falling to nearly a third of its mid-1914 value by November 1920. After what were being referred to a decade later as the two post-war 'Boom Years', this produced great economic difficulties. The position was to alter dramatically in the next twelve months, however, and inflation fell quickly. Nowadays we are conditioned to an on-going inflation, and consider the country is doing well if the *rate* of inflation falls. In 1921, however, the actual cost of living decreased, so that, by the end of that year, the value of the pound had increased again to just half its 1914 value. Everyone was hoping that it would continue this process and regain its pre-war value, but it did not quite achieve this, although, overall, there was to be a continuing, but slower, downward trend in the cost of living during the period in which we are interested.

The effect of these changes on the Great Western's profitability was considerable, their working expenses having increased by almost 200% in 1920 compared with 1913, while wages and salaries had risen by 39% during the previous year alone. Fares and freight rates had all been increased, but, as the cost of living index subsequently fell, these were also reduced somewhat. Wage rates were similarly in a considerable state of flux, some of the proposed changes sparking off a short strike throughout the railways during September 1919, while there was a second among locomotive crews on the railways in January 1924, followed, less than a month later, by another in the docks. All in all, the Great Western, like the other main line railway companies, was facing an unprecedented challenge to get back on its feet again.

The railways of those days were not helped by being 'Common Carriers', which placed on them the legal burden of having to transport, at fixed and published tariffs, every item offered, however difficult or obnoxious it might be to handle, as long as it could be made to fit inside the loading gauge. The ability enjoyed by B.R. today to adjust their fares and charges up or down according to what they consider each specific market sector will bear thus represents a degree of freedom totally unknown to the railways in the inter-war years.

Under the 1921 Act the GWR, alone among all the British companies, retained its own name and basic organisation. The legislation laid down that the larger railways became constituent companies of the appropriate new group, with power to appoint directors to the new board. The remainder were only subsidiary companies, without such rights, although the financial details for even the smallest such railway had to be agreed by the Railway Amalgamation Tribunal and accepted by its own shareholders. The Great Western was thus in a unique situation, but the original Bill had given them an even stronger position, since it was named as the *only* constituent company in the group. This was changed during the Third Reading in Parliament, after it had been successfully argued that six of the Welsh railways rated constituent rather than subsidiary status, so each of the companies in the table below duly appointed a director to the enlarged GWR board. The percentage of the 1921 dividends on these companies' ordinary shares is also shown, and the list is arranged in descending size of this figure. For comparison, the Great Western's dividend was $7^{1}/_{4}$%, which was one of the arguments put forward for these companies to be given constituent status.

	Dividend (%)
Barry Railway	10
Rhymney Railway	9
Alexandra (Newport & South Wales) Docks & Railway	$7^{1}/_{4}$
Taff Vale Railway	4
Cardiff Railway	1
Cambrian Railways	Nil

Between them the six constituent companies' capital came to 29% of the issued capital of the GWR, but together they only made 24% of its net income in 1921. Their total route mileage was just 17% of the Great Western's, the Alexandra Docks & Railway having only just over nine miles of line. Taken together, however, the five South Wales railways in the list served the very important coalfields and industry in their area. It should not be forgotten that, during the period in which we are interested, railways derived approximately two-thirds of their revenue from freight and mineral traffic, underlining the importance of these South Wales companies to the general financial well-being of the enlarged GWR. The effect on the passenger train services of their amalgamation with the Great Western was, however, small, but we will examine this in more detail in a later chapter.

In contrast to the five constituent South Wales railway companies, which were enmeshed in the highly competitive business of serving the coal industry by means of a compact network of lines that linked the mines with the railways' own docks, the Cambrian Railways were a rural undertaking. They handled comparatively little freight and mineral traffic, and their 300 route miles straggled across the thinly-populated areas of central and northern Wales. They served many of the Welsh coastal resorts, however, and, with the increasing holiday business generated by the railways between the wars, the Cambrian was to play a part in the development of the Great Western's train services during this period.

It is often thought that the Grouping began overnight on 1 January 1923, but, as we have already seen, the Great Western had by that time already absorbed no less than nineteen other railways, including the six constituent companies. Elsewhere the Lancashire & Yorkshire and London & North Western Railways also amalgamated at the beginning of 1922, in anticipation of the formation of the London Midland & Scottish Railway in 1923, but the Western Group got on with the amalgamations under the 1921 Railway Act far more quickly than the other companies. With the exception of the Cambrian, the finances of the Great Western's constituent companies were in good shape, although their assets were not universally of the same high standard as the GWR's. When the boiler inspectors from Swindon went to examine the motive power on the Barry Railway, for example, a third of their stud of 148 locomotives was immediately stopped for urgent repairs. The potential business from the collieries of South Wales was also to decline during the inter-war years, and, with this, some of the usefulness of the extensive dock systems along the north coast of the Bristol Channel, but in 1923 all that lay in the future.

On 1st January 1922, in addition to the six constituent ones, the Great Western also took over the first five of the subsidiary companies. These were as follows, the percentage dividends for each of the companies in 1921 being included in the table:

	Dividend (%)
Port Talbot Railway & Docks	9
Rhondda & Swansea Bay Railway	6
Penarth Harbour, Docks & Railway	$5^{1}/_{4}$
Cleobury, Mortimer & Ditton Priors Light Railway	2
Princetown Railway	nil

With the first part of the amalgamation complete, the enlarged GWR board then set about the task of incorporating the remaining subsidiary companies into their system. This was achieved in three separate stages, taking place at half-yearly intervals, as follows:

	Dividend (%)
Absorbed as from 1st July 1922	
Bury Port & Gwendreath Valley Railway	10
Vale of Glamorgan Railway	$4^{5}/_{32}$
Wrexham & Ellesmere Railway	$3^{1}/_{2}$
West Somerset Railway	$2^{3}/_{4}$
Ross & Monmouth Railway	$1^{3}/_{4}$
Brecon & Merthyr Tydfil Junction Railway	nil
Lampeter, Aberayron & New Quay Light Railway	nil
Neath & Brecon Railway	nil
Absorbed as from 1st January 1923	
Mawddwy Railway	4
Penarth Extension Railway	$3^{3}/_{10}$
Gwendraeth Valleys Railway	nil
Liskeard & Looe Railway	nil
Llanelly & Mynydd Mawr Railway	nil
South Wales Mineral Railway	nil
Teign Valley Railway	nil
Welshpool & Llanfair Light Railway	nil
Didcot, Newbury & Southampton Railway*	nil
Van Railway	Not available

*Absorption only approved on 22 February 1923, but back-dated.

Absorbed as from 1st July 1923

Exeter Railway	nil
Forest of Dean Central Railway	nil
Midland & South Western Junction Railway	nil

It will be seen that the eagerness with which these subsidiaries were welcomed into the fold was not unconnected with their financial profitability, and even before this, the Great Western had, in many cases, already been working the railways concerned, so was only too well aware of their revenue potential, or lack of it. As a result, when the shares of the old companies were exchanged for those in the GWR, the differences between the absorbed companies were very clearly displayed. The Gwendreath Valleys Railway, for instance, was simply purchased for £17,000 in cash, but they did better than the Van Railway, which was in the hands of receivers, and just had its shares cancelled. Where exchanges took place, the deals were very diverse, those holding Bury Port & Gwendreath shares, for instance, getting 143% of their holding in GWR ordinary stock, whereas the shareholders of the Teign Valley Railway only got $5^{1}/_{2}$%. Even more unusual was the situation with the Forest of Dean Central Railway. This had long ceased to exist, and had already presented the GWR with problems at the end of the nineteenth century, when it wanted to renew its working lease of the line. It had to go to the Crown to get one. The Great Western was still owed a large debt by the defunct company, and, as the rights of the only other creditors came after its own, with the agreement of the Railways Amalgamation Tribunal, the GWR just assumed control of the line.

Taken as a whole, nineteen out of the twenty-six companies absorbed into the Great Western were in Wales or the Marches, while another five were in the West of England, but only two of these had any potential to take advantage of the rising holiday traffic. In addition to these there were two cross-country lines, the Didcot, Newbury & Southampton, and the Midland & South Western Junction, both of which pottered for quite long distances through southern England. However these two routes ran across rather than along the general flow of traffic, although the former was to be considerably up-graded in World War II prior to the invasion of Europe.

Having thus briefly summarised just over eighty-five years of the Great Western's history, it is now possible to turn to the task of looking at its routes and traffic in more detail.

In the days before our study starts, a 'City' class 4-4-0 climbs Filton Bank out of Bristol with an express for the North of England. This stretch of line was quadrupled in the years between the two World Wars.

The GWR station at Vine Street in Uxbridge in August 1919, showing a steam railmotor and a train of 4-wheeled suburban stock.

Ealing station in August 1919, looking west along the fast lines, with a parcels train in the down relief line platform. The subsequent developments on the overbridge have made Ealing Broadway, as it now is, a very different station to this semi-rural scene.

One of the surviving Brunel wooden viaducts on the Falmouth line at Ponsanooth, in June 1920.

CHAPTER TWO

THE MAIN ROUTES

Although the physical geography of that part of the country through which the Great Western Railway ran has not changed in the last half-century, the advent of high-powered diesel traction has markedly decreased the apparent severity of gradients, while modern track systems have eased the speed limits over curves, points and crossings, as well as on the straight stretches. At the same time the development of new industries and communities has markedly altered the economic geography of the area it served. In addition, route rational-isations and the closure of branch lines have made great changes to the one-time Great Western system, so, in order to appreciate the somewhat different conditions under which the GWR operated between the two World Wars, we must now make a lightning tour over their major routes to get an impression of what they were like at that time. To do this it is most convenient to work in a clockwise fashion, starting with the line between Paddington and Penzance.

PADDINGTON – EXETER – PLYMOUTH – PENZANCE
(via Westbury and Castle Cary)

Although the Great Western Railway only ran as far west as Bristol in the first instance, its associated companies – the Bristol & Exeter, South Devon, and Cornwall Railways – continued Brunel's broad gauge westward to Falmouth, while the standard-gauge track on the older West Cornwall Railway, running between the River Fal and Penzance, was reluctantly mixed. All these companies were to be absorbed by the Great Western in 1876, but, as we have already seen, the development of this prime holiday route really stemmed from the early days of the twentieth century, and its full realisation was to follow the opening of the line via Westbury in 1906.

It was from Westbury too that the Great Western threw off its twenty-five mile line to Salisbury, while twenty miles further west a longer line branched southwards from the West of England line at Castle Cary to reach the port of Weymouth, thirty-nine miles away on the coast of the English Channel. This provides an interesting example of the way in which the importance of the GWR's routes changed over the years, since the line to Weymouth from Thingley Junction, just west of Chippenham on the original Great Western line to Bristol, was opened throughout in 1857. By the 1920s it had become less important than the line to the West of England, although it did serve the port from which their Channel Islands' shipping services operated. Castle Cary itself gained prominence indirectly in the early 1930s, however, when the opening of the Westbury and Frome cut-offs saw the timetable entry 'Via Castle Cary' replacing 'Via Westbury' one for those services using this route.

The 'Cornish Riviera' from Paddington to Penzance thus travelled over a number of different lines with varying antecedents, and a remarkably good idea of their characteristics can be obtained from a study of their gradient profiles. For the first thirty-six miles west to Reading we follow Brunel's superbly-engineered original line, which had been quadrupled well before the time at which our study starts. Only in the vicinity of Sonning Cutting, just east of Reading, were there any gradients steeper than five feet per mile, this change possibly being dictated by the less stable ground conditions here, which have from time to time caused a number of earth slips, necessitating lengthy and expensive engineering work to rectify.

Apart from this imposing deep cutting, where cost considerations brought the tracks rather closer together than elsewhere on the London–Reading stretch, the spaciousness of the four-track layout is noteworthy, and in particularly noticeable from the cab of a locomotive, as the author found when he made a footplate trip on a 'Castle' a quarter of a century ago. The wide open spaces also reduce the sensation of speed, and on his first-ever journey in one of the 'InterCity 125' units, along this stretch of line, it was only the reading of his stopwatch that confirmed that we were actually doing 125 mph. In earlier days too the route was noted for the quality of its riding, and, on the opening page of John Buchan's *Mr Standfast*, the hero, in the days of World War I, sets the scene for the reader, 'As we slipped up the Thames valley on the smooth Great Western line ...'. With that author's close Oxfordshire connections, this would have been no idle phrase, but one of those useful remarks that help establish the credibility of the fictional hero for the knowledgeable reader. Now that the line has four-aspect colour-light signalling and the approach tracks to the terminus have been rationalised, after 1993 they will be able to handle hourly peaks of twelve HSTs, plus four of the new 100-mph Heathrow electrics in each direction, in addition to the suburban services.

Back in the 1920s there was already a lot of industrial and residential development along this artery which, it must be remembered, was the Great Western's *only* main-line out of Paddington until the opening of the direct line to Birmingham in 1910. Mention should especially be made of the extensive trading estates at Slough and Hayes, both of which were served by their own railway systems. The preserved Hudswell Clarke 0-6-0ST *Slough Estates No. 5* on the Yorkshire Dales Railway provides a reminder of the sort of motive power used on these lines, and dates from as late as 1939. Less obvious to the passenger was the Brentford Branch, swinging south-eastwards from Southall to reach the Great Western's extensive docks on the banks of the Thames. Although now truncated after the demise of rail-to-water transfers at this point, most of the branch is still open, and serves one of the important terminals for today's stone traffic from the quarries of Somerset.

Southall was also the site of the locomotive depot that provided much of the motive power for the suburban services along the Thames valley. The main-line locomotives for services out of Paddington were based at Old Oak Common, the new sheds being opened three miles from the terminus in 1906 as a replacement for those at Westbourne Park. Closer in still were the facilities on the down side at Ranelagh Bridge, which were used by main-line locomotives from outlying parts of the system during their short turn-rounds between up and down workings. Going west there was also a locomotive depot at Slough, and this was followed by the more extensive one at Reading, set in the triangle between curves off the Berks & Hants and the original main line to Bristol.

Reading, thirty-six miles from Paddington, was an extremely important centre for the Great Western. The town was a very busy one, and its passenger revenue in the 1920s and 1930s was very much greater than any other station along the Thames Valley. In those days the Southern Railway had its own station a hundred yards or so from the GWR's 1870 frontage block, which is now a Grade II Listed Building. The Southern station had belonged to the South Eastern & Chatham Railway, although it was also used by the London & South Western's services that travelled over their own tracks as far as Wokingham station, six and three quarter miles out. The last-named company also owned five chains (110 yards) of the link between the SE&CR and GWR systems. This was extensively used for through trains, and will feature considerably in our story, but the layout was not such a convenient one in those days, having subsequently been considerably improved during World War II.

The Great Western Signal Department was based at Reading, and there were extensive freight yards on the country side of the original main-line to Bristol. Local industry provided considerable business for the railways, the well-known biscuit manufacturers, Huntley & Palmer, having a link at board level in the person of Ernest Palmer, who joined the GWR as a director in 1898. He became Deputy Chairman eight years later and continued in that office until the end of 1943, by which time he had become Lord Palmer, having been elevated to the peerage for his services to music. There was another Reading industry which, although it did not generate business in quite the same quantities, was nevertheless a well-known sight for all travellers on the GWR. This was Sutton's Seeds, whose fields of flowers enlivened the view from the line on the approach to Reading.

For expresses to and from the West of England, the east-to-south curve just beyond Reading station imposed quite a severe restriction, and the locomotives then had to recover speed up the 1 in 307 climb through Reading West. The tree-lined cutting provided a splendid setting for a 'King' working hard, and the site was used with great effect by railway photographers, notably Maurice Earley. After leaving the Basingstoke line at Southcote Junction, the Berks & Hants snakes its way up the valley of the Kennet, paralleled also by the Kennet & Avon Canal for the next thirty-odd miles to Savernake, which marks the summit of both railway and waterway as they both squeeze through the Marlborough Gap.

Industrial activity has long been present in the lower part of the valley, but thins out as the downs creep in on the twisting railway, where, even today, the 'InterCity 125s' have to reduce speed for the curves. Newbury, with its race course, was an important centre, where the Didcot, Newbury & Southampton crossed the main line, and the branch to Lambourne struck off northwards. It was nevertheless very much a country town, and years later, when Gerry Fiennes was trying to speed up passengers changing trains when he was the Western Region general manager in the 1960s, he was gently reminded by the guard that this was not the done thing – "Sir, we do not blow whistles at people from Newbury"!

In the days of steam, the fireman on a heavy down West of England express had to work hard all the way to Savernake summit, the 'Riviera' in 1925 being booked to take $73\frac{1}{2}$ minutes for the 70.1 miles from Paddington when the overall time for the non-stop run to Plymouth was two minutes over the four hours. The next twenty-five miles to Westbury were very much easier, and on many trains the dropping of a slip portion there then made a worth-while difference to the load behind the tender. At Patney & Chirton the original single-line Berks & Hants Extension continued to the right on its own way to Devizes, while the expresses could then romp down the sweeping curves of the 1900 line along the north face of the downs, with the white horse coming into sight shortly before Westbury was reached. Going east, the five and a half mile climb from Lavington to Patney & Chirton, most of it at 1 in 222, was hard work for an up express.

Westbury is now the hub of the Somerset stone traffic, but in steam days it also played an important motive-power role, standing as it did on the junction between the West of England, the Chippenham–Weymouth, and the Bristol–Salisbury lines. The first-mentioned of these three had been the last to arrive, so the junctions did not provide the optimum layout for non-stop trains, which led the Great Western to construct a three and a quarter mile cut-off around the station area in 1932, while a similar new line at Frome, six miles further on and only two-thirds the length, saved nearly a quarter of a mile and avoided an even more severe speed restriction.

On the next stretch to Castle Cary trains have to climb to Brewham Summit, before benefiting from falling gradients as steep as 1 in 81 towards Bruton. Down trains could not take full advantage of the impetus available from the descent because of curves, and the climb was a particularly difficult one for those in the up direction. After the restriction over the junction at Castle Cary, expresses again had the benefit of the gentle gradients and sweeping curves of a twentieth-century stretch of line, although the short bore of Somerton Tunnel, having been built to standard-gauge dimensions, can cause quite appreciable ear strain if two 'InterCity 125s' should pass inside it.

Although the alignment of the Durston–Yeovil branch was followed by the 1906 line from Curry Rivell Junction, regrading work enabled it to be taken flat out, it even being claimed that a 'King' had reached over 100 mph on the descent to the levels of the Somerset wetlands, although the detailed timings did not bear this out. As the line approached the old route via Bristol it cut the corner to Cogload, where the junction was originally a flat one between the two twin-track routes. As part of the extensive development work carried out by the GWR in the 1930s with the aid of cheap government funding, the Taunton bottleneck was quadrupled. This took place over the full eight miles between Cogload and Norton Fitzwarren, the junction for the lines to North Devon and North Somerset. As part of this work a flyover was built at Cogload, which still remains, although the junction itself has recently reverted to a twin-track one, now worked from the power box situated nearly thirty-seven miles away at Exeter.

With the converging routes on both sides, Taunton was also an important railway centre, its 1948 allocation of locomotives being half as many again as the total at Exeter. There were also extensive goods facilities, with a separate freight line bypassing the passenger station, while the area had an appreciable amount of industry, a notable example being *The World's most famous Semi-Stiff COLLAR*, made by Van Heusen and advertised on the spine of contemporary issues of *Bradshaw*.

Although latterly thought of as branches, the Great Western's routes to Minehead and Barnstaple were, as we will see, much more of secondary main-line status in the 1920s and 1930s, with more than one set of daily through carriages in each direction between London and Ilfracombe. The Minehead line was the shorter of the two, but undoubtedly had the edge on scenery, which can still be enjoyed from the train as most of its twenty-two and three-quarter mile length is now operated by the West Somerset Railway. Climbing steeply to the wooded summit at Crowcombe, it then descends to the Doniford stream and reaches the coast at the busy port of Watchet, worked intensively by the GWR in the period under review. Hill-dodging takes the line inland again past Washford, with the ruins of Cleeve Abbey, to regain the coast at Blue Anchor. From here to the terminus was a particularly busy holiday area in Great Western days, and the preservation society is able to benefit from the generous extensions made to the facilities at Minehead between the two World Wars to accommodate the growing amount of traffic, while four new crossing loops were installed to facilitate the increased number of trains being worked over the single line.

The North Devon line had much more of a year-round operation, although it did provide the GWR with a link to the port and holiday resort of Ilfracombe over Southern Railway tracks from Barnstaple Junction. Only a few years ago, during the author's last visit to the town, the painted sign, high up on the wall of a building in the main street, still proclaimed the whereabouts of the one-time GWR booking office. The Great Western had its own terminal station in Barnstaple, not well sited for the town centre, and half a mile outside it there was a connection to the Southern line that had followed the Taw valley at the end of its way from Exeter. An east-to-south spur had been built in 1905 to permit through running from Taunton straight to the LSWR's Junction station, and we will see later how this was used for through trains in the period under review. In the 1930s the line was doubled from the junction as far as the first station at Milverton, and table-exchanging equipment was provided at loops along the line to speed up the passage of non-stop trains.

Immediately beyond the divergence of these two routes at Norton Fitzwarren, the main line began its climb into the Blackdown Hills, with the triangular-section Wellington Monument dominating the view to the south-west. The climb steepens to 1 in 80 before

Whiteball Tunnel, which produced plenty of sound effects from the labouring locomotive on the front of a heavy steam-hauled express, even if a special 2+5 'InterCity 125' set in 1985 effortlessly shot into the bore at no less than 96 mph. On summer Saturdays bankers would be standing by at Victory Siding just beyond Norton Fitzwarren, but to stop and put one on the back of a struggling express was always likely to take more time than would be lost by battling on, unless the train was in danger of stalling completely on the bank.

Devon is reached in the middle of the tunnel, and the next twenty miles are easy for down trains as they sweep along the Culm valley, where extra platform loops were put in at several stations in the 1930s to facilitate the running of more and faster trains. Curvature beyond Cullompton causes a slight check, but since early in 1988 speeds of up to 100 mph are permitted for much of the distance. The approach to Exeter is marked by the junction with the Southern's line from North Devon and North Cornwall at Cowley Bridge, and then follow the extensive Riverside freight yards. St. David's station is situated well away from the city centre, below the sandstone outcrop that here forms the left side of the valley of the Exe. At the time unders discussion, St. David's, like most of the Great Western's main stations in the west country, was an 'open' one, but this was changed just before World War II, reportedly because it was getting too difficult to conduct a full ticket check between here and Taunton on the faster trains. Prior to this, the centre island platform had always been 'closed' because it was used by the Southern's trains, and that company provided its own ticket collectors at the foot of the stairs from the footbridge.

Southern trains for Waterloo diverged from Great Western metals at the west end of St. David's, and, being so close to the busy station, this flat junction was even more disruptive than the one at Cowley Bridge. The position was made worse by the need to assist most trains up the 1 in 37, which required additional paths for the returning bankers, although the disruption was minimised at peak periods by putting a couple of them on the front of a down train, to work them back to St. David's. There were two schemes at different times to do away with this problem altogether, by eliminating the flat junctions. The first, in 1904, was a London & South Western initiative to avoid their boat trains having to make the mandatory stop at St. David's. The second scheme was put forward by the GWR for government support in 1935, and would have involved a high-level Southern Railway platform to the west of the Great Western ones.

We now enter the tracks of the one-time South Devon Railway, the layout of which still suffers from Brunel's 'Atmospheric Caper'. Although this form of traction started at Exeter, the first twenty mile stretch to Newton Abbot was virtually level along the banks of the Exe and Teign estuaries, or above the sea wall from Dawlish Warren to Teignmouth. West of Newton, however, there are the worst of all the gradients on the way to Penzance, the short tunnel on the top of the Dainton gable being humped-back, with gradients of 1 in 36 and 1 in 37 on opposite sides of the approach. At the start of this climb, there was the junction for the Kingswear line, serving the main seaside resorts of Tor Bay. This is one of Devonshire's finest natural features, and faces almost due east, so the high ground behind it provides shelter from the prevailing winds. It has thus long been one of the country's premier resorts, even attracting William of Orange as long ago as 1688! The South Devon Railway served it by means of a branch from Newton Abbot, so trains for this destination miss the steep gradients on to Plymouth that were a legacy from the atmospheric system. Nevertheless, to get over the ridge to the terminus at Kingswear on the bank of the River Dart requires a bank that is as steep as 1 in 60, and there is a nasty short climb eastwards out of Torquay.

Newton Abbot was thus an important junction, and many trains were divided or combined at this point, the station being enlarged and rebuilt in the 1920s, when a grateful local authority paid for the public clocks. There was a lot of freight activity too, being supplemented by ball clay traffic off the Moretonhampstead branch. Newton Abbot had the second largest allocation of locomotives in the West of England, being only exceeded by that at Laira. One important duty was the provision of assistant locomotives for banking duties between there and Plymouth.

In spite of being virtually level, the twenty mile stretch from Exeter to this point could cause operational difficulties at peak periods, as services booked to stop at Dawlish or Teignmouth produced a disproportionate gap between trains. To overcome this problem, and at the same time reduce the difficulties caused by having to run comparatively slowly along the weathering sandstone cliffs, the Great Western decided to build a cut-off line in the 1930s. It would have involved four tunnels, one of them one and a half miles long, and gradients as steep as 1 in 150. Some land was purchased but World War II stopped the project, and it was never resurrected.

Beyond Dainton the main line descends into the Dart valley, crossing the river at Totnes before climbing to the fringes of Dartmoor on gradients little easier than those surmounted earlier. The next station, at Brent, was the junction for the Kingsbridge branch which had various through sections to and from London. The final descent to the estuary of the Plym involved the two mile Hemerdon Bank, much of it at 1 in 42, which was a formidable obstacle for eastbound trains, especially when autumn saw the leaves falling off the trees in the woods alongside the line. On the outskirts of Plymouth were Laira sheds, the largest in the West of England, which were built in 1901 in the triangle with the South Western's lines into their Friary station, and extended in 1932. That railway had running powers over the Great Western from just beyond North Road station to this point, its route from Cowley Junction at Exeter taking its trains over the northern flank of Dartmoor, so that, as at Exeter, those bound for London were running in the opposite direction from the Great Western's.

The Plymouth area was a very busy one, stimulated to a considerable extent by the naval activities there. Both the Great Western and Southern routes ran through the immediate hinterland behind Devonport Dockyard, and this enabled both of them to operate extensive suburban services. A plethora of new halts was built on their main lines, although these had reached their peak in the days before our study. The fact that the railways bridged some of the nearby estuaries gave them a considerable edge over road transport before the highway crossings were also built, an advantage that is still enjoyed by the former Southern branch to Gunnislake.

The completion of the Royal Albert Bridge across the Tamar estuary at Saltash, and the opening of the Cornwall Railway in 1859, saw the national railway system at last serving every one of the English counties, but it should not be assumed that there were no railways in Cornwall prior to this. There were many earlier lines, dating back to the opening of the Bodmin & Wadebridge Railway in 1834. These had been built for local services, and in most cases worked down to a port on the coast. By contrast, the Cornwall Railway ran along the spine of the county, and thus crossed many of the earlier lines at right angles. In several cases these were subsequently integrated into the Great Western as branch lines, and will thus feature in our study of this type of train service in Chapter five.

To make its way along the length of Cornwall, the main line has to follow a hilly course across the volcanic intrusions that are such a feature of the county, but which were also responsible for the mineral business the county provided for the railway. While tin and copper ores won from the deep mines of the Redruth and Camborne area were mainly sent away by sea, the kaolin industry, whose china clay pits still dominate the countryside around St. Austell, used the Great Western to move its products both to the deep-water railway port at Fowey as well as 'up country'. The longest of the Cornish branches, from Par to Newquay, owed its origin to the Cornwall Minerals Railway, started privately by Squire Treffry of Fowey over his own land in the late 1830s, but the railway facilities at Newquay were extensively modified between the two World Wars to handle the summer holiday crowds, many of them brought to the resort by lengthy through trains from London and elsewhere. Newquay was also served from the west by the line from Chacewater via Perranporth, opened in the 1900s.

Although the Great Western's main line through Cornwall had a lot of climbing to contend with, the maximum gradients were less than those over the South Devon banks, so loco-motives were permitted to take heavier loads west of Plymouth. 'Kings' were, however, barred from Cornwall because of the weight restrictions on Saltash Bridge. The maximum single-handed load allowed was 420 tons, for the 'Castles', but this was 105 tons more than they could take up the Devon inclines, and sixty more than the 'Kings' could handle over the worst pitches east of Plymouth. Curvature was virtually continuous too in Cornwall, although the opening of the diversion between Saltash and St. German's in 1908, bypassing several of Brunel's timber viaducts, was to produce the 'only straight mile in Cornwall', where today's HSTs frequently manage a brief 80 mph fling. In the 1920s and 1930s trains were limited to a maximum of 60 mph anywhere west of the Tamar, which prevented them from rushing the banks, although there were often curvature restrictions in the dips, such as those to 45 mph through Lostwithiel and Par. The Cornwall and West Cornwall Railways were both built as single lines, but by the time of the grouping there were two tracks as far west as Scorrier, and our period of study was to see the line being doubled throughout, except for the short stretch over Saltash Bridge.

READING – SWINDON – BATH – BRISTOL – TAUNTON

We must now retrace our steps eastwards to return to Brunel's original route for Bristol, which we left at Reading. At the time our main study commences, this was quadruple as far as Didcot, although additional tracks were to be provided on some other sections east of Swindon during the 1920s and 1930s. Didcot itself was very much a railway operating town, with extensive facilities being provided alongside the main line, including the depot where all the forage was prepared for the Great Western's horses. By the time of the grouping, some of these installations had become a railway enclave, sited between the old line to the north from the western end of the station and the avoiding lines used by non-stop trains to and from Oxford. This site, still without road access, is the centre for the extensive preservation activities carried out by today's Great Western Society.

Standing at the junction with the Great Western's original line to the Midlands, Didcot handled a lot of freight traffic. Although the present-day massive power station, with its numerous Merry-Go-Round coal trains, was not even thought of at that time, the large Royal Ordnance Factory slightly further west produced a lot of traffic for the Great Western. Several of the pannier tanks based at Didcot were provided with spark-arresting chimneys to enable them to work safely among its extensive stores and buildings. Didcot itself was a very small community, and the Great Western had to build a special hostel there for engine crews during World War II, when the railway activities in the area increased very considerably, and had included the construction of a new marshalling yard at Moreton Cutting, two miles to the east.

Swindon, just over seventy-seven miles from Paddington, is one of the earliest railway towns in the country, having been chosen in the early days of the GWR as the location for its locomotive works. From this green-field beginning a vast enterprise had sprung up, the extent of which can best be appreciated by a visit to the Great Western Railway Museum and the associated preserved cottage nearby. This and the beautifully-restored Railway Village provide an insight into the paternalism that followed in the wake of the vertical integration of the GWR's activities. This was a very characteristic policy of so many railway companies in the days when they needed to retain a large force of trained and loyal staff to carry out functions that were not available to be bought in from outside. In 1924 the railway employed as many as 14,000 people in Swindon, and thus dominated the town, whose daily timetable was regulated by the coded blasts from the massive hooters that rose high above the Works, fed by the steam pipes from the boilers.

Most items that moved on the GWR probably came to Swindon every few years, which meant there was much for the passing enthusiast to see from the train, with, perhaps, some of the unusual crane tanks *Hercules*, *Cyclops*, and *Steropes* next to the buffer-stops on the long sidings between the running lines and the shops. All this activity also made Swindon an important traffic centre, which was supplemented by the fact that it marked the junction for the original line to South Wales via Gloucester. There was also the Highworth branch going off north-eastwards, as well as the Midland & South Western Junction's main line that crossed the Great Western, and was provided with a connecting spur at Rushey Platt.

After the opening of the South Wales & Bristol Direct Railway in 1903, trains for the Severn Tunnel left the original main line to Bristol at Wootton Bassett Junction, eight miles further west, beyond which the latter descended the 1 in 100 Dauntsey Incline. This was the first point out of Paddington where the gradients became at all significant, and was followed by the longer stretch at the same inclination through the 1.8-mile bore of Box Tunnel, the first such structure that Brunel had to construct on the way to Bristol. It is noted for the legend that the rising sun is supposed to shine directly through it on 9th April – Brunel's birthday – but this has been disproved by a recent careful examination of the physical data by Phil Atkins, the Librarian at the National Railway Museum. He showed that the actual dates for direct illumination are 6th and 7th April, and this was duly tested in 1988 when the BR engineers were able to arrange for a party of us, including representatives from France and Switzerland, to view the phenomenon from the lineside at dawn. While this legend has little to do with Great Western train services between the wars, they were undoubtedly affected by the steep eastbound climb through the tunnel, whose bore in those days used to be completely obscured by smoke and steam.

Halfway on to Bath from the exit of the tunnel is Bathampton, the junction with the line from Westbury, now used by the 'Super Sprinters' working the hourly BR 'Express' services between Portsmouth and Cardiff, which, as we will see in the next chapter, have a long history. At Bath the Great Western managed to make a very sympathetic passage for the railway through the centre of the ancient city, with its splendid architectural history that spans the centuries from the Romans to the Regency period. Curves make it necessary to ease back on the speed, and even today no exceptionally fast running is possible over the remaining twelve-mile stretch of the original Great Western Railway, before we reach its western terminus at Bristol.

Great changes took place in this busy railway centre during the 1920s and 1930s, with Temple Meads station, used jointly by the GWR and LMS, being enlarged to cover more than twice its previous area, while the longest platform was extended by nearly 50% to a length of over a quarter of a mile. The goods station, partly underground, was also considerably extended in the same period, so that more than 400 wagons could be handled under cover. One of the last changes was the provision of six and a half miles of quadruple track, stretching from Filton Junction in the north to Portishead Junction in the west, which was invaluable on busy summer Saturdays. Although Brunel's great train-shed at Temple Meads still remained in daily use at that time, it lost its tracks in the post-war rationalisations, which has now enabled the building to be restored and admired as an exhibition hall. The station area was also equipped with power signalling, but, as at Paddington, the colour lights only acted as 'armless' semaphores rather than being of the multi-aspect type which are now so familiar. In addition to its maritime activities, Bristol was an important manufacturing centre, and provided much freight business for the railways, even if the Bristol Company's aircraft and buses usually moved out of the city under their own power. The Somerset coalfield was also situated not very far away to the south, and this also produced an important flow of mineral traffic.

West of Bristol, the line descended to the Somerset plains, and there were no gradients of note over the remaining forty miles to Cogload Junction, where the route from Reading via Castle Cary, already described, trailed in on the left. Almost half way along this stretch is Weston-super-Mare, an important resort and residential area on the coast of the Bristol Channel. It was originally served by a one and a half mile branch off the main line, worked by horses, but a four-mile loop was constructed later. This enabled through trains to call at the station, although an additional mile was added to the resulting journey between Worle and Uphill Junctions.

WOOTTON BASSETT – SOUTH AND WEST WALES

The 1903 South Wales & Bristol Direct Railway, which commenced at Wootton Bassett Junction, eight miles west of Swindon, was one of the earliest twentieth-century lines to be laid out for high-speed running, the best Brunel traditions of inclination and alignment being supplemented by the provision of platform loops either side of the through lines at intermediate stations. In spite of the difficulties of the terrain, a ruling gradient of 1 in 300 was adopted, significantly less than that on the direct Birmingham line, so it was not an unduly difficult proposition for the new generation of standard locomotives then being provided by Churchward. Even so, considerable earthworks were required, and the ridge of the Cotswolds had to be pierced by the two and a half mile tunnel at Chipping Sodbury, which, having been built to standard-gauge dimensions, puts an aerodynamic limit on the speeds allowed for today's HSTs. The Midland line from Gloucester to Mangotsfield was crossed by the lofty viaduct at Westerleigh, where, in due course, a triangular connection was constructed to enable Great Western trains from Birmingham via Stratford-on-Avon to regain their own metals. This was a flat junction, although the connection with the Midland at Yate was a flyover.

Extensive freight yards were constructed at Stoke Gifford, on the site of today's Bristol Parkway station. West of here, the tracks had climbed out of the depths of the Severn Tunnel on long gradients of 1 in 100, so trains for London could be marshalled to utilise their motive power fully for the long trundle to Acton or elsewhere. Stoke Gifford Junction still marks the point where westbound trains via the South Wales & Bristol Direct split for their alternative destinations. Those going to Bristol have just over five miles to travel to Temple Meads down Filton Bank, two miles of which are inclined at 1 in 75, while the line straight ahead leads to the busy port at Avonmouth. In the 1920s and 1930s this increasingly replaced the older facilities in the centre of Bristol in importance as it became more difficult for the new, larger ships to navigate the Avon Gorge. South Wales traffic follows the third line, the east-to-north curve at Stoke Gifford, to begin the long descent into the murk of the Severn Tunnel. Up and down tracks separate over this stretch, to minimise the severity of the up-hill gradients, while from the more open down line the traveller can look away to the west to see the distant docks and industry at Avonmouth, only some of which is of post-war origin.

Emerging on the Welsh side of the river, the main line climbs up under the earlier route via Gloucester and Chepstow, which then joins it on the left. Immediately beyond is Severn Tunnel Junction, where there was a large locomotive shed as well as the yards – extended in the inter-war period – to hold freight traffic awaiting paths forward into England, especially through the tunnel. Because of the difficulties of sighting signals in the reduced visibility of the smoky depths, the tunnel had to be worked as a single block section, which put a limit on the number of trains that could be moved through it. It was not until the middle of World War

II that this restriction became intolerable, and signals with specially-intense lamps were installed to provide an additional block section.

For the next thirty miles westwards from Severn Tunnel Junction there is little in the way of gradients to contend with as the line makes its way along the South Wales coastal plain. In the period covered by this book there was little in the way of major lineside industry until Newport, the Llanwern steel complex with its coal and ore terminals being a post-war development. The railway crossed the Usk just above the first road bridge at Newport, opposite Maindee on the left bank, where there was a triangular junction with the line which traversed the Marches northwards to Hereford and Shrewsbury. This formed the North-to-West route for a number of important cross-country trains, which we will be discussing later. Newport, where the station facilities were extensively improved over a seven-year period, finishing in 1930, was also the site of the first major docks on the Bristol Channel, those of the pre-grouping Alexandra (Newport & South Wales) Docks & Railway, on the western side of the river, being reached from Ebbw Junction at the far end of the twin Hillfield tunnels from the station. There was a very important locomotive shed here too, the largest on the GWR in Wales.

The rising ground of South Wales that is cleft by the coal-mining valleys begins west of Newport, and the main line is pushed south-westwards towards the capital city of Cardiff. At Newport the first of the branch lines start to extend their tentacles north-westwards, this edge of the coalfield being dominated by the Great Western's own lines, rather than those it acquired in 1922. Most of the mining area lay between the one-time broad-gauge South Wales Railway that was absorbed by the Great Western in 1863 after being leased by them from the time of its completion, and the LNWR 'Head of the Valleys' route from Abergavenny Junction to Merthyr. The whole area was a mass of lines, many of the valleys being served by two separate railways, cut into the steeply-sloping hillsides, one on each side of the river. If one of these lines should disappear up a side valley, it was as likely as not that another would appear through a tunnel from the next valley to take its place. Such was the cut and thrust of the railway development in South Wales, with the different railway companies vying with each other to secure as much traffic as possible and funnel it down to their ports on the Bristol Channel.

All these lines, big and small, passed into the Great Western's hands at the grouping, but, because of the complexity of the landscape and the location of the individual collieries and multitude of small steelworks, there was little they could do in the way of rationalisation, although at Cardiff, the main hub of the business, the rebuilding of the General station was completed in 1934 to match the other civic developments going on in the Welsh capital. The new facilities also enabled the Great Western to integrate their own passenger services more effectively with those of the former Taff Vale and Rhymney Railways. From here the main line turns inland and does not regain the coast until Margam, where it swings north-westwards around the sweep of Swansea Bay, and passes through Port Talbot and Neath *en route* to Swansea. However, the principal station in that city was on a spur, rather than the main line, which continued westwards from Landore, just over a mile away up the valley. Considerable changes took place here during the period of our study, with the through train services being worked into and out of the extended High Street station instead of merely having connections from and to the city-centre terminus. There were again extensive dock installations in the area, one of the developments of the 1920s being the oil-refining activities of the Anglo-Persian Oil Company that were to result in the huge oil and chemical complex at Llandarcy that we know today.

To cross the base of the Gower Peninsula the line from Swansea to West Wales had to surmount a nasty gable, with gradients as steep as 1 in 50 on the climbs to Cockett, although the Swansea District Lines, opened just before World War I, ran further inland between

Court Sart and Llandilio East Junctions, and were skilfully engineered to have no appreciable banks that were steeper than 1 in 120. This route was built primarily for the easy passage of coal trains from the mining areas west and north of Swansea, although it was used for the Ocean Liner specials between Fishguard and London, in addition to some local services. Beyond Gowerton the main line regains the coastal plain, and there are no gradients worth bothering about for the next forty miles. Mining and industry petered out beyond the explosives factory at Pembrey, and the line followed the bank of the Tywi estuary to the market town of Carmarthen. Now a dead-end terminus, it used to form an end-on junction with the line to Aberystwyth, but then, as now, through trains for the west could bypass the station by the south side of the triangle, and call, if required, at the Junction station instead, until it closed in 1926.

Whitland marks the first division in the railway routes that serve the three main termini in western Dyfed, the southern line taking trains through the resort of Tenby to Pembroke Dock. Ten miles further, at Clarbeston Road on the 1906 cut-off, the tracks diverge for the destinations on the north side of the deep-water inlet of Milford Haven, and for Fishguard, on the coast of Cardigan Bay. At the time of our study, on the line to the town of Milford Haven there was a branch after Johnston that went to Neyland, where certain of the expresses from London then terminated. In those days, a ferry link across less than half a mile of water took one to Pembroke Dock on the opposite shore, but these two places were separated by a roundabout journey of over fifty miles by rail.

SWINDON – GLOUCESTER – CHELTENHAM

Once again we must retrace our steps eastwards to reach the starting point of the next of the Great Western's main lines as we study them in clockwise order. This takes us back to Swindon, whence we follow the tracks to Gloucester and Cheltenham, the first part of which formed the GWR's route into South Wales prior to the opening of the Severn Tunnel. The line leaves the original route to Bristol at the west end of Swindon station, and consequently threaded its way initially between parts of the Works, before continuing through Kemble, with its twin branch lines to Cirencester and Tetbury. It then dives under the ridge of the Cotswolds at Sapperton, to emerge into the valley that leads through Stroud down to the flat lands of the Severn. In the 1900s the section west of the tunnel, from Chalford to Stonehouse, had seen the appearance of numerous new halts served by an intensive service of steam railmotors.

At Standish Junction the line joined the one-time Midland route to Bristol, which is followed as far as the edge of Gloucester, a city whose pattern of stations has always left much to be desired as a result of the way in which the railway system developed. From the point of view of our own story, the GWR station lay on the original line to South Wales, which necessitated a reversal for trains to Cheltenham that called there, although the non-stop services could cut across the eastern side of the triangle to pick up the onward route at Engine Shed Junction, which corresponds to the present Barnwood Junction. The Midland had a loop that took their northbound trains from Tuffley Junction into their station, south of the Great Western's, and they could then regain the through lines at Engine Shed Junction without reversing. In the route rationalisations of the post-World War II era, it was the Midland station that was closed, so reversals are still necessary for those North-East–South-West trains that stop at Gloucester.

From the passengers' point of view, the railway layout at Cheltenham in the inter-war days was no better than that at Gloucester. The six-mile stretch of line between the two places was jointly-owned, and, prior to the opening of the GWR's 1906 line to Birmingham, their only

31

station at Cheltenham had been the terminus at St. James'. This was situated just over a mile from Lansdown Junction where the Midland's own tracks diverged from the joint line, their own Lansdown station being less than a quarter of a mile from the junction. The new Great Western line was not able to enter St. James', and had to join the former line just over a quarter of a mile outside the terminus, with a new station, Malvern Road, being constructed just south of this point. Things were thus far from easy for passengers wanting to change off the Midland for stations to Honeybourne and Stratford-on-Avon. Landsdown Junction also marked the divergence of the GWR's branch to Kingham, which was additionally used by the Midland & South Western Junction's trains for Swindon and Andover, and these latter trains, just to be awkward, continued to use the LMS station after grouping.

Although there were thus two routes from Cheltenham to London, via Kingham and Gloucester, neither was particularly direct, and, as we will see in Chapter four even when the 'Cheltenham Flyer' was the fastest train in the world, it often left St. James' behind a tank engine, and its progress as far as Swindon, including the reversal at Gloucester, was nothing remarkable. To overcome these constraints, in October 1928 the GWR introduced a road service, using fifteen-seater 'armchair cars', between Cheltenham and Oxford, where there were rail connections to and from London. Nineteen years later, this service still had a whole page devoted to it in the autumn 1947 timetable, the last to be produced by the Great Western.

DIDCOT – OXFORD – WORCESTER – HEREFORD

Having conveniently reached England's oldest university city by road, we can continue north-westwards by rail through the Cotswolds to Evesham, Worcester and Hereford. The idea of a branch to Oxford from Didcot was included in the first GWR bill, and from that point later Great Western lines were to run through Birmingham to the Dee, as well as to the other destinations just mentioned. However, by the period we are studying, the Great Western's principal services to the North-West had been switched to the 1910 route via Bicester, although the longer route via Oxford was still integrated into the same pages of the timetable.

There is nothing very remarkable about the line from Didcot, other than the fact that the bridge across the Thames at Appleford was not strong enough to take the 'Kings'. Oxford, in addition to having its university and the car assembly plants at Cowley, was an important railway centre between the wars, with an appreciable locomotive allocation. The line from Princes Risborough trailed in at Kennington Junction, a couple of miles south of the station, this branch serving the motor factories at Morris Cowley, which provided a lot of business for the railways, even in the 1920s and 1930s. The LMS terminal station was next door to the Great Western one, but in those days there was only an indirect connection between the two systems through interchange sidings. It was during World War II that a proper junction was provided, situated slightly further north, and this subsequently enabled the line to Bletchley to be worked from the GWR station. The LMS's was then closed to passengers and became a coal depot, which serves as a reminder that a city the size of Oxford used to require a large quantity of solid fuel for heating, as well as a supply of coking coal for use in the local gas works throughout the year, all of which arrived by rail. Nearby too was Frank Cooper's marmalade factory, the aroma from which would spread across the tracks during the Seville orange season, and whose products, like the majority of the other manufactured food supplies in those days, were distributed by rail.

At Wolvercote Junction, a couple of miles north of Oxford, the Banbury and Evesham lines split, the latter climbing gently along the valley of the Evenlode. Kingham marked the junction with the branches to Banbury and Cheltenham, which were also linked by a direct spur, bypassing the station, which was used by the 'Ports to Ports Express' which will feature at length in Chapter four. Addlestrop was the next station, one of the few to be commemorated in verse prior to the days of John Betjeman, with the summit beyond Moreton-in-Marsh. After the dip through Blockley comes the final short climb to Campden, with the fine racing stretch beyond that includes four and a half miles at 1 in 100 down. Just before World War II, No.4086 *Builth Castle* achieved a 100 mph maximum here, the first fully-authenticated three-figure speed recorded on the GWR, although it is highly probable that *City of Truro* also managed the 'ton' descending Wellington bank with an Ocean Mail special in 1904.

On the edge of the Vale of Evesham, the route of the 1906 line from Birmingham to Cheltenham was crossed, with a spur giving direct access from the Oxford direction towards Stratford, while others from the north and south swung up into Honeybourne station to provide connections. There is nothing much in the way of gradients as far as Worcester, the whole Vale being a highly fertile area that produces considerable quantities of market-garden produce as well as fruit. In the month of August 1928 no less than 2608 wagons were loaded in Evesham goods station, mainly, no doubt, with plums, and as many as 214 them were filled on a single day. Just before Worcester the GWR line crossed over the LMS one from Cheltenham, and a south-to-west curve enabled their trains to be routed through Worcester and Droitwich to regain their own metals at Stoke Works Junction, just south of the Lickey Incline. These trains called at Shrub Hill station, but those from Paddington followed two different routes from this point. Some of them also continued to Droitwich, before travelling via Kidderminster and Stourbridge Junction to Wolverhampton. The others went to Foregate Street, and then on to Hereford over the steeply-inclined line through the Malvern Hills. There are two single-bore tunnels at Colwall and Ledbury, the former being renewed during the period of our study. Hereford lies on the Newport–Shrewsbury route used for the GWR's North-to-West services, and we will return to this in due course.

PADDINGTON – BICESTER – BIRMINGHAM – SHREWSBURY – CHESTER-BIRKENHEAD

We now come to the last of the Great Western's main routes out of London, the 1910 line to Birmingham, which split off the original Bristol road at Old Oak Common West Junction, just three miles after leaving Paddington. Some six miles further on it was joined by the Great Central's line out of Marylebone, the tracks from here to Ashendon Junction being jointly owned. As far as West Ruislip, London Transport's Central Line now parallels it on the west side, but this was only opened after World War II, although work had started on its construction in the late 1930s, under GWR auspices, using the government's cheap loan facilities. At the time in which we are interested, therefore, the local services along the line were still provided by the main-line railways, the majority by the LNER out of Marylebone.

Between Milepost No 7 and No 21 there is quite a lot of climbing to be done, which was an important consideration since many of the Birmingham trains were very heavily loaded all the year round. Going south this was one of the fastest stretches on the whole line, with 'Kings' regularly working their trains into the 80s. In the northbound direction, however, full advantage could not be taken of the easier grades over the five miles on from Beaconsfield to rush the final climb to Saunderton because of the speed restrictions through High Wycombe and West Wycombe stations. These were a relic of the first railway here, which was the roundabout route to Oxford from Maidenhead via Bourne End and Thame.

The central stretch of this, between High Wycombe and Princes Risborough, was taken over and doubled to become the new line. While the curves through the towns could not easily be straightened, it was possible to ease the gradients over the summit at Saunderton by constructing the second track on a completely different alignment which included a short tunnel.

Beyond Princes Risborough the whole of the line as far as Aynho Junction, six miles south of Banbury, was constructed this century, the first stretch as part of the Great Western & Great Central Joint, but the final eighteen miles were purely Great Western, and not completed until 1910. It is all well laid out, both horizontally and vertically, and the 'Kings' on the heavy Birmingham two hour expresses were able to give a good account of themselves up and down the lengthy 1 in 200 banks. There was not a lot of industrial activity along the line of the sort that put an appreciable amount of business on rail, although the new station at Bicester did provide accommodation where huntsmen could change before and after their day's sport with one of the local packs of hounds. One month the *Great Western Railway Magazine* published a letter of thanks from the Prince of Wales for the facilities provided for him during the previous hunting season.

At Aynho the old route to Birmingham via Oxford is joined, our quick journeyings over the Great Western's main routes having not, so far, covered the fifteen miles from Wolvercote Junction to this point. The line ran along the valley of the Cherwell, shared for its whole length with the Oxford Canal, and, at the time of writing, these modes of transport are currently being joined by the new M40 motorway extension. Predominantly rural in nature, the area nevertheless had two major industrial installations, the cement kilns at Shipton on Cherwell, between Kidlington and Bletchington, built in the late 1920s and 1930s with equipment that arrived by railway, and the ironstone mines served by the branch from King's Sutton running westwards towards Kingham.

The old main line from Banbury to Birmingham was also well laid out, with gradients of generally similar inclination as far as Leamington, another important spa town, which the Great Western drew to passengers' notice by incorporating that three-letter word into the name given to their station, where virtually every express stopped. Less than two miles further on, just before Warwick station, comes Hatton Bank, a climb of over six miles at around the 1 in 100 mark. Shortly before the top is the triangular junction with the Stratford-on-Avon branch, which so often these days sees the passage of steam specials out of Marylebone. Beyond lies the southern Birmingham commuter belt, well served by suburban services in the years between the wars. Nine miles of track between Lapworth and Olton were quadrupled in the early 1930s, the new underbridges being tested by running four 'Kings', side-by-side in coupled pairs over them one Sunday morning, at speeds of up to 60 mph. At Tyseley the Henley-in-Arden line trailed in from the left, which handled the through trains by the 1906 route from Cheltenham, as well as its own suburban services. Many of the latter terminated at Moor Street station, alongside the GWR main line where it crossed the LMS route into New Street, just south of Snow Hill tunnel.

Impressive though the recreated Snow Hill station may be, it is still a single-ended surburban station, whereas, in the inter-war years, the Great Western's was one of the main hubs of that railway's passenger activities. Birmingham, the 'City of a Thousand Trades', developed into an exceedingly important business, manufacturing, and cultural centre after the arrival of the railways, although in 1937 the passenger revenue generated in the Great Western's Birmingham Division was 3% less than that from their Bristol one, and both came well behind London. However, the number of season tickets issued in the Birmingham Division was 87% of those in the London Division, although their total revenue was only 32% of London's. The Great Western expresses to the north all continued on to Wolverhampton Low Level station, which was where the 'Kings' from Stafford Road shed would come off in favour of something smaller for the next stage of the journey to the north. In contrast to the residential areas traversed by the line south of Snow Hill, these twelve and a half miles lay through the very centre of the industrial Black Country, and speed was low because of the curvature and numerous junctions.

Wolverhampton was the location of the Great Western's second locomotive factory, which had been entirely responsible for their 'Narrow-Gauge' stock in the days when Swindon looked after the seven foot gauge locomotives. Even after 1892 Wolverhampton continued to play an important role in overhauling locomotives, a new factory having been completed there in 1932 using low-interest government loans, which only ceased operations in the 1960s. Beyond here the industrial activity along the line slackened in intensity, as the railway passed through the corner of Staffordshire into Shropshire. The Great Western's lines in this area had a complicated history, and its trains did not reach Shrewsbury over its own metals, as its line turned northwards at Market Drayton Junction, just beyond Wellington. These finally terminated at another Market Drayton Junction, on the line from Shrewsbury to Crewe, just over four miles from that great railway centre, the creation of the LNWR, into which the Great Western had running powers. Another LNWR line from Stafford joined the Great Western at Wellington, and the continuation to Shrewsbury was over joint GW and LNWR metals. Lines of similar joint ownership were also used by the Great Western trains to leave Shrewsbury for Buttington on the Cambrian, and all the way south to Hereford on the North-to-West route to Newport and the Severn Tunnel.

North of Shrewsbury the Great Western changed character again over the final forty-two and a half miles of its own line to Chester, with frequent breaks of gradient, and then colliery subsidence slowings over the nine miles between the Dee viaduct at Cefn and Wrexham. At Chester the trains for Birkenhead had to reverse, being taken forward over the metals of the Birkenhead Railway, another GWR/LNWR joint company, to terminate right on the banks of the Mersey beneath the overall roof of Woodside station. This was again an exceedingly busy maritime area, while the Wirral itself was also heavily industrialised, Port Sunlight, Harold Lever's soap factory alongside the line, having celebrated its centenary in 1988. There were docks on the Cheshire side of the Mersey too, as well as ship-building yards, not to mention the resort of New Brighton. A short walk from Woodside took passengers to the Mersey ferries, while the GWR's London services called at Rock Ferry to make connections with the Mersey Railway's electric trains running to and from Liverpool Central under the estuary.

SHREWSBURY – ABERYSTWYTH AND PWLLHELI

Although the Cambrian Railways were by far the least profitable of the six constituent companies that joined the GWR in 1922, they were the only one that possessed anything in the way of long-distance lines. Their main route to the Cambrian coast stretched for over a hundred miles from Buttingdon to Pwllheli, with a further fifteen running southwards from Dovey Junction to Aberystwyth. The Great Western reached Cambrian metals at Buttingdon over the sixteen-mile GWR/LMS joint line from Shrewsbury, which gave them a massive additional length of track to be exploited by the new combined management and with the backing of a company whose share issue totalled £140,000,000. Most of this route was single, with frequent passing loops, and gradients that were severe in places. Until the middle of World War II, the bridges were not strong enough to take anything larger than 4-4-0s on passenger trains, so no high overall speeds could be achieved. After the first summit on the joint line between Westbury and Breidden, the profile was not unduly difficult as far as Moat Lane, but beyond this there is a nine-mile climb to the summit at Talerddig. Once over the pass the line plunges down into the Dovey valley, with the worst three miles being inclined as steeply as 1 in 52/56, which made the twelve-mile bank a formidable obstacle for London-bound trains.

Machynlleth was the operational centre of the line, with an allocation of well over twenty locomotives, and from there the line continues alongside the estuarine salt marshes to Dovey Junction. This particular station was built solely for interchange purposes, with nothing more than a footpath to link it with the outside world. There are two unusual humps in the gradient profile on the approach to Aberystwyth, with a mile or more of climbing at 1 in 75 on both sides of each, but these presented no great obstacles, even for the small locomotives used on the 'Cambrian Coast Express' and other through trains. Aberystwyth station was extensively rebuilt in the mid-1920s, the new restaurant being provided with a sprung floor for the benefit of those attending the tea dances that were held for holidaymakers and local residents nearly every week during the season. This resort was also the terminus of the narrow-gauge Vale of Rheidol line, now also part of the GWR, which ran inland to the well-known beauty spot at Devil's Bridge, from where there were at one time cross-country GWR trips with special road vehicles to the summit of nearby Plynlimon. The narrow-gauge line did not run into the main station during the time we are studying, but used its own terminus until after World War II.

At Dovey Junction the line to Pwllheli turns away to the north, crossing the estuary to follow the twisting sea wall below the 900-foot ridge that runs out to the headland above the port and holiday resort of Aberdovey. Here the line turns northwards, passing the end of the Talyllyn Railway at Towyn, as the name of that town was spelt at that time. As this book is an historical study, this convention is adopted throughout as distinct from a guide to the present-day railway system. Cross-references are however given to any *fundamental changes* in station names that have occurred in the last sixty years, but this has not been done when the present-day Welsh spelling is obviously very closely related to the one quoted.

Continuing northwards along the coast, the line has to climb steeply to traverse the unstable cliffs at Friog on the western end of the Cader Idris *massif*, where there was a serious accident in 1933. From here it descends past Fairbourne, with its miniature railway, to what was called Barmouth Junction until its 1960 change of name to Morfa Mawddach. This was where the line from Ruabon via Llangollen and Bala Junction joined the coastal route, the former having been the Great Western's own property as far as Dolgelly. This was only seven and a half miles away at the head of the estuary, which the coastal railway had to cross by the imposing Barmouth Bridge. For much of its 800 yard length the single track is supported by wooden piles driven into the mud of the estuary, but there is a steel section at the Barmouth end, with an opening span over the navigation channel, which gives it a very characteristic silhouette.

Between the world wars the facilities at Barmouth station were very much more extensive than they are now, and many of the trains from the south terminated there at that time. The continuation along the coast to Pwllheli is a magnificently scenic run, but presents no particular operational difficulties, other than those inevitably associated with a long stretch of single-line railway. The overhead connection with the narrow-gauge Festiniog Railway still remains at Minffordd, but in pre-war days there was also the physical link with the LMS at Afon Wen, three stations before the terminus. Although this line joined the Cambrian facing towards the east, there were through carriages off certain LMS trains to Pwllheli as well as to Portmadoc.

SHREWSBURY – HEREFORD – NEWPORT AND THE SEVERN TUNNEL

The last of the Great Western's major routes that we must consider is the one from Shrewsbury to Newport through Ludlow, Hereford and Pontypool Road. This 'North-to-

West' route used joint GWR/LMS tracks for the first fifty-one miles south from Shrewsbury. A 'Castle' coming on to a train from Manchester or Liverpool at this point would be faced with the steep thirteen-mile climb to Church Stretton, set in the valley between ridges of hills that tower to over 1500 feet on both sides. This is the first of three major summits on the line, and, as the railway descends past Wenlock Edge, Craven Arms is reached, the junction for the London & North Western's Central Wales line that in pre-war days continued as far west as Carmarthen. Our route takes us along falling gradients through the Teme valley as far as Wofferton, after which the railway switches to that of the Lugg, without any appreciable climbing being necessary to cross the watershed between the two rivers.

Hereford was served by three different Great Western routes, in addition to the joint line (and that outpost of the Midland's empire, the line to Three Cocks Junction). The railway geography meant that the GWR services that called at the passenger station at Barrs Court then had to continue southwards over the two-mile purely LNWR link between Rotherwas and Red Hill Junctions. Part of this is inclined as steeply as 1 in 92, and the climbing continued at 1 in 104 as the line headed for the Black Mountains. After dropping down to Pontrilas there begins the next six and a half-mile slog to the second major summit at Llanvihangel, appreciable lengths of it being as steep as 1 in 100. The southern side of this gable is even steeper, with gradients of up to 1 in 82 through Abergavenny Junction station, which were thus against the flow of northbound freight traffic from the South Wales docks and mines. Trains could not rush the dip at Penpergwn, six and three quarter miles on, in either direction because of the lengthy speed restriction there, which also hampered those tackling the final major summit at Pontypool Road. This was a somewhat broken climb, with a slightly downhill stretch through Nantyderry and just over a mile of 1 in 141 down before Little Mill, which *could* be taken at full tilt.

There were speed restrictions at Pontypool Road, which were particularly severe going north, and then came progressively slower limits as the train circled the hill-fort at Caerleon and finally negotiated the triangle at Maindee, beside the River Usk, to join the South Wales line, heading for the Severn Tunnel. All in all the North-to-West route was a hard one from the locomotive point of view, and it was not until after World War II that 'Kings' were permitted to operate these services. However, even then, few would then have imagined that the route would become the only one over which *King George V*, the only working example of the class, would operate in the 1970s and 1980s, thanks to the joint preservation efforts of the Hereford cider firm of Bulmers, Swindon Corporation (later Thamesdown District Council) and the National Railway Museum.

PADDINGTON STATION

As well as examining the characteristics of the Great Western's main routes, we must also have a look at the hub of their system – Paddington station – the gateway for so many journeys to the west and north. When our story opens, major reconstruction work was already in progress there. The 1850s cast-iron columns supporting the three unequal roof spans had been suspect for some time, and at the cross-platform transepts wire bonds had been used for strengthening, but full replacement of all the vertical members with steel girders was necessary. This work was carried out one row at a time, and required excavation down to well below platform levels for the foundations. Starting in October 1922, the row between Platform Nos 2 and 3 was tackled, and the work was successfully accomplished without the breakage of a single pane of glass, in the following April, ready for the busy summer season. From October 1924, similar procedures were followed with the columns between Platform Nos 7 and 8, which were much more awkwardly placed between a pair of tracks, so the new foundations had to be built under lines that remained in operation.

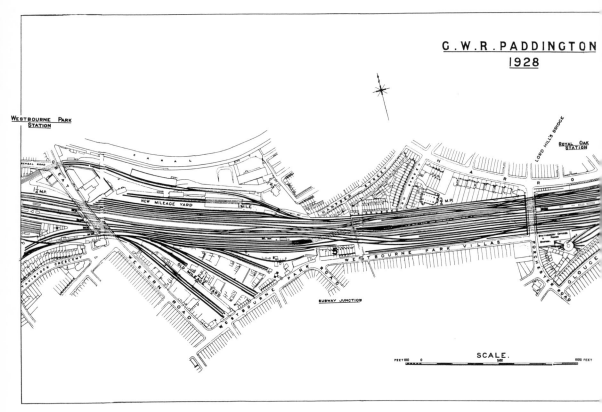

The layout of Paddington station and its approaches in 1928, as shown in the report from the Chief Engineer's Office referred to in the text.

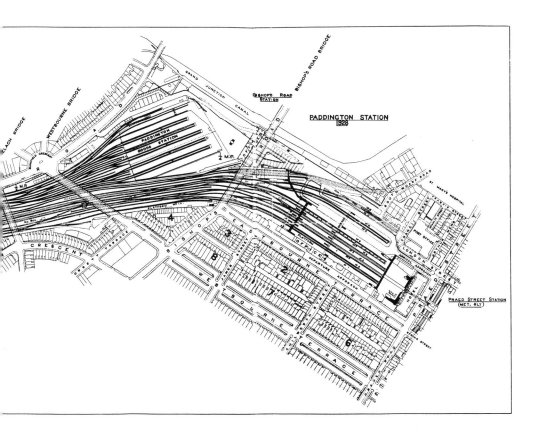

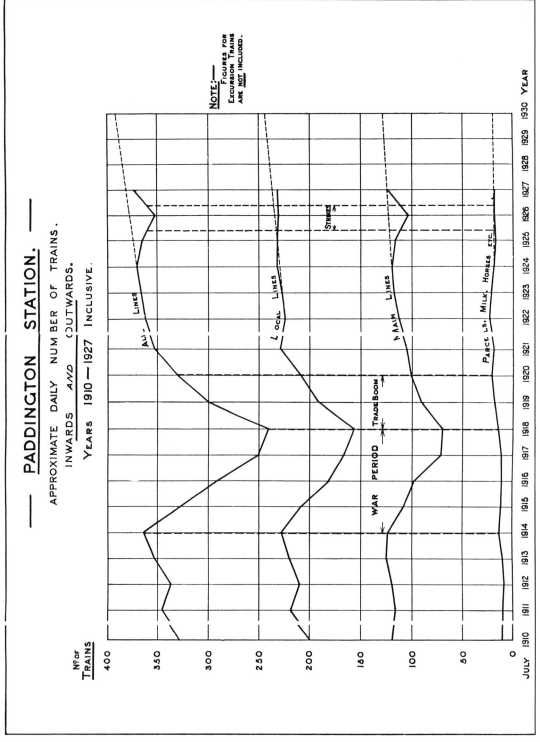

The growth in numbers of trains, as shown in the 1928 report from the Chief Engineer's Office.

However, plans for a much more radical rebuilding were being prepared, and a report, *The Future of Paddington Station* duly appeared from the Chief Engineer's Office in September 1927. This spelt out the problems as follows:

OBSOLESCENCE OF EXISTING STATION

To the casual observer, the loss incurred in working by the obsolescence of the existing layout may not be apparent. It is therefore advisable to note the chief causes. They are:–

(1) Delays and congestion on No. 1 platform due to the concentration of the Station business thereon and the two-way movement of traffic this feature necessitates.

(2) Short length of platforms. The length of many trains today exceeds the platform length; consequently, adjacent shorter trains are locked in position until a long train standing on their controlling points is cleared. The lengthening of platforms within the existing layout and the number of trains that can be brought alongside platforms at certain periods in the day's working has reached practicable limits.

(3) The existence of the Subway and Hammersmith & City Lines in their present central position between Westbourne Park and Bishop's Road Stations constitute main obstacles to increase of accommodation in the Station Yard.

(4) Inadequacy of Parcels traffic accommodation. This is a long standing and increasing trouble. The present layout can only provide palliatives at heavy cost.

(5) The obstruction of the Lawn area by parcel and mail traffic to the detriment of its proper use by passengers.

(6) Insufficiency of the number of platforms to deal with growing traffic. No extra lines are possible within the boundaries of the present Station.

(7) The Up main line at present must cross the Up and Down Relief lines on the level, a factor which prevents improvement of the train services.

(8) All Down trains emerge from the Station Yard by one line only, due to the limited width of the 'bottle neck' at the Station entrance, which precludes the laying of a second Down line.

(9) Taxi-Cab traffic nearing the Down approach in busy times is blocked back a considerable distance through congestion caused by want of manoeuvring space alongside the Station buildings for both Parcels and Cab traffic.

(10) Inadequacy of Office accommodation and its defective distribution and arrangement for supervision purposes.

Due to the foregoing and other less apparent causes, the conclusion is inescapable that the present Station has passed the stage when minor alterations and additions can improve its working and that in fact the time has arrived when entire reorganisation and a measure of expansion must be put in hand, if matters are to be prevented from going from bad to worse.

Information on the growth of traffic at the station was included in the report, and has been reproduced in the diagram on page 40. This shows that the total number of trains using the station daily was expected to reach 385 in 1928, and the upward trend indicated an annual increase of 1%. Of the total, 125 were mainline services, and the rest local ones, except for a fairly-constant twenty per day conveying parcels, horses, milk, etc.

The changes put forward to overcome these problems were drastic, but they were not, in the end, to be carried out in the form proposed. In this book we must concentrate on those aspects of the plans that affected the operation of the train services, so can therefore skate over the proposal to replace Brunel's train-shed with a reinforced concrete one, and the suggestion for a 300-foot high clock tower on the southern façade. (It is convenient from the descriptive point of view to make the slight assumption that the alignment of the station platforms is east and west.) In 1928 there were twelve long platforms beneath the main station roof, as there are to the present day, but only Platform Nos 1, 2 and 3 at that time extended anywhere near Bishop's Road Bridge. None of them actually reached it, while platforms four to seven did not even get as far as half-way to the bridge from the end of the overall roof. The electric services had their own pair of short through platforms, situated partially under the Bishop's Road Bridge, with a through track between them, which was used for the locomotive changes that took place here on services to and from Liverpool Street.

The report recommended the provision of no less than 18 long platforms, varying in length between 1,000 and 1,320 feet from the row of buffer-stops all of which were in line. The outermost two were solely for parcels traffic, which meant that Platform No 1, from many points of view the 'prime site' in the station, would no longer be available for passengers. The General Offices would occupy the block on the Praed Street side of the station, with the hotel moving round to the south-east corner, where the rest of that particular frontage was entirely given up to the handling of parcels, with office accommodation located above it. Entrance and exit for passengers would be via a new road, opposite London Street, slightly north of the present exit. This led to the wide Departure Roadway between Platform Nos 13 and 14, from which taxis and other vehicular traffic would continue down the station to make a right-handed, 180 degree turn over a bridge across tracks Nos 14 and 15 and exit via the Arrival Roadway between Platform Nos 15 and 16. At the end of the bridge they were to be joined by the incoming taxis that had entered by the elevated road over the parcels platform on the north side of the station, as they still do.

The GWR's first preference was to banish the electrified Hammersmith & City lines from the station altogether. They would go into tunnel at Ladbroke Grove before even transgressing on to the surface of any GWR property, and the tracks would continue underground to join the Inner Circle at a new junction, *south* of Paddington Praed Street station. This would obviously have had many advantages for the Great Western, but the passengers would also have benefited. As things still persist today, anyone travelling towards Paddington along the north side of the Inner Circle, including all those from Liverpool Street, King's Cross and Euston stations, can catch any train. It matters comparatively little whether they finish up at Praed Street or Bishop's Road London Underground stations, since access is equally easy to the main-line platforms at either end. However, those who arrive at Paddington, and make the transfer in the opposite direction, have to choose one or other of these stations to go for, and the number of trains thus available for them to catch is reduced. The 1928 report did show an alternative alignment for the electrified lines in roughly their original positions, and that was to be the final choice, and it remains like this today, although the current proposal for a BR underground link between Paddington and Liverpool Street would transform the whole railway network of the capital.

In 1929 came the Wall Street crash and resulting Great Depression, which was to affect the Great Western's plans very considerably, and very little of the report's detailed proposals were finally to be implemented. The Hotel and Platform No 1 remained, as, in fact, did all the others within the overall roof, complete with their staggered buffer-stops. The Parcels Platform, No 14, set back from the line out of Platform No 1 on the country side of Bishop's Road Bridge, was supplemented by others built into the enlarged parcels area behind it, and major changes were made to the electrified tracks at Bishop's Bridge station. The through line was done away with, and two new island platforms provided, with all four tracks being electrified. The Hammersmith & City trains normally just used the outer faces of these (Platform Nos 13 and 16) and the centre pair were for the Great Western's steam-operated suburban services. Room was found for a short, dead-end locomotive spur on the north side at the city end of Platform No 16, just where the Grand Junction Canal, hidden behind the containing wall of the station, makes a sharp turn to the north-west. This was used for the electric locomotives waiting to take over the through trains to Liverpool Street during the morning rush hour.

On the main-line side, Platform Nos 1 to 11 were all extended, up to, under or beyond Bishop's Bridge, and full-length trains can stand in any of these without fouling other movements, except those in and out of parcels Platform No 12, which can only be reached by using the external portion of Platform No 11. The whole of the permanent-way layout over the first three-quarters of a mile was completely remodelled in the 1930s, with additional improved arrangements for moving trains of empty stock to and from the carriage sidings at Old Oak Common, which were themselves extended. Movements in and out of the station were controlled by two new power-operated signal boxes, on the arrival and departure sides, but there was a serious design fault with their equipment, as the Arrival Side one was badly damaged by fire in November 1938, and the same thing also occurred at the neighbouring Westbourne Bridge box only a month later. Considerable ingenuity was needed to overcome the short-term operating problems that resulted, but the overall changes enabled the Great Western to operate many more services into and out of its London terminus, without destroying its unique, and much admired, character.

The west end of Slough station in August 1919. The Windsor branch curves away to the left behind the locomotive sheds. One of the local tank locomotives, complete with shunter's wagon, is at work in the goods yard, beyond the white-washed cattle dock.

4-6-0 No. 4099 *Kilgerran Castle* on a down West of England express near Frome in August 1938.

'Saint' class 4-6-0 No. 2939 *Croome Court* on a Torquay–Sheffield express leaves the Frome Cut-off at Clink Road Junction in August 1937. The original line through the station is on the right.

Strap Lane Halt, with its wooden platforms and small timber shelters, was situated at the summit of Brewham bank. 4-6-0 No. 5016 *Montgomery Castle* completes the 1 in 107 climb from the Witham direction with an express for Plymouth, before descending the steeper grades towards Bruton.

4-6-0 No. 6015 *King Richard III* on a down express for Penzance passes the end of the down platform loop at Dawlish Warren in April 1939. The assortment of vans, two of them 'Siphons', behind the tender will be noted.

Even in the middle of the summer, paths had to be found for local freight trains along the coastal stretch from Dawlish Warren to Teignmouth. Pannier tank No. 5760 was photographed leaving one of the tunnels in July 1936.

Par station in 1922, looking west. On the left, a coach for Newquay has been dropped off the rear of a down main-line train, while a rake of clerestory stock stands in the curved Newquay line platform. The nearest vehicle is a 6-wheeler, while the vacuum reservoirs on the roof of one of the others indicate that it is a slip coach. In the distance on the far right can be seen the works and shed of the former Cornwall Minerals Railway at St. Blazey.

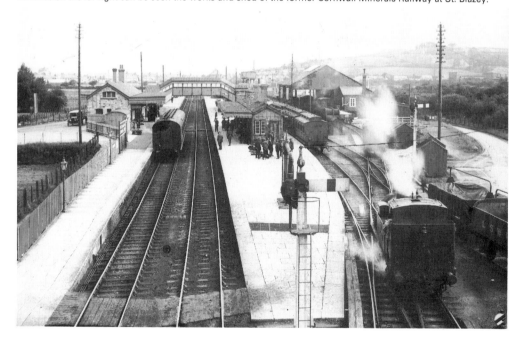

On a bright morning in January 1936, Dean goods No. 2456 heads a lengthy Bristol–Salisbury freight towards Bathampton. To judge from the smoke from the guard's van, the stove has been got going nicely to keep out the chill of a cold morning.

A Churchward Mogul, No. 6322, on a Cardiff–Portsmouth train at Bathampton. The first coach is one of the Dean clerestories, with its characteristic bogie suspension. These trains were important enough to rate destination boards on the coach roofs.

A very deep cutting was constructed by the Bristol & Exeter Railway at Uphill, south of Weston-super-Mare, to prevent any sudden gradients interrupting the easy passage of the line over the Somerset wetlands. 2-8-0 No. 2854 works a down goods for Laira through it in May 1936. The splitting signals for the junction at the south end of the Weston loop can be seen beyond the left-hand of the two parachute water-columns.

Near Hullavington on the South Wales & Bristol Direct, 4-6-0 No. 4043 *Prince Henry* heads an up train from Bristol. The photograph was taken after October 1931, as the locomotive had been fitted with 'Castle' type outside steam pipes.

The junction for the Barnstaple and Minehead branches at the west end of Norton Fitzwarren station in June 1921, before the quadrupling which was carried out using the government's low-interest finance.

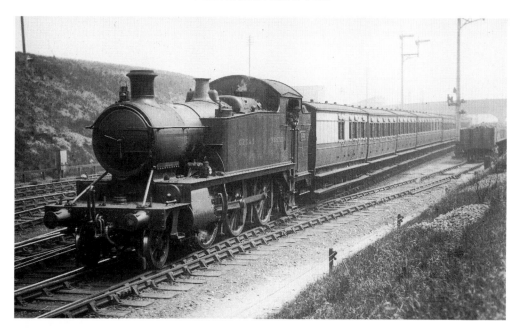

Contrasts at Handsworth Junction in the 1920s. This was to become the site of The Hawhornes Halt, opened on Christmas Day 1931 to serve the West Bromwich Albion football ground.

2-6-2T No. 3138 heads along the main line with a local from Snow Hill to Wolverhampton, the height of the locomotive dwarfing the 6-wheeled coaches.

A Birmingham–Stourbridge Junction local takes the left-hand line at the junction, hauled by the former Midland & South Western Junction Railway, inside-cylinder, 4-4-4T No. 18. One of two built by Sharp Stewart in 1897, it became GWR No. 27 after Grouping. It had been rebuilt in 1925 with one of their standard boilers, and worked in the Kidderminster district for the last 4 years of its life.

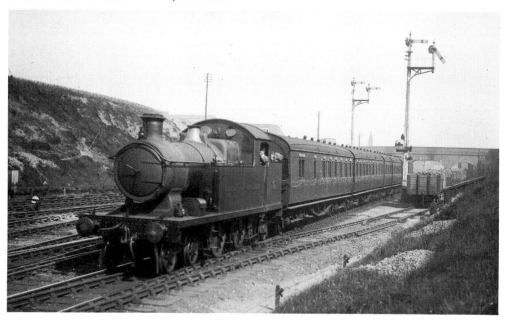

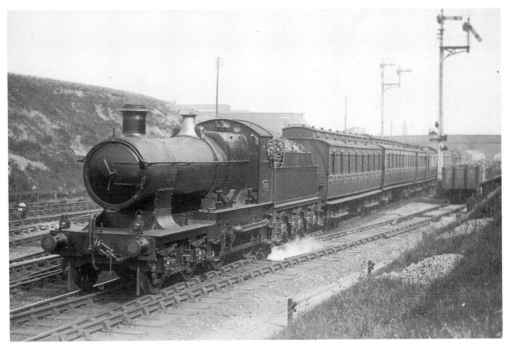

'Bulldog' 4-4-0 No. 3420 on an express for Hereford or beyond, with three clerestory coaches immediately behind the tender. Note the lofty signals to permit the driver to sight them from well beyond the overbridge in the background. Short repeating arms are provided on the right-hand post at carriage-roof level.

4-6-0 No. 5036 *Lyonshall Castle* on a down express for Penzance passes Stonehouse LMS station in June 1936.

4-6-0 No. 2912 *Saint Ambrose* on a down Weymouth express near Frome in September 1937.

4-6-0 No. 6021 *King Richard II* eases the down 'Torbay Express' round the curve on to the sea wall at Dawlish Warren in July 1936. The work going on to strengthen the sea defences can be seen. A special siding has been laid from the end of the down platform loop in the distance to terminate outside the retaining wall on the right to convey the large stone blocks used to reinforce the wall.

2-6-0 No. 4310 heads an up goods train out of the tunnel just south of Wood End Platform on the Tyseley–Bearley line.

CHAPTER THREE

MAIN LINE PASSENGER SERVICES

Before commencing our examination of the Great Western's train services in detail, we should try to obtain an over-view of the way in which the railway's business was split up, in order to judge the importance of the different parts. The Library at the National Railway Museum has a copy of the extremely useful book of statistics listing the business done at each of the GWR's stations. As a starting point certain figures have been extracted, which are presented in Table 3.1. These are for each of the eleven Divisions under which the railway operated in the grouping era, details for 1937 are given which, from all the companies' points of view, was a 'golden year', coming after the Great Depression, and before the looming war-clouds started to affect the country. (The GWR dividend on their ordinary shares went up to 4% for 1937.) In the table the annual sales of ordinary and season tickets, and the total passenger revenue that resulted are given.

Table 3.1. Great Western Railway. Passenger Revenue by Divisions, 1937

| Division | Tickets issued | | | Ordinaries per Season | Revenue | |
	Ordinary	Seasons	Total		£	Pence (p) per ticket
London	22,883,841	302,820	23,186,661	76	3,066,371	13
Bristol	6,336,123	53,849	6,389,972	118	1,020,871	16
Exeter	2,214,797	45,443	2,260,240	49	468,572	21
Plymouth	3,163,935	38,374	3,202,309	84	609,322	19
Gloucester	1,516,961	9,928	1,526,889	153	242,983	16
Cardiff	6,419,465	108,930	6,528,395	59	702,748	11
Swansea	2,606,435	19,459	2,625,894	134	431,195	16
Worcester	1,403,333	22,681	1,426,014	62	194,604	14
Birmingham	7,628,487	264,381	7,892,868	29	991,520	13
Chester	1,824,154	10,453	1,834,067	175	285,830	16
Central Wales	1,013,545	10,777	1,024,322	94	137,829	13
	57,011,076	887,095	57,898,171	62	8,151,845	14

Source: *Great Western Railway, Traffic Dealt with at Stations and Goods Depots*

From this basic information there are calculated two sets of derived figures: the number of ordinary tickets issued per season ticket, and the average price paid per ticket. A certain amount of caution must, however, be used when interpreting these, since we do not know the sort of season tickets that were being bought half a century ago. They could be weekly, monthly, quarterly, or for longer periods still, and the mix could thus easily have differed between Divisions. The same *caveat* also applies to the figure worked out for the average price per ticket, since all types of season ticket are given equal importance in making that calculation. The table shows the average price per ticket in terms of our present-day decimal currency, and, on the same basis, the 1937 rate per mile for a third-class single ticket was 0.625p (1¹/₂d in old currency). Monthly returns, which were calculated as a fare plus one third, worked out the same as the old 1d/mile rate for Parliamentary Trains. If all tickets were third-class returns, the average length of each journey over the whole system would have been thirty-three miles.

From the point of view of understanding the development of the company's train services, there are a number of significant conclusions to be drawn from the table. London was clearly the busiest division, and its revenue represented 37% of the whole. The next busiest was Bristol, but the London Division issued three-and-a-half times the number of tickets, although it only took three times the revenue. The proportion of season tickets issued was much higher in London than Bristol, which is what one would expect, but the entries for Exeter are surprising. Its ratio of season tickets to ordinaries was the highest anywhere on the system, apart from the Birmingham Division, and had the highest average price for each of its tickets (21p compared with the overall average of 14p).

The Plymouth Division covered Cornwall, and its overall revenue was appreciably more than that of the Exeter Division next door. Although not shown in the table, Paddington itself had a revenue of £1,549,923 in 1937, which represents almost exactly half of that generated in its Division, and there the average cost of a ticket was 57p (equal to 137 miles travelling at 1d/mile), which reflects the large proportion of originating main-line business, as one would expect. The revenue totals at Exeter St. David's and Plymouth (North Road and Millbay combined) were £98,398 and £273,334 respectively, and the average fare in both cases was in the range 40–41p (ninety-six to ninety-eight miles), so there was clearly a lot of custom from passengers going to London, as well as away from it. There are a lot more comparisons that could be made from these figures, but space does not permit a more detailed analysis.

A railway's public passenger timetables are not only a sales catalogue for their services, but also provide an important insight into the way in which the company views its whole operation. We will thus start our examination of the Great Western's main routes with a quick look at their own July 1921 timetable, a paper-covered publication of foolscap format, printed in chocolate on cream, which cost six old pence, or two-and-a-half new pence. Inset in the back of the 192 pages were a series of maps showing the GWR lines in different parts of the country, plus their bus and shipping routes. At the top of the title page appeared the names of the Company Chairman and the Deputy Chairman, with those of the Principal Officers below them:

General Manager	Felix J. C. Pole	*Supt. of the Line*	R. H. Nicholls
Secretary	A. E. Bolter	*Chief Goods Manager*	E. Lowther
Chief Accountant	Ralph Cope	*Chief Mechanical*	
		Engineer	G. J. Churchward
Solicitor	A. G. Hubbard	*Chief Engineer*	W. W. Grierson

This was then followed by the address and telephone (Paddington 7000) of the General Offices, and a commentary on the new and changed services that were included in the new timetables.

On the inside of the cover was the guide to the tables, with the seven 'Main Lines' at the top, followed by the 206 'Local and Branch Lines'. The latter were arranged in alphabetical order, but many of them only referred to the two end stations in the table concerned. Each branch appeared only once, being listed under the name of the station furthest from the main line, with 'Abbotsbury and Weymouth' forming the first entry, and 'Ynysybwl and Pontypridd' the last. There were also certain non-GWR lines included in the list of branches, including some of those belonging to the LSWR in Devon. Such was the stability, or perhaps the conservatism of the Great Western, that anyone with a copy of their last timetable, dated 'October 6th, 1947 (and until further notice)', would instantly recognise the 1921 document, which still only cost sixpence. Slight changes in cover design and names of the chief officers took place over the intervening quarter-century, and the postal address of the general offices had changed from 'London W' to 'London W.2', but the phone number was the same. The contents list had also migrated to the title page, replacing the commentary on the changes made to the services in the new issue, and the order of listing the Main Lines had also altered very slightly, but these changes were post-war ones. Back in 1921 the list was not laid out in either alphabetical or geographical order, so this presumably represented the order of importance attached to them at that time by the railway.

The headings were as follows:

London and Reading
    London, Ealing, Staines, Uxbridge, Windsor and Eton, Maidenhead, Henley-on-Thames and Reading

London and the West of England
    Reading $\left\{ \begin{array}{l} \text{Westbury} \\ \text{Bristol} \end{array} \right\}$ and Taunton
    Reading, Oxford, Swindon, Bath, Weston-super-Mare and Taunton
    Reading, Newbury, Westbury and Taunton
    Taunton, Exeter, Torquay, Plymouth, Newquay, Falmouth and Penzance

London and the Berks and Hants and Weymouth Lines
    Reading, Newbury, Westbury, Yeovil, Dorchester and Weymouth

London, Swindon and South Wales
    Reading and Swindon
    Swindon, Badminton, Bristol, Newport, Cardiff, Swansea, Tenby, Neyland and Fishguard
    Swindon, Stroud, Gloucester, Cheltenham, Hereford, and Chepstow

London and Banbury, Birmingham and the North
    London, Wycombe and Princes Risborough
    Princes Risborough, Banbury, Leamington Spa, Birmingham, Wolverhampton, Shrewsbury, Chester and Liverpool
    Oxford and Banbury

London and the West Midland Line
    London, Reading, Didcot and Oxford
    Oxford, Chipping Norton, Evesham and Worcester
    Worcester, Droitwich, Kidderminster, Dudley and Wolverhampton
    Worcester, Malvern and Hereford

West of England, Bristol, and South Wales and $\left\{ \begin{array}{l} \text{Birmingham} \\ \text{North of England and Scotland} \\ \text{Midland Line and Scotland} \\ \text{Great Central Line} \end{array} \right.$

With the coming of the grouping era, changes were clearly needed, and were duly made: the third and fourth of the final subheadings were altered to 'LMS Line and Scotland' and 'L.& N.E. Line' respectively!

It is thus easy for us to make our study of the changes in the GWR's train services in the 1920s and 1930s on a common basis, while those who want to look into the pre-grouping situation in greater detail are aided by the availability of the July 1922 *Bradshaw*, in reprint form and enlarged format, from David & Charles.

As already mentioned, there were some 5000 separate trains every day on the Great Western at the time we are studying them, and there is no way in which we can hope to do more than look at a handful of the more important. For the reason just given, July 1922 is taken as representing the situation at the time of the grouping, and compared with those services of July 1939. Ideally it would be interesting to make some summer/winter comparisons, but this would take too much space. The summer services were the busiest, and were thus used by far more people, particularly the thousands who travelled by the Great Western for their annual summer holiday. We will also largely be concentrating on the down trains out of Paddington although not exclusively, because it is much easier to follow the development pattern of the services over a particular route when dealing with the departures from a single station, rather than from a string of main-line and branch-line starting points all the way through the West Country.

Synthesising the train services of sixty-odd years ago from the contemporary public timetables does, however, have its problems. While there was a certain amount of criticism about the size of print when the current BR tables were introduced, one only has to wade through a pre-war *Bradshaw* to realise how much the standards of presentation has improved. Looking back, the most significant change has been the adoption of a bold type face for the times of through trains, which gives an immediate indication of any changes required. While *Bradshaw* did not use heavier type, the GWR's own timetables did, but only as a means of identifying the times at the larger stations whose names were similarly in bold type.

Between the two world wars there was a trend for more trains to be marked with the TC symbol to indicate 'Through Carriages', but elsewhere one had to undertake a careful study of the two tables concerned and then make an educated guess whether there was a through service or not on the basis of the time spent at the junction station. The same problems applied to the railway company's own timetables, and these limitations were clearly realised, as in the late 1920s the Great Western's devoted four full pages at the back to a list of through carriages. As far as the main lines were concerned, in the summer of 1927 they covered the situation in the following words:

Through Carriages are run on the principal Express Trains between the following places:-

LONDON AND –

ABERYSTWYTH	DROITWICH SPA	MALVERN	SWANSEA
BARMOUTH	EXETER	NEWPORT	TAUNTON
BATH	FALMOUTH	NEYLAND	TENBY
BIRKENHEAD	FISHGUARD	OXFORD	TORQUAY
BIRMINGHAM	GLOUCESTER	PEMBROKE DOCK	WEYMOUTH
BRISTOL	HEREFORD	PENZANCE	WOLVERHAMPTON
CARDIFF (General)	KIDDERMINSTER	PLYMOUTH	WORCESTER
CHELTENHAM SPA	KINGSWEAR	PWLLHELI	WREXHAM
CHESTER	LEAMINGTON SPA	SHREWSBURY	

Also between BRISTOL, PONTYPOOL ROAD, HEREFORD, SHREWSBURY, CHESTER, BIRKENHEAD and CREWE, LIVERPOOL, STOCKPORT and MANCHESTER, and BRISTOL and CHELTENHAM, BIRMINGHAM and WOLVERHAMPTON.

There then followed a list of 103 different stations, each of which had one or more significant through workings on weekdays, ranging from Worcester Shrub Hill's 9.35 a.m. to Aberystwyth on Fridays and Saturdays, to the thirty-five separate entries for Oxford, many of which were to multiple destinations and involved more than one train each. Even when the through carriages were indicated in the tables themselves, the information was always printed sideways in the columns, while the notes could be several pages away and spread all round the margins. As an example of the complexity of these, the Torbay table in 1939 had no less than seventeen letters or symbols identifying various versions of trains that only ran on Saturdays.

It was very rare to include the departure or arrival times of these through services at the ends of their journeys on intermediate sheets, and, although references were given to as many as nine other pages on which the continuation times appeared, these were by no means always complete, as we will see. Bearing in mind the much more complicated railway system that existed at that time, the business of finding one's way by train from one part of the country to another was far less user friendly than it is now, and many people still have difficulties doing so! It is also quite within the bounds of possibility that some through workings have been omitted or inadvertently implied that they existed, when, in fact, an intermediate change was required.

In 1924 the GWR adopted the principle of 'Clock-face' departures from London and certain provincial cities, thus introducing an arrangement which we take for granted today, although we will see later that even in 1939 there were still many deviations from this practice. However, for most of the years we are studying, the standard times for departures from Paddington were as follows:

Trains to	Minutes past Hour
Birmingham and the North	10
Bristol	15
West of England and Weymouth	30
Worcester and West Midland line	45
South Wales	55

In the up direction, the standard time for departures from Birmingham was on the hour, while trains from Bristol and Cardiff both departed at fifteen minutes past the hour.

With that preamble, we will now turn to our examination of the main-line routes, in the order in which they appeared in the timetables of the period, as listed above.

LONDON AND READING

Although certain long-distance trains called at Reading between the two world wars, as they still do now, in this section it is primarily the suburban services in which we are interested. Commuting along the Thames Valley increased markedly over this particular period, as the following selected figures show:

Table 3.2.

	Number of season tickets sold in year	
	1923	1937
Ealing Broadway	15,960	53,248
Southall	6,617	15,404
Langley	635	1,495
Iver (opened in December 1924)	–	3,939
Slough	4,768	9,644
Maidenhead	5,205	10,968

Although the GWR data do not differentiate between season tickets issued for the up and down directions, it is a fair approximation to assume that the majority were for daily journeys to and from Paddington. Beyond Reading the numbers of commuters fell off quickly, the totals along the Berks & Hants dropping to less than 100 per station, although the old main line was somewhat busier with this sort of traffic, Tilehurst and Pangbourne issuing 638 and 981 season tickets, respectively, in 1937.

In the up morning commuter period in 1922 the first train was the 6.20 from Reading, which stopped at Slough to set down, and reached Paddington at 7.10. This was the 8.40 p.m. sleeper from Penzance, stopping at Tilehurst as well as Didcot, and was followed by the 7.14 and 7.30 originating trains from Reading. The first called at all stations to Slough, and the latter to Maidenhead, with a subsequent stop at West Drayton. The arrivals in Paddington were at 8.20 and 8.28. The next up train also started at Reading, at 8.0, and ran fast from Maidenhead, to be followed by two non-stop Reading–Paddington workings. The 8.20 was the 7.8 from Oxford, and the last service to reach London before 10.0 was the 8.47, which originated from Didcot. There were other, shorter-distance trains, and the following table summarises the whole service, the workings starting from the stations shown, except the three marked ones from Reading.

Table 3.3. Up Morning London Suburban Service – July 1922

Origin	Departure times	No. of trains
Reading	6.20†, 7.14, 7.30, 8.0, 8.20†, 8.47†	6
Henley	8.50	1
Marlow	8.33	1
Maidenhead	8.0, 8.54	2
Windsor & Eton	6.22, 7.28*, 8.36, 8.47	4
Slough	5.28, 7.0	2
West Drayton	5.49, 6.16, 8.27, 8.48, 9.4*, 9.17, 9.33*	7
Hayes & Harlington	7.5, 7.17	2
Southall	5.30, 6.50, 7.50, 7.57, 8.8, 8.16*, 8.21, 8.28, 8.33, 8.55, 9.8	11
		Total 36

* These trains ran through to Liverpol Street, as will be described later.
† Trains originating west of Reading.

By 1939 the position had changed very considerably, the service having been improved by the arrival of the new 61XX class 2-6-2 tanks, of which seventy were built between April 1931 and November 1935, specifically for the accelerated London suburban services. All of them were allocated to London Division depots, out as far as Didcot, and the sets they hauled on these services were mainly of new non-corridor stock. They would not, of course, be rostered for workings such as the 7.10 from Oxford, which would have been in the hands of a 4-6-0. The service in the summer of 1939 had become as follows:

Table 3.4. Up Morning London Suburban Service. July 1939

Origin	Departure times	No. of trains
Reading	6.15, 7.15, 7.33, 7.50†, 8.0, 8.20†, 8.50†	7
Henley	8.50	1
Marlow	8.34	1
Maidenhead	7.5	1
Windsor & Eton	6.20, 6.45, 7.28*, 8.10, 8.37, 8.47	6
Slough	5.30, 6.42	2
West Drayton	5.51, 6.18, 8.27*, 8.50*, 9.12	5
Hayes & Harlington	5.25, 6.40, 7.52*, 8.16, 9.5	5
Southall	8.5, 8.16*, 8.28, 8.33	4
		Total 32

* As with the 1922 services, these trains ran through to Liverpool Street.
† Trains originating west of Reading.

It will be seen that, although the number of trains had actually been reduced by four, the number of services operating from further out in the country had increased markedly, those originating from Southall dropping from eleven to just four. The Penzance sleeper did not appear, while the 7.50 and 8.50 departures from Reading had originated at Swindon, and the 8.20 was the through Oxford train, now leaving two minutes later, but still being booked into Paddington at 9.0 after its forty minute non-stop run from Reading.

On the suburban workings, the accelerations were very marked. In 1922 the 7.0 a.m. all-stations train from Slough to Paddington took no less than fifty-five minutes, whereas the 7.5 from Maidenhead in 1939 was making the same stops in from Slough in just forty-eight minutes, and the 8.10 from Windsor managed it in only forty-five. The through services from Marlow and Henley had, however, not changed very much in overall speed, the former being

Table 3.5. Evening Thames Valley Commuter Departures from Paddington
(July, Mondays – Fridays 4.30 p.m. to 6.30 p.m.)

1922			1939		
Time	Destination	Stops	Time	Destination	Stops
4.30	Windsor	Fast to Slough			
			4.33	Reading	Iver, Slough & all stns
4.35	Slough	All stations	4.35	Slough	All stations
4.50	High Wycombe	West Drayton, Maidenhead	4.50	Maidenhead	West Drayton only
5.0	Didcot	Reading and all stations			
5.3*	West Drayton	All stations	5.3	West Drayton	All stns except Westb. Park
5.5	Weymouth	Taplow (slip), Reading			
5.8	Maidenhead	All stns except Westb. Park	5.8	Didcot	Reading and all stns
			5.10	Maidenhead	All stns except Westb. Park
5.15	Bristol	Twyford and Reading	5.25	Bristol	Twyford (slip), Reading
5.18	Maidenhead	Slough only	5.18	Reading	Slough, Maidenhead
5.20	Hayes	All stns except Westb. Park	5.20	Hayes	All stns
			5.32	West Drayton	All stns except Westb. Park
5.33	West Drayton	Semi-fast			
5.36*	Windsor	All stns except Westb. Park	5.36*	Windsor	All stns except Westb. Park
			5.37	Didcot	Langley, Slough, Twyford
5.40	Didcot	Slough, Reading and all stns	5.40	Windsor	Iver, Slough
5.42	Slough	All stns except Westb. Park	5.42	Slough	All stations
5.45	Marlow/High Wycombe	West Drayton, Maidenhead	5.45	High Wycombe	Non-stop to Maidenhead
			5.52	Southall	All stns except Westb. Park
5.53	Southall	Semi-fast			
			6.4	Southall	All stations
6.5	Malvern	Taplow (slip), Reading	6.5	Oxford	Non-stop to Reading
6.7	Southall	All stns except Westb. Park			
			6.8	Marlow	Taplow, Maidenhead
6.12	Henley	Slough, Twyford			
			6.13	Henley	Slough, Twyford
6.15*	Southall	All stns except Westb. Park			
			6.16	Maidenhead	Iver and all stns
			6.17	Hayes	All stations
6.20	Windsor	Semi-fast	6.20	Windsor	Semi-fast
6.27	Southall	All stns except Westb. Park			
			6.28	Hayes	All stations
6.30	Plymouth	Reading (slip)			

* Through workings from Liverpool Street
Only the stops on the main line have been indicated.

two minutes quicker, but the latter remained the same. Another alteration was that several of the earlier workings had become third-class only by 1939. In 1922 the only one to be so indicated in the morning rush hour was the 6.3 a.m. Maidenhead–Hayes. Its 1939 counterpart left three minutes later and also had no first-class accommodation, but, in spite of putting in extra stops at Burnham and Iver, it was five minutes faster overall.

The evening down peak can be looked at in a different way, by listing the trains in departure order from Paddington, which appears in Table 3.5 on page 61. Overall there was one extra working during the two-hour period in 1939, compared with 1922, but, the pattern had generally been recast, although there were a few trains that were still running at the same times after a lapse of seventeen years. Overall speeds with the stopping trains still varied quite considerably in 1939, the 4.35 taking sixty-one minutes to Slough, although the 5.10, which only missed out Westbourne Park, managed it in forty-five. The 4.35 in 1922 had done the trip in fifty-five minutes, while the next similar workings, the 5.8 and 5.36, got there in fifty minutes only. The number of slip workings in the period covered by this survey had dropped from the 1922 total of three, with the remaining one in 1939 being at Twyford, although it was off a Bristol train that left Paddington ten minutes later than the Weymouth express of seventeen years earlier. The overall London–Twyford time had improved from twenty-eight to twenty-five minutes.

Mention has been made of the through trains between the GWR and the 'Widened Lines' of what, by 1939, had become the London Passenger Transport Board. Although the Great Western's own condensing tanks worked the through freight services to Smithfield, the passenger trains had their motive power changed at Paddington (Bishop's Road) in each direction. This involved some smart and dextrous work by the shunters, who would have been working from ground-level on the electrified tracks. The services were worked by Great Western tank engines and some of the Metropolitan Bo-Bo electric locomotives. Because of the central conductor rail, the GWR locomotives equipped with ATC had to have that moved out of the way. Their contact shoes were modified so that, as they went over a special ramp on the approach to the electrified lines, they were automatically raised and clipped up out of the way. Similar arrangements caused them to drop again when they returned to their own tracks. Only those of the main-line company's locomotives that actually worked through on to the LT lines had to be equipped with trip-cocks to apply the brakes if they over-ran a signal.

These workings only took place at peak hours, and in 1939 one of them was even withdrawn during the August holiday period. Going up in the morning, in 1922 there were seven through trains to Liverpool Street, with a further two in the afternoon. The latter did not run on Saturdays, the five- and a half-day working week at that time necessitating major changes to the whole suburban timetable on those afternoons and evenings, although the up commuter trains ran much as usual in the mornings. The westbound workings from Liverpool Street in 1922 thus included two mid-day Saturdays-only workings (12.26 and 1.29), and four Saturdays-excepted ones in the evening (4.43, 5.15, 5.55 and 6.18). While several of the contra-flow workings were advertised in the public timetables, there were some unbalanced empty-stock ones.

These Great Western's services were different from the steam-hauled ones off the Great Northern and Midland, which only worked as far as Moorgate, where there were terminal platforms where stock could be left between peaks. At Liverpool Street there was only room for the stand-over electric locomotive, and the train would return to Paddington very quickly after arriving. The running time between Bishop's Road and Liverpool Street was seventeen minutes, and the first through train in the morning, the 8.19 from Paddington, was off back at 8.44, after a layover of only eight minutes. The 1939 service comprised five morning eastbound workings and four in the opposite direction. In the evening peak there were no eastbound passenger-carrying services to match the two return trains that left Liverpool Street at 5.15 and 6.19 p.m., Saturdays-excepted. The Saturdays-only westbound services were at 12.27 and 1.29, the former being the one that did not run in August.

While on the subject of these electrified suburban services, the Great Western's own direct involvement with this form of motive power should not be overlooked. Although the Western Region will not have any electrified lines until the completion of the new Heathrow link in 1993, from 1906 the GWR were part owners of forty multiple-unit electric trains, which were shared with the Metropolitan Railway. These operated through Bishop's Road station at Paddington on the services to Hammersmith and Addison Road, Kensington – now Olympia. The junction between the two routes was west of Latimer Road station, but the LT service to Olympia by this route finished in 1940 after air-raid damage, although the line was not formally closed until after their link in the opposite direction from Earls Court had come into use in December 1946. The Great Western stock book had continued to record the multiple-units until they were withdrawn in 1938, in spite of the Hammersmith & City line having been handed over to the new London Passenger Transport Board five years earlier.

Before finally leaving the Paddington suburban scene, mention should be made of the services between Paddington and Greenford. There is a choice of route between the two stations, with the roundabout one via West Ealing and the Greenford Loop being traditionally the busier. In 1922 there were approximately thirty workings a day in each direction to and from Paddington by that route, with roughly half that number over the direct line via Brentham, virtually all the services being by auto trains. By 1939 the number of trains over each route had increased very considerably, with upwards of forty-five via West Ealing and forty via Brentham. In spite of the adoption of 'clock-face' timetabling for main line trains out of Paddington in 1924, the same arrangements never applied to the suburban services, either on this route or by the main line to Reading.

All these extra workings that began during our period of interest would have been too much for Paddington to cope with, so the West Ealing trains mainly ran to and from Ealing Broadway, while the others started at Westbourne Park or even Old Oak Lane Halt. The services by the direct route were, however, scheduled to run all the way into and out of Paddington on Sundays. It is an indication of the increased capacity of the modern railway that the West Ealing services have been extended to and from Paddington again in the last few years, and are now on a regular-interval basis, running twice an hour in each direction. On a recent journey a single-unit diesel railcar took just seven- and a-quarter minutes from Bishop's Road to Ealing Broadway, which should be compared with over ten minutes allowed in 1922.

LONDON AND THE WEST OF ENGLAND

Although the Great Western timetables split the longer routes into a series of separate tables, starting at the London end, it is easier to build up our understanding of the train services as a whole by dealing with the extremities first, so we will commence our study of the West of England line with those between Paddington and Penzance.

In the two summers in which we are interested, the through trains on ordinary weekdays were as shown overleaf in Table 3.6.

It will be seen that the starting times of the first three trains of the day did not change over our period of study, and, indeed, the first two of them had a much longer ancestry altogether. The 10.30 down was the 'Cornish Riviera Express', the flagship of the Great Western's services, dating back to 1904, and we will be devoting a section of the next chapter to studying it in detail. The 5.30 a.m., however, went back to the days of the Broad Gauge, when it was

Table 3.6. London–Penzance Services

1922	a.m.	a.m.	a.m.	p.m.	p.m.	ngt.	
Paddington dep	5.30	10.30	11.0	2.0	10.0	12.0	
Penzance arr	3.35	5.0	6.10	10.10	7.40	11.32	
1939	a.m.	a.m	a.m	p.m	p.m	p.m	a.m.
Paddington dep	5.30	10.30	11.0	1.40	3.30	9.50	1.35
Penzance arr	3.35	4.55	6.35	9.30	10.55	7.25	8.52

known as the Newspaper Express. By 1922 that type of business was being dealt with by the overnight trains, but the 5.30 still pottered its way to the West of England via Bristol, stopping at such unlikely places as Durston, Wellington, Teignmouth (but not Dawlish), and every station in Cornwall except Doublebois, Probus & Ladock, Carn Brea and Marazion.

The 11.0 from Paddington was the summer relief to the 'Riviera', when the premier service traditionally ran non-stop to Plymouth and left the following train to make many intermediate calls. Its first stop was in Somerset, at Taunton, followed by Exeter, Teignmouth, Brent and Plymouth in Devon. At the last of these it spent no less than twelve minutes (compared with the 'Riviera's' seven), and then called at twelve intermediate stations in Cornwall. It had been twenty-five minutes faster back in 1922, but made a lot less stops at that time, only calling at Exeter and Plymouth North Road before Par. Beyond this point the stopping pattern was almost identical, although the schedule in 1922 missed out the one at Scorrier. In spite of this, the train took seven minutes longer over the concluding forty-five miles, which was perhaps dictated by the stretches of single-line that still existed in those days. On Saturdays in 1939, the 11.0 ran non-stop to Plymouth, by which time it was fifteen minutes up on its ordinary weekday timing, and the gap had widened to twenty minutes by Penzance, with three more stops being cut out.

In 1922 there was only one train to Penzance after the 11.0 a.m., which left three hours later, and then took a whole hour longer to get to Penzance. The 1939 equivalent left at 1.40 – a non-standard departure time for a West of England express – but was twenty minutes faster than the 1922 working, and included a portion for Kingswear too, except on Saturdays. The last daytime working in 1939 left Paddington at 3.30 and took only seven hours twenty-five minutes to get to Penzance, twenty-five minutes faster than the 1.40 and three-quarters of an hour quicker than the 12.10.

After this we come to the overnight services, the first of which, with the Penzance sleeping cars, ran via Bristol. Between 1922 and 1939 its starting time had come forward by ten minutes, but the overall journey was five minutes faster, in spite of a conditional call at Marazion – 'Stops to set down from Bristol and beyond on informing the Guard when joining the train'. There was also a Monday-morning stop at Keyham, just after 4.30 a.m., to set down only, presumably for the benefit of naval and dockyard personnel returning from leave. On the other hand, the second overnight train had been scheduled to run one and a half hours later by 1939, but it had lost its sleeping cars in the process. In 1922 these had only gone as far west as Plymouth.

The earlier train was also involved in the longest through working in the country at that time. This was the celebrated Aberdeen–Penzance through coach, which had been introduced in 1921. The following year it was setting off from the Granite City at 9.45 a.m. via the East Coast Route, and collected a through coach from Glasgow at Edinburgh. South of York it followed the Swinton & Knottingley Joint and the Great Central to reach the GWR at Banbury. From there it continued via Oxford, and the north-to-west curve at Didcot, to Swindon. Here it arrived at 11.30, thirteen and three-quarter hours after leaving Aberdeen, and the through coach was then attached to the Paddington–Penzance sleeper, to continue its westward journey half an hour later. With more than eight further hours travelling still ahead before reaching journey's end, relief was in sight for passengers to Cornwall, as long as they had been able to act on the timetable instruction, 'Passengers may secure Sleeping Car accommodation between Swindon and Penzance by notifying any Station Master en route before 3 aft. on the day required'. There was a corresponding west-to-north through coach, leaving Penzance on the 11.0 a.m. in 1922, which got to Swindon via Westbury in this direction, and finally arrived in Aberdeen at 7.30 the following morning.

In the up direction, the through trains between Penzance and Paddington were as follows:

Table 3.7. Penzance–London Services

1922	a.m.	a.m.	noon	p.m.		
Penzance dep	10.0	11.0	12.0	8.40		
Paddington arr	4.45	6.50	9.0	7.10		
1939	a.m.	a.m.	a.m.	a.m.	p.m.	p.m.
Penzance dep	9.0	10.0	10.15	11.10	1.30	9.30
Paddington arr	4.30	4.40	6.15	6.50	9.0	7.20

The 1922 service looks extremely sparse, but, for those prepared to change at Truro, there was the Truro and Kingsbridge Express, complete with Luncheon and Tea Car, which could be caught off the 8.0 a.m. from Penzance. The arrival in London was at 4.35. A two-hour earlier start, plus a change of train, thus resulted in an arrival that was only ten minutes sooner, so would presumably only have been of interest to those who could not get seat reservations on the 'Riviera'. In each of the years studied there was a London train that was combined with one for the North of England. In 1922 this was the 12 noon from Penzance, which split at Plymouth, the London portion, now with a Tea and Dining Car, departing a quarter of an hour after the train for Manchester and Liverpool. After admiring the beauties of North Road station for a full half an hour, they took four hours-fifty minutes to reach Paddington, travelling the Great Way Round via Bristol.

The corresponding working in 1939 was the 10.15 a.m. from Penzance, and the train, complete with restaurant car, ran through to Bristol before splitting, having acquired the Kingswear–Manchester section at Exeter. The restaurant car continued to Liverpool, the coaches for that destination being combined with those for Birkenhead, but passengers for London only had a Buffet Car for the remainder of the journey, which now took an extra quarter of an hour from Plymouth. The 8.40 p.m. in 1922 and the 9.30 in 1939 were the sleeping car trains, both of which ran via Bristol.

Looking at the changes in the services that took place between 1922 and 1939, we find that, in the down direction, the number of trains via Castle Cary had doubled from two to four, but for passengers going to London the direct services had only increased by one. This did, however, mean that the number of trains in each direction was now matched, with five running direct, and two via Bristol, one of them the overnight sleeper. While there may have been more services in 1939, they were not always quicker, although that could not be said about the 'Cornish Riviera Express', which in the up direction was the 10.0 a.m. departure from Penzance.

With reference to Table 3.8, shown overleaf, we will now look at the London–Plymouth services, which were more frequent than those all the way to Penzance.

In Broad-Gauge days there were twice as many trains between London and Plymouth compared with those that went all the way to Penzance, but in the 1920s and 1930s the same ratio was not maintained. By 1939 Plymouth nevertheless had three additional trains of its own, which was the same *number* of extra ones they had prior to 1887. All but three of the services have already been discussed, and these can be identified from their London

Table 3.8. Paddington–Plymouth Services

1922	a.m.	a.m.	a.m.	a.m.		
Paddington dep	5.30	7.30	10.30	11.0		
Plymouth arr	12.16	2.15	2.37	3.16		
	p.m.	p.m.	p.m.	p.m.	ngt.	
Paddington dep	2.0	4.15	6.30	10.0	12.0	
Plymouth arr	7.6	10.5	12.25	4.25	7.11	
1939	a.m.	a.m.	a.m.	a.m.		
Paddington dep	5.30	7.30	10.30	11.0		
Plymouth arr	12.25	1.40	2.30	3.40		
	p.m.	p.m.	p.m.	p.m.	p.m.	a.m.
Paddington dep	1.40	3.30	5.5	6.30	9.50	1.35
Plymouth arr	6.33	8.5	10.25	12.29	4.20	6.10

departure times. Our examination will be confined to the extra ones, which ran in the early morning and late afternoon, all of them via Bristol.

Neglecting those energetic enough to catch the 5.30 'Newspaper Express', passengers for Plymouth were clearly prepared to rise much earlier in the morning than those for Penzance, as the 7.30 left three hours before the 'Riviera'. In 1922 it had the same overall timing to Plymouth as the 5.30 a.m., but by 1939 thirty-five minutes had been cut off its schedule, although it still took five hours and five minutes for the journey. The 6.30 p.m. was even slower, taking almost six hours, and needed an extra four minutes in 1939 compared with 1922. By the end of the 1930s the 5.5 p.m. was running as well, and this took the rather more presentable time of five hours twenty minutes, even though that was still three-quarters of an hour longer than the 3.30 p.m. from Paddington to Penzance, which had appeared in the interim. On the whole, passengers for Plymouth thus got a faster service when they were prepared to share trains with those going further west. Although one could travel from Waterloo at the same fare, the best the Southern could do in 1939 was the 'Atlantic Coast Express', which took five hours and three minutes to North Road, while their last service was the 3.0 p.m., which took twenty-six minutes longer, so there was no real competition except for those who wanted to enjoy the view across northern Devon from the Okehampton area.

Having examined Plymouth's services from London, we will now look at the GWR suburban workings in the area, most of which took place over the main line. Even by 1922 these motor-train workings had passed their peak, there having at one time been fifteen stations and halts along the main line on the fourteen and a half miles between Plympton and St. Germans, exclusive of those mentioned. One of them, at Mutley, was only half-a-mile east of North Road station. The Great Western steam rail motors were used between Saltash and Yealmpton, as well as up the branch to Tavistock, but by 1939 the services were all in the hands of pannier tanks, working push-pull with autocars, some of which were conversions from the old rail motors. All these workings were third class only, which makes them easy to pick out in the main-line timetables, although there was a separate table for the Plymouth suburban services, which had disappeared from *Bradshaw* by 1939.

These workings across the Tamar into Cornwall provided an important link with Saltash, a town of greater antiquity than Plymouth, and in 1906 Defiance Platform had been opened, three-quarters of a mile further west, just where the line swings round the headland between the Tamar and Lynher estuaries. Moored off here was HMS *Defiance*, one of the Royal Navy's old sailing men-o'-war, which was used as a training ship, and the halt was built to improve communications between the ship and the naval authorities at Plymouth. In 1923 the passenger revenue generated here amounted to no less than £3,657, which was slightly greater than that from the whole of the Fowey branch. In 1922 fourteen up trains called at the platform, of which five only appeared in the suburban timetable, most of them being motor-trains. Saltash was better served, there being thirty-six down trains that called there in 1922, a significant proportion of them continuing along the main line further into Cornwall, although one of the motor-trains worked as far as Menheniot.

For much of the day, the motor trains shuttled backwards and forwards between the limits of Defiance Platform and Plympton, sometimes going into Millbay terminus and out again, and on other trips cutting across the viaduct on the triangle just west of North Road. Only a few workings went the full distance, the timetable clearly being designed to provide the necessary local services, but not to let them get in the way of the main-line trains. Plympton had eight down main-line services and fourteen suburban workings, the majority of the former being the all-stations Plymouth–Newton Abbot trains that ran at frequent intervals throughout the day between 8.45 a.m. and 9.18 p.m. There were seven workings in each direction between Millbay and Yealmpton, with an additional late one on Saturday evenings. On the main suburban shuttle there were also the usual changes in the services on Saturdays, as we saw in the London area. The other branch radiating eastwards from Plymouth was the one to Tavistock and Launceston, and there were ten workings in each direction in 1922, only four of which went beyond Tavistock. These trains did not appear to call at Lipson Vale and Laira halts before they turned off the main line at Tavistock Junction, the site of some important freight yards.

By 1939 there had been many changes in the area. Several of the halts had gone, Defiance Platform closing in 1930, although the shelter was still there over fifteen years later. Mutley, so close to North Road that was clearly visible from the platform end, disappeared as part of the station rebuilding that started just before World War II. The service to Yealmpton was withdrawn in 1930, although the line was to be reopened after the wartime blitz only to close for good in 1947. Saltash only had thirteen down services and sixteen in the up direction, and there were long gaps in the middle of the day when the main-line trains had a clear run of the single-line bottle-neck across Saltash Bridge. Even so, as the regular travellers knew only too well, there were many occasions when the 'Saltash Motor' was put into the loop at St. Budeaux to give other more important traffic priority across the Tamar.

At the other end of the suburban area, Plympton was still served by the all-station main-line trains, there being nine calls in the down direction in July 1939, but it had lost all its rail motor shuttles. This was doubtless due to bus competition, which was not so effective in the western direction because of the barrier of the Tamar, then only crossed by the clanking ferry. It is worth remarking that, even with the Tamar Road Bridge, in the summer of 1988 there were still twelve down and ten up trains that called at Saltash, whereas Plympton station had closed to passengers nearly thirty years earlier, in March 1959.

While the Yealmpton branch was given a short reprieve by World War II, the conflict caused the still-birth of an extremely ambitious new suburban railway scheme in the Plymouth area, put forward by the GWR in 1935. This would have involved a completely new branch line from St. Germans to Looe, where the Great Western were already building a hotel to rival their existing one in Cornwall, the Tregenna Castle at St. Ives. Instead of having to box the compass between Liskeard and Coombe Junction and then potter along the slow and tortuous route down the valley to Looe, the new line would have been much more direct, but only at the expense of three tunnels, including the 2,288-yard one at Seaton, and the 343-yard Keveral Viaduct, 144 feet above the stream. The new terminus would have been on the eastern edge of the town, near the hotel. It was proposed to run a commuter service between Looe and Plymouth using streamlined diesel railcars, which would also have served the new intermediate station and halt on the line, as well, presumably, as St. Germans and Saltash. The scheduled time overall was to have been only thirty-five minutes. Although some work was done on the ground, construction stopped at the beginning of the war, and never recommenced.

To continue our study of the GWR's West of England services, we must now look at those which ran to Torbay, leaving the main line to Plymouth at Aller Junction, a mile west of Newton Abbot. There were a lot of trains between Newton Abbot and Paignton, many of them continuing for the further six and three-quarter miles to Kingswear, but our examination will confine itself to those that ran through from east of Newton, and we will use their arrival time at Torquay as a means of identification. The trains concerned are shown in Table 3.9.

Table 3.9. Arrival Times of Through Trains at Torquay
(Ordinary summer weekdays)

| 1922 | | 1939 | |
Arrival time	Origin (Dep time)	Arrival time	Origin (Dep time)
p.m.		p.m.	
2.7	Paddington (9.15 a.m.)	1.0	Wolverhampton (7.10 a.m.)
–	–	1.32	Paddington (9.0 a.m.)
–	–	3.15	Swansea (9.45 a.m.)
3.15	Birmingham Snow Hill (10.15 a.m.)	3.40	Paddington (12.0 noon)
3.35	Paddington (12.0 noon)	4.20	Wolverhampton (10.40 a.m.)
–	–	–	–
4.25	Wolverhampton (10.35 a.m.)	5.18	Liverpool Lime St (9.10 a.m.)/ Manchester London Rd (9.25 a.m.)
5.49	Manchester London Rd (9.25 a.m.)	6.1	Paddington (1.40 p.m.)
–	–	6.45	Bradford Forster Sq (10.25 a.m.)
6.45	Paddington (2.0 p.m.)		
7.3	Bradford Market St (10.12 a.m.)/ Manchester London Rd (10.40 a.m.)	–	–
–	–	7.32	Paddington (3.30 p.m.)
–	–	9.49	Paddington (5.5 p.m.)
–	–	10.50 FO	Glasgow St. Enoch (10.10 a.m.)
–	–	11.27 FO	Paddington (7.15 p.m.)
–	–	–	–

It will be seen that there were seven such trains on an ordinary summer weekday in 1922, of which three started from Paddington. Two of the others had used the Great Western's Birmingham–Cheltenham link, while the last through train of the day had travelled via the Midland's line to Bristol, over which the GWR had running powers between Gloucester and Yate for its own services. The train from Bradford left from what *Bradshaw* referred to as Market Street station, which was their own means of identification for what we now know as Forster Square, that name being officially adopted by the LMS in 1924. This last train also conveyed through carriages from Manchester London Road, which travelled over the North-and-West route from Shrewsbury, and were combined with the Liverpool to Plymouth train as far as Newton Abbot. There was also an earlier train from Manchester London Road to Torbay, leaving at 9.25 a.m.

Moving on to 1939 we find there were now ten down trains on an ordinary weekday, with an additional pair on Fridays. Five of these worked through from Paddington, the first three of which corresponded with similar workings in 1922. The 'Torbay Express' still left Paddington at noon, and had been slowed by five minutes, but the other two original workings had both been speeded up, as well as leaving somewhat earlier. The 9.0 a.m. departure, corresponding to the 9.15 working in 1922, had been accelerated by twenty minutes, while the 1.40 p.m. (formerly the 2.0) had had its journey time cut by twenty-four minutes. The additional workings from London left Paddington at 3.30 and 5.5 p.m., the first of them giving a very presentable overall time of four hours and two minutes. The second of the trains from the West Midlands (the 10.35/10.30 from Wolverhampton) ran in virtually the same timings as in

1922, but the earlier Birmingham departure had been altered to work through from Wolverhampton, and left much earlier in the day. The LMS train from Bradford was now running by itself, and it too had been speeded up, this time by thirty-one minutes overall. It had also been named the 'Devonian' in 1927, and a decade later had benefited from the general accelerations over their Birmingham–Bristol route that followed the well-known trials runs with the 'Jubilee' *Rooke*. The Swansea–Torbay train was also a new working compared with 1922, and it is worth mentioning that this was the route pioneered by the Great Western air services in 1934. Haldon–on the high ground inland of Dawlish–was used as the airport for Torbay.

There is no space for a detailed examination of the peak summer Saturday services, and that subject has already been ably covered by David St. John Thomas and Simon Rocksborough Smith in *Summer Saturdays in the West*. However this book would not be complete without some indication of the way in which the Great Western's train services were augmented at week-ends. Table 3.10 thus lists the peak summer Saturday through trains to Torquay, which can then be compared with those already given for ordinary week-days. The

Table 3.10. Arrival Times of Through Trains at Torquay
(Summer Saturdays)

1922 Arrival time	Origin (Dep time)	1939 Arrival time	Origin (Dep time)
–	–	*a.m.*	
–	–	3.0	Sheffield (6.21 p.m.)
–	–	5.15	Paddington (12.20 a.m.)
–	–	6.15	Colne (6.55 p.m.)/
			Manchester Victoria (8.55 p.m.)/
			Liverpool Lime St (9.25 p.m.)
–	–	6.25	Manchester London Rd (10.0 p.m.)
–	–	7.2	Bradford Forster Sq (8.15 p.m.)
–	–	11.15	Bristol (8.20 a.m.)
		p.m.	
–	–	12.15	Bristol (9.40 a.m.)
p.m.	–	12.50	Paddington (8.50 a.m.)
1.18	Paddington (7.30 a.m.)	–	–
–	–	1.26	Birmingham Snow Hill (8.10 a.m.)
–	–	1.47	Paddington (9.0 a.m.)
2.7	Paddington (9.15 a.m.)	–	–
–	–	2.35	Cardiff (10.55 a.m.)
–	–	2.45	Paddington (10.55 a.m.)
3.15	Birmingham Snow Hill (10.15 a.m.)	3.10	Birmingham Snow Hill (10.10 a.m.)
–	–	3.20	Swansea (9.45 a.m.)
3.35	Paddington (12.0 noon)	3.40	Paddington (12.0 noon)
–	–	4.0	Manchester London Rd (8.5 a.m.)
–	–	4.20	Bristol (1.40 p.m.)
4.25	Wolverhampton (10.35 a.m.)	–	–
–	–	4.30	Manchester London Rd (9.10 a.m.)
–	–	4.45	Wolverhampton (10.55 a.m.)
–	–	5.13	Liverpool Lime St (9.10 a.m.)
–	–	5.18	Cardiff (12.55 p.m.)
–	–	5.25	Manchester London Rd (10.20 a.m.)
–	–	5.40	Paddington (1.30 p.m.)
5.49	Manchester London Rd (9.25 a.m.)	–	–
–	–	6.15	Liverpool Lime St (10.20 a.m.)
–	–	6.25	Nottingham (11.10 a.m.)
–	–	6.35	Bradford Forster Sq (10.25 a.m.)
7.3	Bradford Market St (10.12 a.m.)/	–	–
	Manchester London Rd (10.40 a.m.)	–	–
–	–	7.10	Paddington (3.25 p.m.)
–	–	8.10	Manchester London Rd (10.40 a.m.)
–	–	9.15	York (1.30 p.m.)
–	–	9.49	Paddington (5.5 p.m.)
–	–	10.50	Glasgow St. Enoch (9.20 p.m.)

way in which the peak had grown over the years between 1922 and 1939 is particularly marked. When our study starts there were the same number of through trains (seven) on a Saturday as on the other week-days, although their origins were somewhat different. By 1939 the Monday–Thursday total had risen to ten, but this swelled to no less than thirty-one on Saturdays. Like all the similar information referred to in this book, these were the trains that appeared in the public timetables, and there were additional ones that also ran on certain weekends, some of which did not even appear in the normal working timetables, but were covered by the weekly notices.

Having now discussed the cross-country trains running to Torquay, it would be as well to complete the West of England picture by listing those in Table 3.11 that served Plymouth and Cornwall, which can be identified by their westward departure times from Newton Abbot. In certain cases the train had a portion for Torbay, and this is indicated by an asterisk, which will permit a cross-reference to Table 3.6. It should not be assumed that there were through coaches from each of the originating points to all the destinations shown. This applies to the Torbay branch too, the 5.23 from Newton Abbot in 1922, for example, having coaches from Liverpool and Birkenhead, which had thus far been combined with the Manchester to Torquay through carriages.

Table 3.11. Cross-Country Trains for Plymouth and Cornwall

1922

Departure from Newton Abbot	Destination	Origin
a.m.		
3.32	Penzance	Aberdeen/Glasgow Queen St.
p.m.		
4.0	Penzance*	Wolverhampton
5.23	Plymouth*	Liverpool Lime St./Birkenhead
6.40	Plymouth*	Liverpool Lime St.
11.29	Plymouth	Glasgow Central

1939

Departure from Newton Abbot	Destination	Origin
a.m.		
3.25	Penzance	Aberdeen/Glasgow Queen St.
9.16	Penzance	Glasgow St. Enoch/Liverpool Lime St./Manchester London Rd.
p.m.		
2.20	Newquay/Penzance	Wolverhampton
4.5	Penzance*	Wolverhampton
5.3	Newquay/Penzance*	Liverpool Lime St./Birkenhead/Manchester London Rd.
7.50	Plymouth*	Liverpool Lime St./Birkenhead/Manchester London Rd.
10.30 FO	Plymouth*	Liverpool Lime St.
11.32 FX	Plymouth*	Liverpool Lime St./Birkenhead/Glasgow St. Enoch

* Trains combined with portion for Torbay

Over the seventeen years these workings increased from five to seven, but the number continuing west of Plymouth had increased by a factor of two and a half, and Newquay now had as many through coaches as had worked to Penzance in 1922, which underlines the growth of the north-coast resort in the 1920s and 1930s. It is interesting to note that the through carriages from Glasgow to Plymouth changed their starting point from Central to St. Enoch during the period under study (and thus followed the Glasgow & South Western's route to Carlisle rather than the Caley's), and, just to be awkward, in the LMS section of the 1939 *Bradshaw* they were only shown as going as far west as Bristol. Two of the recommendations of the Royal Commission on Transport in the early 1930s were that joint or over-lapping lines should be merged into one of the groups, and that all competitive traffic should be pooled, but the GWR and LMS still to some measure continued to compete between Birmingham and Bristol. In the case of the through coaches from Glasgow, the LMS may well have worked on the basis that, by avoiding reference to this facility, passengers going to the West of England would travel via Euston.

Before leaving South Devon, it is worth taking a quick look at the all-stations services that ran between Exeter and Plymouth throughout the day. In 1922 these were as given in Table 3.12.

Table 3.12. Local Trains on Main Line in Devon in 1922

1922		a.m.	a.m.	a.m.	a.m.	p.m.	p.m.	p.m.	p.m.	p.m.
Exeter	Start		6.40	9.0	11.10			6.5	6.45	
Newton Abbot	Finish								7.38*	
	Start	7.28				2.40	4.15			8.10
Plymouth Millbay	Finish	9.32		11.30	11.46	4.10		8.35		9.35
Saltash	Finish						6.7			
Truro	Finish	11.39								

* Train continuing over Torbay line
† Train starting from Taunton

This gave no less than eight down trains calling at virtually all the nine intermediate stations between Newton Abbot and Plymouth Millbay, which is a type of service that has now completely disappeared, with Totnes being the only station currently open on this thirty-three mile stretch.

Moving on seventeen years, the picture had changed considerably, with even more such services.

Table 3.13. Local Trains on Main Line in Devon in 1939

1939		a.m.	a.m.	a.m.	a.m.	a.m.	p.m.	p.m.	p.m.	p.m.	p.m.
Exeter	Start	6.45		8.0		9.30	10.5†	11.25		1.25	1.5
Newton Abbot	Finish			8.47*		10.16*	10.58*	12.12*			2.4
	Start		8.25		9.23				12.20		
Plymouth Millbay	Finish	8.57	9.28		10.50					1.30	3.35
		p.m.	p.m.	p.m.	p.m.	p.m.	p.m.	p.m.	p.m.	p.m.	
Exeter	Start	4.20	3.45	5.15	6.10	6.50	8.5	7.50	9.15	10.12	
Newton Abbot	Finish	5.36	4.29*		6.56	7.34*	9.46	8.34*	10.0*	10.53*	
Plymouth Millbay	Finish	5.36		7.11			9.46				

* Trains continuing over Torbay line
† Train starting from Taunton

As will be seen, the number of such workings had more than doubled, and no less than nine were workings from Exeter through to the Torbay line, while the eight daily workings still continued between Newton Abbot and Plymouth, although their timings had changed somewhat. Bearing in mind the few passing loops available *en route*, this represents a very intensive use of the available line capacity.

Moving further up country, we will now examine the train services on the North Devon and West Somerset lines. These left the one to Exeter and points West two miles west of Taunton, which was used as the junction station in both cases, rather than Norton Fitzwarren where the lines actually diverged. In 1922 there were two through services from London to Ilfracombe and Minehead off the 9.15 a.m. and 12.5 p.m. trains out of Paddington, the first of which also had a portion for Torbay. On the North Devon line these only called intermediately at Wiveliscombe, Dulverton, and South Molton, although the loops at the other stations had to be taken slowly enough to exchange tablets by hand. In the opposite direction the 11.45 a.m. from Ilfracombe and 12.55 p.m. from Minehead combined to reach London at 5.30, but there are no indications in *Bradshaw* of a second up through working, the other limited-stop train from Barnstaple, and the 4.35 from Minehead, both *connecting* with a Plymouth, Torquay and Exeter express that got to Paddington at 9.0 p.m. The 12.5 from Paddington and the 11.45 up from Ilfracombe were shown as having connections 'by Road Motor' for Lynton and Lynmouth at Dulverton. It was still possible to continue the long way round to Barnstaple Town and then catch the narrow-gauge Lynton & Barnstaple Railway, but the Southern Railway were to close that in 1935.

There were seven trains each way on the Barnstaple line on an ordinary week-day in 1922, while on Fridays there was one extra down limited-stop, third-class only working, and three in the opposite direction. A late-night train ran as far as Wiveliscombe on Saturdays, which then returned as empty stock. There were also seven daily workings in each direction over the West Somerset line in 1922, with an additional Fridays-only one, but there was no Sunday service on either branch. The situation had, however, altered by 1939, with two up and one down Sunday workings on the Barnstaple branch, while the Minehead line now had six Sunday trains in each direction. Another change was that Minehead was now shown as the connecting point for the road services to and from Lynton, while Lynmouth was reached '(by Cliff Rly), ten minutes later', although the margin in the opposite direction was fifteen minutes.

On ordinary week-days in 1939 there were still only seven workings in each direction over the North Devon line, with an eighth from Taunton to Dulverton and back, which, like many of the other trains, now also called on request at Morebath Junction Halt, which had been opened to improve the connections with the Exe Valley branch. The 9.0 a.m. provided a through working to Ilfracombe and Minehead, the restaurant car from Paddington going as far as Barnstaple, which, however, was not reached in time for the same vehicle to be used on the corresponding return working that day. The overall timing was a big improvement too, with the London–Barnstaple stretch taking only four hours thirty-five minutes compared with five hours-seven minutes in 1922, while the Ilfracombe time dropped by thirty-five minutes to just five hours twenty-eight minutes. The Fridays- and Saturdays-only train at 12.5 p.m. from Paddington was better still, and ran non-stop between Taunton and Barnstaple Junction, cutting the time to three hours forty-seven minutes, and only taking five minutes over the five hours to Ilfracombe. (The Southern's 'Atlantic Coast Express' took exactly five hours from Waterloo.) By this time the tablet-catchers had been installed for the loops on the branch, and the section from Norton Fitzwarren to Milverton doubled. There was some acceleration too of the stopping services, trains in 1922 having taken as long as two hours-twelve minutes from Taunton to Barnstaple GWR, but as little as one hour-forty minutes seventeen years later.

On Saturdays there were a lot more through GWR trains between London and Ilfracombe in 1939. The first left Paddington at 12.20 a.m., and the stock was then presumably available to return as the 9.5 up, neither of them having restaurant cars. The 9.50 a.m. from Ilfracombe utilised the car that had stood at Barnstaple overnight. This was followed by the 11.0 and 12.0 departures, the second conveying a restaurant car, but this again crossed with the first similar down Saturday working, which was the 9.35 from Paddington. The last through workings of the day were the 12.5 and 5.30 from Paddington, having a restaurant car and a buffet car respectively, both of which went through to Minehead, although the timetable indicated that

Ilfracombe passengers could get lunch on the former. The 9.35 from Paddington, but not the 12.20, also had a through section for Minehead.

The workings at Barnstaple were rather interesting. In 1922 the public timetable in most cases shows the arrival at Barnstaple Junction as being only two minutes later than at the GWR station in Victoria Road. It would take longer than that just for a second locomotive to come on the back after the train's arrival in the Great Western terminus, let alone give time to work it over the curved one and a half miles of the Barnstaple Junction Railway between the two stations. Clearly the trains were taking the east curve, but stopping to drop off the coaches for the GWR station, a separate locomotive being necessary for them to be hauled the last few hundred yards. The Fridays-only trains were not shown to call at the Junction station in either direction, and were presumably re-engined at Victoria Road during a reversal there, it being standard practice for GWR motive power to run through to Ilfracombe.

By 1939 more of these trains were shown as reversing in Barnstaple GWR station, the shortest standing time being just five minutes, while the running times for passenger and freight trains between the two stations was also five minutes. The 12 noon from Ilfracombe to Paddington joined up outside the Great Western station, as the two departures from Victoria Road and the Junction stations were both shown as being at 12.47. The former included the restaurant car, and presumably ran clear of the west end of the curve coming from the Junction station, to allow the Ilfracombe section to head for the GWR station and then propel its coaches on to the back of the others. Unlike the Southern, the Great Western did not use Buckeye couplings, having only toyed with them on a minor scale in the 1920s, so all the numerous through portions of trains on and off the many branch lines would have had to be coupled or uncoupled by hand.

During World War II the east curve at Barnstaple GWR was taken out of use, and all trains reversed in the terminus. As far as the author can recall, most of the locomotives ran round in both directions, so were usually operating tender first over the link line with the Southern. Great Western locomotives nevertheless continued to work trains to Ilfracombe to maintain route knowledge, but there were not any normal through passenger trains. After nationalisation Barnstaple GWR became Victoria Road station, but was closed in 1960, all trains running straight through to and from the Junction via the east curve for the line's last six years.

Minehead and the other resorts served by the West Somerset line became extremely busy during the period between the two world wars, and the railway facilities and services were increased to match. While the number of trains on the North Devon line virtually remained the same between 1922 and 1939, those to and from Minehead increased from seven to ten, plus one up and two down ones on Fridays only. The 9.0 a.m. through train from Paddington got to Minehead a whole hour earlier than the 9.15 had done in 1922, so there had been a saving of no less than forty-five minutes *en route*. On the branch itself the overall time came down from seventy-five to sixty minutes for trains making all nine intermediate stops (including the one at Norton Fitzwarren just on the Taunton side of the junction), while the one limited-stop train a day in each direction managed it in fifty-five minutes.

The study of the GWR's West of England services is now nearly complete, but we must conclude with a survey of the trains between Paddington and Bristol, which was Brunel's original route, although the following tables also include those that ran via Badminton and also the 2.45 from Paddington that made its way to Bristol by way of Devizes. As most of the trains also served Bath, I have included the arrival times in that city too, a pair of which were by slip coach in 1922.

It will be seen from Table 3.14, shown overleaf on page 74, that the fastest trains of the day were the 11.15 a.m. and 1.0 p.m., which got to Bristol in the even two hours, non-stop, while passengers in the slip coaches for Bath had arrived a quarter of an hour earlier in each case.

Table 3.14. London–Bristol Services in 1922

		a.m.	a.m.	a.m.	a.m.	p.m.	p.m.	p.m.
Paddington	Dep.	5.30	7.30	9.0	11.15	1.0	1.10	2.45†
Bath	Arr.	8.5	9.53	10.39	1.0s	2.45s	3.52	5.27
Bristol Temple Meads	Arr.	8.27	10.15	12.2	1.15	3.0	4.15	5.49
		p.m.	p.m.	p.m.	p.m.	p.m.	ngt	
Paddington	Dep.	4.15	5.0	5.15	6.30	10.0	12.0	
Bath	Arr.	6.14	7.1	8.4	8.27	12.35	2.47	
Bristol Temple Meads	Arr.	6.35	7.35*	8.26	8.52	12.57	3.15	

* Stapleton Road station. s By Slip Coach. † Via Devizes.

The 6.30 p.m. Bath and Bristol Express also did not make any intermediate stops before Bath, although it did drop slip portions at Reading and Chippenham. Even so it managed to take twelve minutes longer to Bath than the other non-stops, and twenty-two minutes more to Bristol. The 5.0 p.m. train was a South Wales Express that followed the pre-1903 route to the Severn Tunnel, turning right at Feeder Bridge Junction, half-a-mile outside Bristol Temple Meads, to ascend Filton Bank after calling at Stapleton Road. Another interesting feature was the fact that the 7.30, 9.0 and 1.10 from Paddington all stopped at Ealing Broadway, to pick up only.

Turning now to 1939, the services were as shown in Table 3.15.

Table 3.15. London–Bristol Services in 1939

		a.m.	a.m.	a.m.	a.m.	a.m.	p.m.	p.m.	p.m.
Paddington	Dep.	5.30	7.30	8.55	10.0	11.15	1.15	1.18	2.45†
Bath	Arr.	8.7	9.48	–	–	12.57	2.57	3.54	5.28
Bristol Temple Meads	Arr.	8.30	10.7	11.19	11.45	1.15	3.15	4.15	5.53
		p.m.	p.m.	p.m.	p.m.	p.m.	p.m.	ngt	
Paddington	Dep.	4.15	5.5	5.15	6.30	7.55	9.50	12.0	
Bath	Arr.	6.20	6.48	8.2	8.28	–	12.33	2.47	
Bristol Temple Meads	Arr.	6.39	7.5	8.22	8.49	10.17	12.55	3.15	

† Via Devizes

Compared with 1922 there are two extra trains to Bristol, which were effectively the 10.0 a.m. and 7.55 p.m. departures from Paddington, but I have excluded the 9.15 a.m. from Paddington via Bath. This was because it was overtaken by the 'Bristolian', a new high-speed service which was introduced as part of the GWR's centenary celebrations in 1935, and described in the next chapter. The 7.55 p.m. was a South Wales express which slipped a portion for Bristol. It also called at Stapleton Road on its way down Filton Bank, and then continued to Taunton, stopping at most intermediate stations. The 8.55 a.m. was similar, but only ran as far west as Weston-super-Mare. Bath, on the other hand had one train less compared with 1922, but the 11.15 and 1.15 trains stopped there instead of dropping a slip portion, and were three minutes faster. The overall two hour timings to Bristol were maintained, in spite of the extra stop. The 5.5 also made Bristol in two hours with just the one stop at Bath, which was an appreciable improvement over the schedule of the 5.0 in 1922.

Finally we must spare a paragraph for the 2.45 p.m. from Paddington, which throughout followed its own unique route to Bristol via Newbury, Devizes and Bradford-on-Avon, stopping also at Hungerford, Savernake and Holt Junction, as well as Freshford '... to set down from Devizes or beyond on informing guard at Devizes'. The working survived World War II, and the author travelled on it in 1949, when there were ten coaches to Newbury and four thereafter. No. 5937 *Stamford Hall* managed a maximum of 74 mph at Manningford Halt and another of 73 mph through Woodborough before we slowed to diverge to the right at Patney & Chirton, and continue over the rest of the old Berks & Hants Extension. Back on Brunel's original main line we even maintained the tradition, referred to in the 1939 timetable, of calling at Oldfield Park 'three minutes after leaving Bath'. It is worth pointing out that, in spite of the unusual route followed by the 2.45 from Paddington, it only took three hours overall to reach Bristol, and there were several other trains via Swindon which did little or no better, including that relic from the days of the Broad Gauge, the 5.30 a.m. from Paddington, in spite of the fact that it managed to appear in a remarkable number of different timetables, including the one to Birmingham and the North.

LONDON AND THE BERKS AND HANTS AND WEYMOUTH LINES

The Berks & Hants Railway only ran as far as Hungerford, the portion west of there being the Berks & Hants Extension, although the earlier railway also built the line from Southcote Junction to Basingstoke. In the following analysis, therefore, consideration is taken of only those through trains that ran for an appreciable distance beyond Hungerford, and, as will be seen from Table 3.16, there were remarkably few of these. This is in spite of the timetables concerned occupying four and five pages of *Bradshaw* respectively in 1922 and 1939.

Table 3.16. Through Trains over Berks & Hants Line

Departure from Paddington	Departure from Reading	Destination
1922		
a.m.	*a.m.*	
–	8.25	Westbury via Devizes
9.15		Minehead, Ilfracombe, Exeter and Torbay Express
10.15		Channel Islands Express
10.30		'Cornish Riviera Express', including slip for Weymouth
11.0		Exeter, Plymouth, Newquay and Penzance Express
–	11.42	Trowbridge
noon		
12.0		'Torbay Express'
p.m.		
12.50		Minehead and Ilfracombe Express
1.18		Weymouth
2.0		South Devon and Cornwall Express, including slip for Weymouth
2.45		Bristol via Devizes
5.5		Weymouth
5.55		Trowbridge and through carriage to Southampton via Newbury
6.12		Westbury
1939		
a.m.	*a.m.*	
8.30		London and Channel Islands Boat Express
–	8.22	Bristol via Devizes
9.0		London to Exeter, Torquay and Paignton Express (also Ilfracombe and Minehead)
10.30		'Cornish Riviera Limited', including slip for Weymouth
11.00		London to Taunton, Exeter, Plymouth and Penzance Express
	11.50	Trowbridge
noon		
12.00		'Torbay Express'
p.m.		
12.5 FO		London to Minehead and Ilfracombe Express
12.30		Weymouth
1.40		London to Exeter, Plymouth and Penzance Express
2.45		Bristol via Devizes
3.30		London to Weymouth, Exeter, Plymouth and Penzance Express
6.0		Weymouth
7.15 FO		London to Exeter, Torquay and Paignton Express
11.0 FO		London to Plymouth and Penzance Express

However, the Great Western laid them out so that all the cross-connections between Thingley Junction, Westbury and Bathampton appeared in that table, even for trains that ran via Bristol, including the 5.30 a.m. Paddington–Penzance.

It will be seen that in both years there were two morning trains that originated at Reading and ran through to Devizes in the first instance, although their subsequent routing changed. They were supplemented by the 2.45 p.m. from Paddington to Bristol, referred to earlier, and, in 1922, by the 5.55 p.m., which conveyed a through carriage for Southampton. This was detached at Newbury to continue over the Didcot, Newbury & Southampton line. Weymouth had three trains from Paddington in both years, one of them being the Channel Islands Boat Train. Additionally there were two slip-coach workings off West of England expresses in 1922 but just one in 1939. Although one thinks of the Berks & Hants route as carrying a stream of expresses for the West of England, this was not the case on ordinary week-days, there being just seven down passenger-carrying trains a day in each of the years under study. However, no less than twelve extra down expresses were shown in the public timetables as running on Saturdays only in the summer of 1939. There were additionally local services over the Berks & Hants, and in 1939 fifteen down trains of this sort ran between Reading and Newbury.

It is remarkably interesting to compare these services in 1939 with those over the same stretch in the summer of 1988, almost half a century later. In spite of Weymouth being served by an hourly service of electric trains from Waterloo, there were eleven down InterCity workings (plus three more on Fridays only), of which all but two were HSTs. In addition, no less than twenty-two 'local' trains ran in the down direction between Reading and Newbury, giving a total of thirty-three in twenty-four hours. Much of this business has been generated in fairly recent years, as was pointed out in an article by the railway photographer David Canning. Writing in *The Railway World*, he referred to the way in which the number of trains passing his crossing box on the Berks & Hants had increased. When he joined BR in 1968 he had to deal with about twenty-five trains in an eight hour shift, but now it is usual to handle up to sixty on the morning and afternoon turns, with half this number on 'nights'. These movements include freight trains, particularly those conveying stone from the Somerset quarries, some of which weigh well over 2000 tons.

LONDON, SWINDON AND SOUTH WALES

Next in the GWR timetables came the services to South Wales. Table 3.17 opposite lists the expresses as they were in 1922 and 1939. Unlike the West of England, where there had to be different services to many of the resorts, the three most important centres in South Wales could all be served by the same train. The table therefore includes the arrival times at Newport, Cardiff and Swansea, and provides an indication of the ultimate destination in West Wales of those trains that continued beyond Swansea. As mentioned in Chapter two, the arrangements at Swansea altered considerably between 1922 and 1939, with trains reversing there, rather than the city being served by connections to and from Landore.

It will be seen that the total number of trains increased by one between 1922 and 1939, but, uniquely among the routes out of Paddington, the 1924 'clock-face' departure principle had been adopted completely with all the day-time trains. The only one out of step was the overnight sleeping-car train at 9.25 p.m., Although the 8.0 p.m. in 1922 and the 7.55 in 1939 also conveyed sleepers for Fishguard harbour, they provided a 'daytime' service as far as Swansea. As we have seen earlier, the accelerations on the services to the West of England were patchy over the seventeen years under study, but there was a much more consistent

Table 3.17. London–South Wales Services

1922		a.m.	a.m.	a.m.	p.m.	p.m.	p.m.	p.m.	p.m.
Paddington	Dep.	8.45	11.50	1.10	3.35	5.0	6.0	8.0	9.15
Newport	Arr.	11.17	2.27	4.13	6.8	8.8*	8.44	10.33	1.58
Cardiff	Arr.	11.40	2.49	4.35	6.30	8.29*	9.5	10.53	2.28
Swansea	Arr.	1.5	4.30	5.50	7.55	9.50*	10.10	12.10	4.25
Final Destination†		FH	N			FH		FH	N

*Via Bath. † FH = Fishguard Harbour, N = Neyland

1939		a.m.	a.m.	p.m.	p.m.	p.m.	p.m.	p.m.	p.m.
Paddington	Dep.	8.55	11.55	1.55	3.55	5.55	6.55	7.55	9.25
Newport	Arr.	11.23	2.16	4.33	6.16	8.37	9.12	10.27	1.48
Cardiff	Arr.	11.43	2.36	4.53	6.36	8.57	9.32	10.47	2.84
Swansea	Arr.	12.52	3.52	6.10	7.52	10.12	10.40	11.55	3.48
Final Destination†		PD/FH	PD/MH	N	C		FH	FH	N

† C = Carmarthen, FH = Fishguard Harbour, MH = Milford Haven, N = Neyland, PD = Pembroke Dock

trend with those to South Wales. Neglecting the 5.0 p.m. from Paddington in 1922, which ran via Bristol, the overall position changed as follows:

			Average timing			Fastest timing	
Paddington to			1922	1939		1922	1939
		h.	m.	h.	m.	h.	m.	h.	m.
Newport		2	40	2	28	2	32	2	17
Cardiff		3	02	2	48	2	53	2	37
Swansea		4	22	4	01	4	10	3	45

These figures show that the average times to Newport, Cardiff and Swansea improved by twelve, fourteen and twenty-one minutes respectively, but the fastest train of the day achieved a better-than-average acceleration to each of these centres.

In 1922 the fastest schedule to Newport was that of the 8.45 a.m. from Paddington, but the best bookings to Cardiff and Swansea were with the 8.0 p.m. train. Both made just the one intermediate stop, at Reading, but the evening express did not convey local passengers between Newport and Cardiff, which enabled the station time at the former to be cut from six to four minutes and a further minute was saved on the continuation to Cardiff. The connection into Swansea from Landore was much better in the evening than it had been off the 8.45 a.m.

In 1939 the fastest times to all the three places were achieved by the one train, the 6.55 p.m. from Paddington, which ran non-stop to Newport. It was five minutes faster than the 11.55 and 3.55 services, both normally making no intermediate stop, although the second would call on request at Badminton, the *Bradshaw* entry reading 'Sets down at 5.39 aft. 1st class Passengers from London on informing Guard at London'. The class distinction will be noted, and one is left wondering where else, other than London, the passengers might have joined the non-stop train! Between Cardiff and Swansea, the 8.55 a.m. called at Port Talbot, while the 11.55 a.m. and 3.55 p.m. stopped at Bridgend and Neath as well. This was why the 6.55 p.m., non-stop over this stretch, was able to make such a fast time to Swansea. In the case of the 6.55 p.m., the 139-mile non-stop run to Newport was covered at an average of 58.4 mph, which was good going for a 'Castle' with a heavy train.

Before we leave South Wales we should take note of one cross-country service that travelled over part of this route. In recent years the Portsmouth–Cardiff trains have attracted the attention of railway enthusiasts because of the use of the Class 33 Bo-Bos, whose diagrams also included Cardiff–Crewe turns, which thus brought Southern Region locomotives into the very heart-land of the London Midland. From the summer of 1988 these all became part of the Provincial Sector's 'Express' network using the Class 155 'Super Sprinters', and operated hourly between Portsmouth and Cardiff, reversing in Temple Meads at Bristol. The service is of considerable antiquity, however, and even in 1922 there were three through services from Portsmouth to Cardiff, one of which also included a portion from Brighton, complete with 'Luncheon and Tea Car'. These all took the east-to-north curve between Feeder Bridge and Dr. Day's Bridge Junctions at Bristol, to miss Temple Meads, although they did call at Stapleton Road. Additionally there were three more trains from the south coast that only ran as far north as Bristol, one of them continuing to Bridgwater. The restaurant-car train was the fastest overall, taking four and three-quarter hours from Portsmouth & Southsea to Cardiff.

In 1939 the Portsmouth–Bridgwater service had disappeared, but the others ran in much the same pattern. The first two made the overall journey in no more than four hours twenty-one minutes. All three made quite good connections at Bath with trains from Paddington, which thus gave passengers another way of getting from London to South Wales. As would be expected, they were appreciably slower, and did not fill any otherwise empty gaps, only the 6.30 p.m. from Paddington having the advantage of an intermediate stop, at Chippenham, to pick up passengers *en route*.

LONDON AND BANBURY, BIRMINGHAM AND THE NORTH

The tables showing the Great Western's service to Birmingham and the North were split between two sheets, the first covering as far as Birmingham itself, while the continuation to Chester followed next in the timetable, with the services over the Joint Line from the last-named place to Birkenhead being on a third. The London–Birmingham stretch combined the direct route with that via Oxford, although only the Didcot–Aynho section was covered in detail. As in the South Wales case, the principal destinations in the West Midlands and further north were usually served by the same expresses, these are all combined in Table 3.18 (shown opposite). There is one difference, however, between the South Wales and West Midlands services, and that concerns the trains travelling via Oxford. Unlike those to South Wales that ran via Bath, or made connections there, several of these at the two ends of the day provided worthwhile ways of getting from London to the Black Country, and these are shown with an asterisk in the table. Oxford itself is not included, and will appear in the next section, as it was also served throughout the day by trains on the Evesham line.

In 1922, in addition to the 12.15 a.m., which spent six and a half hours pottering its way via Oxford to Chester through the night, there were just the two daytime trains by the old route, leaving Paddington at 6.30 a.m. and 7.30 p.m. The latter was only twenty minutes later than the last train via Bicester, which got to Birmingham one hour and twenty minutes earlier, so would not have been used, except as a last resort, by those travelling to Birmingham. The 7.10 from Paddington was the last of the five two-hour Birmingham expresses, while the other two over the direct line were only five minutes slower. Intermediate stops at Leamington Spa only were made by the fastest trains, whereas the 9.10 also stopped at High Wycombe, and then, like the 6.10 p.m., slipped a portion at Banbury. The 9.10 a.m. followed a very different pattern, being routed over the Greenford Loop so it could call at Ealing Broadway. It had the through carriages for Aberystwyth and Pwllheli, and ran non-stop from Ealing Broadway to Birmingham Snow Hill. For the eight trains over the direct line, there were only two running times to Birmingham–two hours and two hours five minutes–and there was a similar consistency between London and the other main centres.

Table 3.18. London–Birmingham and the North Services

1922		a.m.	a.m.	a.m.	a.m.	p.m.	p.m.
Paddington	Dep.	6.30	9.10	10.15	10.40	12.50	2.20
Birmingham	Arr.	10.28*	11.15	12.20	12.40	2.50	4.20
Wolverhampton	Arr.	10.55*	11.39	12.44	1.9	3.25	4.45
Shrewsbury	Arr.		12.22		1.53		5.33
Chester	Arr.		1.32		3.10		6.50
Birkenhead	Arr.		2.5		3.50		
Final Destination†			P	A/P	A/P		A/P

		p.m.	p.m.	p.m.	p.m.	not	
Paddington	Dep.	4.0	6.10	7.10	7.30	12.16	
Birmingham	Arr.	6.0	8.10	9.10	10.30*	4.1*	
Wolverhampton	Arr.	6.24	8.34	9.45	11.10*	4.32*	
Shrewsbury	Arr.	7.20	9.22	10.45		5.22*	
Chester	Arr.	8.35	10.32			6.45*	
Birkenhead	Arr.	9.15	11.10				

* Via Oxford.   † A = Aberystwyth, P = Pwlhelli
The final destination entries include through coaches

1939		a.m.	a.m.	a.m.	a.m.	a.m.	p.m.
Paddington	Dep.	7.10	9.10	8.40	9.45	11.5	2.10
Birmingham	Arr.	10.26*	11.10	11.46*	12.40*	1.10	4.10
Wolverhampton	Arr.	10.51*	11.35			1.35	4.35
Shrewsbury	Arr.		12.19			2.15	5.21
Chester	Arr.		1.29			3.26	6.41
Birkenhead	Arr.		1.57			4.0	7.20
Final Destination†						A/P	A

		p.m.	p.m.	p.m.	p.m.	ngt	ngt
Paddington	Dep.	4.05	6.10	7.10	7.40	12.10	1.30
Birmingham	Arr.	6.10	8.10	9.10	10.40*	3.50*	4.0
Wolverhampton	Arr.	6.35	8.35	9.43	11.16*		4.32
Shrewsbury	Arr.	7.21	9.24	10.48			5.23
Chester	Arr.	8.34	10.37				6.54
Birkenhead	Arr.	9.10	11.15				

* Via Oxford.   † A = Aberystwyth, P = Pwllheli
The final destination entries include through coaches

Two of the Wolverhampton services got there in two hours twenty-four minutes, one in two hours twenty-five, three in two hours twenty-nine and the remaining pair took six minutes longer still. Four of the seven Shrewsbury arrivals were in three hours twelve or three hours thirteen minutes from Paddington.

Mention must also be made of various cross-country trains that slotted in between the trains from London north of Aynho Junction to fill some of the gaps at the northern end of the route. In 1922, for instance, there were the following trains that continued north of Birmingham, with several others that terminated there, and had called at the major stations along the line from Reading:

Train	Birmingham	Arrival time at Wolverhampton	Birkenhead
	p.m.	p.m.	p.m.
8.22 a.m. Portsmouth & Southsea	1.9	1.37	4.50
9.45 a.m. Bournemouth West	2.24	2.47	5.27
9.45 a.m. Dover Marine	3.13	3.37	6.20

The Bournemouth train included a portion for Manchester London Road, which was detached at Wolverhampton, and left seven minutes ahead of the Birkenhead section to travel via Market Drayton to Crewe.

Turning to 1939 there was one extra train between London and Birmingham, but there were two less travelling over the Birmingham Direct. There had clearly been some quite major changes in the pattern, the 8.40 a.m. via Oxford, for example, having a restaurant car. The 12.50 p.m. from Paddington via Bicester had disappeared, but the two expresses either side of it had closed in by thirty-five minutes, which meant that the mid-day gap in the Birmingham departures was only three hours five minutes, although this was appreciably longer than the one of two hours ten minutes between the 11.40 and 12.50 trains in 1922. Another new train was the 1.30 a.m. for Birkenhead, which, in spite of taking two and a half hours to Birmingham, only required five hours twenty-four minutes overall. This compares with the four hours forty-seven minutes to five hours ten minutes scheduled for the other through trains to the Mersey. This service was shown as connecting with the Isle of Man boat [sic], as did the 9.10 a.m., the 11.5 a.m., and the 6.10 p.m. departures from Paddington, while the 4.5 p.m. was similarly shown as making a connection with the ship for Belfast, due to arrive in Northern Ireland 'at about 7.30' the following morning. The 7.10 a.m. from Paddington connected at Wolverhampton with a train from Worcester which ran through to Crewe via Market Drayton, as did the Manchester section off the train from Bournemouth, which was now combined with one from Portsmouth, except on Saturdays.

Of the six fastest trains between London and Birmingham, only four were scheduled to cover the distance in the level two hours, while the other pair took five minutes longer, but there did not appear to be any clear-cut reason for this in the timetables. The 9.10 a.m. ran non-stop in the two hours, slipping portions at Banbury as well as Leamington Spa. The next train–the 11.5 a.m.–stopped at Leamington, and required an extra five minutes, as did the 4.5 p.m., although the 6.10 and 7.10 p.m. both happily included a stop there in their two-hour bookings. The 2.10 and 7.10 trains each had a Banbury slip, so that town was only missed out by the 11.5 a.m. and 4.5 p.m. trains. It is worth noting that even though the LMS ran some of their expresses to Birmingham in one hour fifty-five minutes, the best overall time to Wolverhampton was by the GWR.

The last direct train from Paddington to Birmingham was still at 7.10, although there was the later one via Oxford, now leaving at 7.40 p.m. It is remarkable that the Great Western scheduled no later trains to this important business centre, only two hours away from the capital. The LMS were no better, with their last train at 7.5 p.m. in 1939, although nowadays the London Midland electric InterCity service out of Euston continues until 23 40. Until 20 40 they run every thirty minutes, but there are still three more that depart at hourly intervals after that. Even with these direct services, one can still leave Paddington at 20 45, change at Reading into the Poole–Edinburgh sleeping-car train and reach Birmingham New Street at 23 44, indicating how much some travel patterns have changed in the last half-century.

LONDON AND THE WEST MIDLAND LINE

Turning to the last of the radial routes operated by the Great Western Railway out of Paddington, this ran through Oxford and the Cotswolds to the Vale of Evesham and the Malvern Hills. As before, it is possible to list the through services for 1922 and 1939 in Tables 3.19 and 3.20 respectively, and those trains that just served Oxford, whether they terminated there or ran through to Banbury and Birmingham are included.

In 1922 there were seven expresses for Worcester or beyond, the fastest being the 1.30 from Paddington which ran non-stop over the 120^1/$_2$ miles in 130 minutes, but dropped a slip coach

Table 3.19. London–Oxford–West Midlands Services in 1922

		a.m.	a.m.	p.m.	p.m.	p.m.
Paddington	Dep.	8.45	9.45	12.10	1.30	1.35
Oxford	Arr.	10.17	11.8	1.58		2.57
Evesham	Arr.	11.21	12.24			4.9
Worcester (Shrub Hill)	Arr.	11.39	12.43		3.40	4.32
Final Destination†		M			H/W	S

		p.m.	p.m.	p.m.	p.m.	
Paddington	Dep.	4.45	6.5	6.55	7.30	
Oxford	Arr.	5.55	7.23	8.28	8.47	
Evesham	Arr.		8.27	10.13		
Worcester (Shrub Hill)	Arr.	7.7	8.45	10.42		
Final Destination†		H/S	M	M*	B	

*Thursdays, Fridays and Saturdays only
† B = Birmingham, H = Hereford, M = Malvern, S = Stourbridge Junction, W = Wolverhampton (via Kidderminster)

for Kingham at 3.2. This was then worked to Cheltenham St. James' via Bourton-on-the-Water, making stops or conditional stops at all the intermediate stations. There were water troughs between Charlbury and Ascott-under-Wychwood, which made such a regular non-stop run feasible, although these installations also contributed to the overall speeds of trains that stopped at Oxford, as they eliminated or reduced the need to take water there, thus reducing the standing time. The 12.10 from Paddington terminated at Oxford after making a number of stops in the lower Thames Valley, but ran non-stop after Reading.

The 7.30 p.m. is the Wolverhampton train that has already appeared in the Birmingham and the North section of this chapter (Table 3.18), and the final destination is shown in this table as Birmingham rather than Wolverhampton. This is to avoid confusion with the 1.30 express that continued from Worcester to Wolverhampton via Kidderminster and Stour-bridge Junction. The other two trains that ran in this direction both terminated at the last-named point, rather than continuing over the final twelve miles to Wolverhampton. The 4.45 p.m. from Paddington ran non-stop over the sixty-three and a half miles to Oxford in sixty-five minutes, and, after a five-minute halt, then covered the fifty-seven and a quarter miles to Worcester in sixty-seven minutes. This made it twelve minutes slower overall than the non-stop 1.30 train. The next-fastest was the 6.5 p.m., which took two hours forty minutes overall, and called additionally at Reading, Kingham, Moreton-in-Marsh and Evesham.

Table 3.20, listing the corresponding details for 1939, contains a lot more services than the 1922 one, but the increase is explained by the extra trains for Oxford, four of which

Table 3.20. London–Oxford–West Midlands Services in 1939

		a.m.	a.m.	a.m.	a.m.	a.m.	p.m.	p.m.
Paddington	Dep.	7.10	8.40	9.45	10.15	11.15	12.15	12.45
Oxford	Arr.	8.44	10.9	11.7	11.20	12.38	2.2	
Evesham	Arr.				12.22			
Worcester (Shrub Hill)	Arr.				12.38			2.55
Final Destination†		B	B	B	H			M/S

		p.m.	p.m.	p.m.	p.m.	p.m.	p.m.	
Paddington	Dep.	1.45	4.45	6.5	6.58	7.40	11.0	
Oxford	Arr.	3.6	5.5	7.25	8.30	9.2	12.30	
Evesham	Arr.	4.13	6.50	8.30		10.37		
Worcester (Shrub Hill)	Arr.	4.37	7.6	8.50		10.58		
Final Destination†		M/S	H/S	M		B		

† B = Birmingham, H = Hereford, M = Malvern, S = Stourbridge Junction

terminated there, as distinct from one in 1922. There were also three that continued northwards via Banbury, and, to maintain the convention adopted for Table 3.19, their final destinations are similarly identified as Birmingham, although none of the through trains via Worcester was shown as running beyond Stourbridge Junction in 1939. In spite of this, the stock was nevertheless probably used for the next local service to Wolverhampton.

As a result of these changes, there was one less through train to Worcester, the equivalent of the 8.45 having disappeared. The first train was now the 10.15, which left half an hour later than the second one had been due out of Paddington in 1922. The crack train of the day however came forward by three-quarters of an hour, and now left at 12.45. In spite of stopping at Kingham rather than dropping a slip portion, it still made Worcester in the same time of two hours ten minutes. It now took ninety-one minutes for the eighty-four and three quarter miles, giving start-to-stop averages either side of Kingham that were both very close to the 56 mph mark. That was an impressive performance over the second leg of only thirty-five and three quarter miles, but the 'Castle' would have had the benefit of being able to romp down Honeybourne Bank, and it was with one such train that had called at Kingham that No. 4086 *Builth Castle* reached an undisputed 100 mph in 1939, as timed by that expert recorder, R. E. Charlewood. In the opposite direction, the up morning train from Kidderminster and Hereford that left Worcester at 8.55 a.m. was scheduled to make two separate runs at more than 60 mph, which was unique in this country when it was introduced five years earlier. The first dash was the twenty-eight minute booking between Moreton-in-Marsh and Oxford, and, after a seven-minute station stop there, it was allowed just an hour for the continuation to Paddington. This gave averages of 60.6 and 63.5 mph respectively.

CROSS-COUNTRY SERVICES

The last section of the Great Western's timetables dealing with their main lines covered the cross-country services from Bristol to the north and north-east, and these have already been touched on quite a lot already. It is not therefore proposed to examine them in any great detail at this point, but it is worth taking a brief look at them in summary form, and also included are some of the other notable cross-country services that cropped up in so many of the Great Western's timetables.

On the North-to-West route from Shrewsbury via Hereford to the West of England, there were six southbound trains every week-day in 1922. All except one of these were timed to take sixty-seven minutes over the fifty and three-quarter miles to Hereford, while the best time for the 120½-mile journey to Bristol was exactly three hours, although the more usual time was six or seven minutes longer. By 1939 the number of through services on ordinary week-days had decreased by one, but there were no less than thirteen on a Saturday, plus another four that went to Cardiff. There had been a significant acceleration too, with two minutes being cut off the standard Shrewsbury–Hereford time, while the fastest train now got to Bristol in three hours dead on ordinary week-days. Somewhat unusually the Saturdays-only workings were, on the whole, appreciably faster, with the best getting to Bristol in two hours forty-eight minutes from Shrewsbury. Many of these services were able to cut out the stop at Pontypool Road, and some ran through Hereford without stopping as well.

Turning now to look at the Birmingham–West of England route via Stratford-on-Avon and Cheltenham, in 1922 there were five through southbound trains a day, with a fifth between Birmingham and Swansea. They all called at Stratford for two to five minutes on their way to the stop at Malvern Road station in Cheltenham at the south end of the Great Western's 1906 line. Overall times between Birmingham and Bristol varied between two hours ten minutes and two hours twenty-two minutes. By 1939 the number of Birmingham–Bristol trains on ordinary week-days had fallen to four, while the one to Swansea now called additionally at Hall Green and Henley-in-Arden *en route* to Stratford-on-Avon. However, as with other West of England services, there had been an explosion of Saturdays-only trains, in this case amounting to another six southbound ones. Many of these did not call at Temple Meads station in Bristol, and probably missed it altogether by taking the avoiding line via St. Philip's Marsh, where locomotives were sometimes changed on the running lines outside the sheds. The additional Saturdays-only mid-day departure from Birmingham left from Moor Street, rather than Snow Hill, which also indicated how busy the main-line station in that city was on summer Saturdays.

The most significant change in the services over this route, however, had been the introduction of the streamlined diesel railcars between Birmingham and Cardiff in 1934. After the experimental introduction of the single-motored No. 1 for suburban services earlier that year, three twin-engined cars, equipped with buffets, were built to provide fast business services on this route. Nos 2–4 only had third-class seating, but a supplementary fare was charged for these journeys. In 1939 the two southbound workings left Birmingham at 9.5 a.m. and 3.40 p.m., and ran non-stop to Cheltenham Malvern Road in an hour flat. While this was faster than any steam-hauled train, the best of those managed the distance in one hour nine minutes, including a five minute stop at Stratford. Stops were also made at Gloucester and Newport, and the overall times to Cardiff were two hours twenty-two minutes and two and a half hours. Going north the morning service left Cardiff at 9.10 and was the fastest of the day, getting through in just two hours twenty minutes, while the 4.50 p.m. departure was five minutes slower. The car that had worked out of Cardiff in the morning put in a mid-day round-trip from Birmingham to Stratford-on-Avon, and took thirty-five minutes each way, inclusive of two stops on the North Warwickshire line.

These cars were not multiple-units, so could not be augmented, which meant that with only forty-four seats they could have severe capacity problems. Five years after their introduction it was thus particularly difficult to trace their workings in the public timetables. They did not appear in any table between Cheltenham and Gloucester, nor on the main South Wales one between Newport and Cardiff, all of which was probably a deliberate move to prevent any short-distance passengers using them. They were about half an hour faster than the through steam trains, the 9.20 a.m. Birmingham–Swansea taking two hours fifty-five minutes to Cardiff. It is of interest to note that the first introduction of the Class 155 'Super Sprinters' on BR's Express services took place between Birmingham and Cardiff in 1988. These operate an hourly interval service over a mixed GWR/LMS route, leaving north-westwards from New Street before swinging left beyond Smethwick to pick up the one-time GWR line from Handsworth Junction to Old Hill and Stourbridge Junction. These trains only take two hours eight minutes to Cardiff, in spite of calling at twelve intermediate stations. 'InterCity 125' units running via Lickey and Bristol Parkway require as little as one hour fifty-two minutes between New Street and Cardiff.

The general deficiencies of the timetable presentation between the two world wars have been referred to previously, but the GWR ones covering the Cheltenham area were probably the worst of any, it being particularly difficult to track down the through services to and from Bristol via Gloucester. One cannot help feeling that this was to avoid having to give away the fact that there were also LMS trains that served the same locations! Even in the late 1940s it was extremely difficult to work out how to get from North Devon to a farming camp at Honeybourne on a summer Saturday, and there were significant annual changes in the services, so one had to go over the whole exercise again every year.

A whole book could be written about the ramifications of the summer cross-country workings that operated on the Great Western in pre-war days, but we will conclude our study of their main-line services with the 10.00 a.m. from Treherbert on summer Saturdays in

1939. This train, of third-class stock, was heading for the seaside resort of Aberystwyth, fifty-seven miles away to the north-west on the coast of Cardigan Bay, but nevertheless set off south-eastwards for 11 miles down the Rhondda Valley to Pontypridd. It then turned to run up the Taff, along another of the one-time branches of the Taff Vale Railway, to Merthyr. This was reached at 11.21, after calling at all the stations so far, and although it had now taken eighty-one minutes to cover twenty-three miles, and was still only eight and a half miles from its starting point as the crow flies, it was appreciably further away from its destination. From here to Talyllyn Junction the tracks of what had been the Brecon & Merthyr prior to grouping were followed, before the train switched to the route of the third and last of the pre-1922 companies it was to use, that of the Cambrian.

Things now speeded up, and stops were only made at Builth Wells, Builth Road, Rhayader and Llanidloes before Moat Lane Junction was reached at 2.36. Twenty minutes were spent reversing here, and then the train, having combined with a portion from Manchester London Road, was off along the Cambrian's line to the coast. Stops were made at Machynlleth, Dovey Junction and Borth, and, six hours twenty minutes after leaving Treherbert, the through coaches rolled to a stand at Aberystwyth. The average speed thus works out at just 22 mph for the 142 miles that had been covered, compared with the fifty-seven miles that separated the two ends of the journey on the map. The geography of its Welsh lines had thus forced the Great Western Railway to haul passengers for two and a half times this distance, but in those days, long before the coming of the car-owning democracy, there was evidently a demand for a through service over such a roundabout route at peak holiday times.

Having now completed our general survey of the Great Western's main-line services between the two world wars, we will turn our attention to the examination of a few of them in greater detail, and the next chapter will concentrate on the story of the company's named trains.

In November 1926 2.4.2T No. 3614 is seen near Twyford on the Down Relief line with a suburban train. The 31 locomotives of this class were constructed between 1900 and 1903, and were originally fitted with water pick-up scoops that could be used in either direction of running. The parallel boiler provided when this particular locomotive was built had been replaced by a coned one with superheater by the time the photograph was taken. *(M. W. Earley Collection, National Railway Museum, York)*

Before the building of the Westbury Cut-off, 4-6-0 No. 6003 *King George IV* on the down 'Cornish Riviera' leans to the curve beyond the junction with the Salisbury line at the west end of the station.

Full of its own importance, 2-4-0T No. 3582 bustles its single coach away from Strap Lane Halt in May 1935 on an up local working.

Piloting of heavy Great Western trains over the South Devon banks was common-place, but double-heading also occasionally occurred elsewhere. In May 1934, No. 4026 *Japanese Monarch* pilots another 4-6-0, No. 5000 *Launceston Castle*, on a down express for Plymouth at Witham.

4-6-0 No. 5066 *Wardour Castle* restarts a down local from Dawlish station. Note the starting signal on the left, which was one of many on the GWR which were sited on the right-hand side of the line because of the driver's position on that side of the cab.

In its streamlined condition, 4-6-0 No. 6014 *King Henry VII* hauls a short down express for Bristol near Chippenham in March 1935.

Some of the Swindon–Bristol locals were used as running-in turns for locomotives leaving the shops after overhaul. Here can be seen express passenger 4-6-0, No. 6023 *King Edward II* just leaving Bathford Halt.

Outside-framed 'Bulldog' 4-4-0 No. 3396 *Natal Colony* on a Westbury–Bristol slow train near Keynsham.

'Star' class 4-6-0 No. 2942 *Fawley Court* on a lengthy local passenger train for Bristol photographed near Badminton in August 1935. The assorted stock and the reporting number on the front of the first coach would indicate that it was probably an excursion.

2-6-2T No. 5126 on an up local at Flax Bourton.

4-6-0 No. 5040 *Stokesay Castle* blasts its way up the 1 in 100 gradient out of the Severn Tunnel towards Pilning with a London-bound express from South Wales. At slow speeds, the design of GWR valve gears resulted in quite high compressions at the end of the piston stroke, causing the cylinder relief-valves to discharge a characteristic plume of steam from the front end.

4-6-0 No. 2928 *Saint Sebastian* on a up express from Shrewsbury south of Lapworth.

The large-boilered 2-8-0s were used on week-end workings at peak periods. Here No. 4704 is seen with a train from Wolverhampton to Weymouth near Hatton.

At Standish Junction the LMS line to Bristol diverged from the GWR's to Swindon and Paddington, while north of that point the two ran parallel as far as the southern edge of Gloucester. *Above:* 4-6-0 No. 4094 *Dynevor Castle* works a northbound West of England–Wolverhampton train, having crossed over from the LMS or to the GWR's own tracks. The height of the GWR signal beyond the bridge should be compared with the lofty Midland ones. *Below:* No. 4090 *Dorchester Castle* heads southwards along the GWR line with a Cheltenham–Paddington express.

4-6-0 No. 5021 *Whittington Castle* heads a North of England–Plymouth express near Brent Knoll, on the level tracks across the Somerset wetlands. The vehicles seem to be of GWR origin, except for the LMS restaurant car.

Streamlined diesel railcar No. 2 slips quietly through the countryside. This was the first of the three cars, all equipped with buffet facilities, that were introduced for the fast Birmingham–Cardiff services.

Two different workings on the service between Cardiff and Portsmouth seen near Bathampton in the late 1930s: 4-6-0 No. 6804 *Brockington Grange*, at the head of some quite modern Southern Railway stock, heads westwards, while the stock behind 4-6-0 'Star' class No. 2940 *Dorney Court* in March 1936 on this Cardiff–Portsmouth working includes one of the GWR's Dean clerestory coaches.

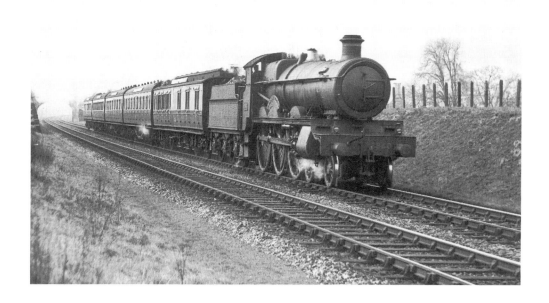

4-6-0 No. 4054 *Princess Charlotte* on a down local train leaves Dawlish Warren in April 1939.

4-6-0 No. 6021 *King Richard II* on an up express from Plymouth on Brewham bank.

4-6-0 No. 5040 *Stokesay Castle* on a down South Wales express near Hullavington.

An up South Wales train near Hullavington worked by 4-6-0 No. 4091 *Dudley Castle*.

4-6-0 No. 4076 *Carmarthen Castle* leaves Westbury with an express for Plymouth in March 1936.

In March 1937, 4-6-0 No. 4057 *Princess Elizabeth* heads a down express for Weston-Super-Mare, near Bathampton.

CHAPTER FOUR

NAMED TRAINS

In the days when stage coaches sped along the turnpike roads and generally-speaking provided the fastest means of travel, the vehicles were named to provide means of public identification. When the Stockton & Darlington Railway was opened in 1825, this tradition moved on to the tracks, as the passenger service for the first eight years was run by private contractors using named horse-drawn carriages between Shildon and Stockton. Because each individual coach was associated with its own scheduled timings, after the building of the trunk lines it was only natural for the fastest trains to acquire names. These were very largely unofficial until the last couple of decades of the nineteenth century, when their promotional use started to be exploited as a marketing tool. Thus the principal West of England Broad-Gauge express became known as the 'Flying Dutchman'. Apart from eighteen months in 1867–69, when it was withdrawn as an economy measure, the down train left Paddington at 11.45 a.m. without a break from 1862 until 1904. It was in the latter year that its ascendancy was eclipsed by the introduction of the 'Cornish Riviera', and, from then on, that train, later to be officially named, became the Great Western's 'flagship', a tradition that still continues eighty-five years later. During the period covered by this book, only a handful of Great Western trains carried names, but, in view of their importance, this chapter is devoted to the study of their story in the years between the two world wars, listed in the order of their introduction.

'CORNISH RIVIERA'

Mention has already been made of the introduction of the accelerated seven-hour Paddington–Penzance service in the summer of 1904. The new train left Paddington at 10.10 a.m., and ran to Plymouth in four hours twenty-seven minutes. This was the longest regular distance to be scheduled non-stop anywhere in the world, and covered the 245.6 miles via Bristol at an average of 55.2 mph. At Plymouth, North Road station was used, rather than the city-centre terminus at Millbay, as a through train to Cornwall could then continue much more easily over the north side of the triangle at the west end of the station. This took place after the usual large-wheeled Dean 4-4-0, or perhaps the de Glehn compound *La France*, had been changed for another 4-coupled locomotive, frequently one of the varieties with 5' 8" inch diameter wheels, for the continuation to Penzance. As the new service was intended primarily for the holiday and tourist market, this influenced its stopping pattern in Cornwall, and it called at Truro, Gwinear Road and St. Erth only. These were all junctions for important branch lines serving the holiday areas around Falmouth, the Lizard (with its pioneering railway bus service from Helston), and St. Ives, respectively, and the limited stopping-pattern of the train was thus tailored to the connections that could be made, rather than being based on the local population served by that particular railhead. (Newquay had not at that time developed into the resort whose holiday-makers were later to out-rank in number those visiting any other town in Cornwall).

The introduction of such a revolutionary new service generated a lot of interest, and *The Railway Magazine* immediately christened it the '3 T.F.', this being an abbreviation for the '3 Towns Flyer', since Plymouth, with the contiguous local authorities of Stonehouse and Devonport, formed what were popularly referred to as the Three Towns. They then arranged that the monthly competition in their July issue should be to find a name for the new train, the prize offered being three guineas (£3.15). In conjunction with the Great Western, it was announced that their General Manager, James Inglis, who had worked as a civil engineer in the Plymouth area for the South Devon Railway as well as in private practice, '. . . has kindly consented to consider the various titles suggested, and the reasons adduced for the choice of such titles, and will award the prize to the person who, in his opinion, has chosen the most suitable title for the new express'.

By the closing date early in August, 1286 entries had been received, plus a further 700 which were sent in error direct to the Great Western, and thus ineligible. After short-listing them, it was found that there were no less than nine which included a reference to 'Riviera', including four that suggested the title 'Cornish Riviera Limited'. However, the two joint winning entries were for 'The Riviera Express', and Messrs Hynam and Shelley, of Hampstead and Hackney respectively, shared the prize. After all this, it is thus somewhat puzzling why the train should have become the 'Cornish Riviera', but, by the time the name had been adopted officially, the Cornish connection was clearly too important a feature to omit, and the train has carried variants of that title to the present day.

It was only really with the coming of main-line electrification that the fastest trains ceased to have their loads limited by the power output of the locomotives, and, as a consequence, prior to that, limited capacity often became synonymous with speed. There was thus a tendency to use the word 'Limited' for titled trains, although such a word can also have disadvantages from a marketing point of view. We thus find that at different times in its career the train under discussion was known as the 'Cornish Riviera Limited' or the 'Cornish Riviera Express', while today it appears in the current BR timetable just as 'Cornish Riviera'. It was, however, always known to the staff simply as 'The Limited' throughout the steam area.

The 'Cornish Riviera' was initially a seasonal service, and, as introduced in the summer of 1904, consisted of six coaches, all of them running the whole way from Paddington to Penzance or vice versa. In its first summer five of the coaches were Dean clerestories, plus the dining car, which was one of the massive 'Dreadnoughts'. When the train reappeared in 1905 it was provided with new stock. This was now all of the 'Dreadnought' type, no less than nine and a half feet wide, and, for the first time with a whole train, electric lighting was used throughout. Another innovation was the abolition of the second-class accommodation. The Midland Railway had started this trend thirty years earlier, and the experiment was obviously a success, as second class as a whole had disappeared from the GWR by World War I, only to make a brief return when some of the absorbed railways brought the practice with them at the time of the grouping in 1922/23. A seat reservation system was also introduced for the first time, which proved increasingly popular, and was to feature on Great Western services long before it became generally adopted elsewhere in this country.

In 1906, the start of the summer services coincided with the opening of the Great Western's new West of England line via Westbury, and this saw the 'Cornish Riviera' being switched to the new route and speeded up. It also became a year-round working, and the down train left Paddington twenty minutes later at 10.30 a.m., which was to become its traditional departure time for the next sixty-six years. With Churchward's more powerful 4-6-0s taking over from his predecessor's double-framed 4-coupled locomotives, it became possible to include slip coaches for Westbury and Exeter, while still only taking four hours ten minutes to Plymouth and six hours forty minutes to Penzance. Although the train was now a regular feature of the GWR timetable, seasonal variations still continued to be made, and, at the start of the following winter, the train added a third slip portion, for Taunton, which also gave a better service for the North Devon and Minehead lines. This practice was also beneficial from the point of view of the operating authorities, since the load of the train was successively reduced as the severity of the gradients increased. As a result, a further three minutes were cut from the time to Plymouth in October 1906, which had stretched to five by the time the train had reached Penzance.

The next change in the train's timing did not take place until 1914, when the schedule beyond Plymouth was cut, enabling the overall journey time to be reduced to six and a half hours, which represented a significant acceleration over the decade since its introduction. Unfortunately this improvement was short-lived, as the wartime restrictions introduced under government control at the beginning of 1917 saw major changes. Its departure time came forward to 10.15 a.m., and, with the withdrawal of slip coaches (and dining cars), stops were made at Westbury, Taunton, Exeter, Newton Abbot, and principal stations to Penzance, which was not reached until 6.0 p.m., seven and three quarters hours after leaving Paddington.

At the end of the hostilities, the Great Western did somewhat better than most of our railways at getting back to pre-war standards of running, and accelerated the 'Riviera' in July 1919, as well as reverting to the traditional 10.30 departure time. A non-stop run was made to Plymouth once more, but took four and a quarter hours for the journey, with slip carriages being dropped off at Taunton and Exeter only. Penzance was reached three hours later. At the beginning of the October timetable that year the train was back to its pre-war schedule, including the three slip portions for Westbury, Taunton and Exeter.

The Great Western were great exponents of slip coaches, but the inclusion of three separate portions in the one train was unique. Each, of course, needed its own guard, and passengers in the slip were unable to get through into the main train to use the dining car. Even after World War II, when returning to Oxford at the beginning of each term, the author remembers changing back into the slip coach for Reading during the Westbury stop of his up West of England express, after having had lunch on the way from Taunton. Although unable to recall it happening, there must have been a particularly thorough ticket check before or during the last booked stop to ensure that no one was left in the wrong portion of the train. With the down 'Riviera' leaving from the open No. 1 Platform at Paddington, it must have required quite a number or staff to ensure that no last-minute passengers for Plymouth or beyond climbed into the rear coach just as the guard was preparing to blow his whistle.

At this time the standard motive power for the 'Cornish Riviera Limited' was one of Churchward's 4-cylinder 'Star' class 4-6-0s, and they had little difficulty with the working. In the autumn of 1921 Cecil J. Allen, then the writer of the monthly 'Locomotive Practice & Performance' article in *The Railway Magazine* which this author now writes, travelled to Penzance and back on the train, by courtesy of Felix Pole. Going down he had a particularly good run behind No. 4003 *Lode Star*, now preserved as part of the National Collection, and on exhibition at the Great Western Railway Museum in Swindon. Leaving Paddington the train weighed 406 tons tare, and this came down successively to 341, 282 and 249 tons as the three slip portions were dropped at Westbury, Taunton and Exeter. These portions comprised two through coaches for Weymouth, one each for Ilfracombe and Minehead, and one for Torquay, respectively. Their start was hampered by fog in the London area, and they departed approximately three minutes late before dropping a further two and a half by Slough. A permanent-way slowing then cost three minutes, so they were eight and a quarter minutes late passing Reading in forty-two minutes fifteen seconds from Paddington. After a maximum of 75 mph down Lavington Bank, Westbury was passed almost nine and a half minutes outside schedule and twelve and a half late, thanks to three more permanent-way slowings.

This represented the nadir of their run, however, and the Old Oak crew – Driver J. Springthorpe and Fireman Belcher – were able to regain all the loss over the remainder of the journey. They attained 82 mph at Bruton, and by the time they slipped the North Devon and North Somerset portions at Taunton were running only six and three quarter minutes late. With a minimum of forty at Whiteball and a maximum of eighty along the Culm Valley, they were only four minutes behind time passing Exeter. A further one and a half minutes were regained by Newton Abbot, and after minima of thirty and thirty-two on Dainton and Rattery Banks, the lateness at Brent was only a minute and a half. Even two signal checks from the London & South Western local train that was booked to run into Plymouth ahead of the express from Lipson Junction to North Road failed to prevent an arrival on time. They took 244 minutes 50 seconds for the 225.7 miles from Paddington, compared with the 247 minutes booked. Allowing for the various checks, the locomotive gained exactly a quarter of an hour on schedule, which was a splendid effort, corresponding to a net average of 58.4 mph.

At Plymouth one of the seven bogies they had hauled over the South Devon Banks was detached before the train continued on into Cornwall behind another 'Star', No. 4025 *King Charles*, later to be renamed *Italian Monarch* when Collet was introducing his 'King' class. Further through coaches were dropped off at Truro (for Falmouth), and at St. Erth (for St. Ives), leaving just four, including the dining car, to roll into Penzance at the end of the journey. With no speed over 60 mph anywhere west of the Tamar, they still managed to gain six minutes net, and the nineteen miles from Par to Truro were covered in twenty-five minutes twenty-five seconds, compared with the twenty-nine minutes allowed. A load of only four to six bogies was, of course, a lightweight one, even for the Cornish switchbacks, and, on Mr Allen's return trip on the 'Cornish Riviera Limited', the train was hauled as far as Truro perfectly satisfactorily by nothing larger than the 2-6-0 No. 5383. A 'Saint', No. 2937 *Clevedon Court* came on there with the Falmouth portion, and ran well to Plymouth. On the round trip through Cornwall the three locomotives, between them, gained no less than thirty-three minutes on schedule.

Finally they had a good return run to Paddington with 'Star' No. 4024 *King James* (later *The Dutch Monarch*), hauling seven bogies to Exeter and nine for the non-stop continuation to Paddington. With Driver Rowe in charge, the terminus was reached just twenty seconds inside the three-hour schedule, in spite of six and three quarter minutes lost through checks of various sorts. From the locomotive point of view the up run was easier with a constant load throughout, there being no way in which slip carriages could be picked up without stopping! The round trip gave an excellent insight into contemporary Great Western performance on the longest non-stop working in the world. C. J. Allen also commented on '. . . the keen interest of all the crew of the train with its welfare; even in the restaurant car the names and merits of all the different drivers were well known, so that to the excellence of the *menus* and the courtesy of the service were added an enthusiasm on the part of the staff that helped make the trip to myself one peculiarly memorable'.

The next step forward with the 'Cornish Riviera' took place in the summer of 1923, when the arrival of a new design of seventy-foot carriages prompted a return to the old chocolate and cream livery that had been discarded for an overall shade of lake in the 1900s. Their appearance was a lot less 'fussy' than had been the case previously, although they still carried a lot of lining-out. In that respect they echoed the locomotives, as at the same time the railway started to re-apply the full pre-war lining out to those used for the express passenger workings. That year also saw the introduction of Collett's 'Castle' 4-6-0s, which gave the Great Western a design that was appreciably more powerful than the best of its previous stud.

It was also perhaps the most attractive-looking of all their passenger locomotives, which was to be further enhanced in due course by the use of the high-sided, 4000-gallon tenders.

From the publicity point of view the Great Western already had the longest non-stop run in the world and the fastest start-to-stop schedule in Britain, but were anxious to capitalise on their latest design, which was cited as the country's most powerful passenger locomotive. Power is the rate of doing work, which is measured in horsepower in this country, but that particular rating is not easily determined in the case of a steam locomotive. It ultimately depends on the rate at which coal can be burnt in the firebox, but that is not the end of the story. Different designs had varying abilities to generate steam by abstracting that heat as it passed through the boiler, while the steam might then be used with more or less efficiency in the cylinders. The journalist always wants a 'one-liner' to catch the readers' interest, so the nominal tractive effort of steam locomotives became the yardstick by which their 'power' was rated in the public press, in spite of the fact that it was a *force*. It represented the maximum pull the locomotive could achieve, but it had the great advantage that it could be calculated from the cylinder dimensions, the driving wheel diameter and the boiler pressure. One of its limitations as a measure of true power can, however, be well indicated by the fact that when Churchward designed the 'Stars' he achieved his target of a locomotive that would be capable of exerting an actual tractive effort of two tons (4480 pounds force) at 70 mph, to do it he had to give it a nominal tractive effort of no less than 25,100 pounds force.

In 1924 the first of the 'Castles', No. 4073 *Caerphilly Castle*, was exhibited alongside the much larger LNER 'Pacific' *Flying Scotsman* at the British Empire Exhibition at Wembley, and, on the strength of its greater nominal tractive effort, the GWR claimed their locomotive as the more powerful. This claim led to Exchange Trials being arranged between the two classes in the following year, which saw a Gresley 'Pacific' at the head of the 'Cornish Riviera'. It managed to work the train to time, but the GWR drivers put on a magnificent show with their own 'Castles' which had taken over the working of this train between Paddington and Plymouth. The two finest recorded trips were achieved by Driver Rowe, who had worked *King James* on C. J. Allen's 1921 up run described earlier. With No. 4074 *Caldicot Castle* he passed Exeter on 2nd May 1925 in 169 minutes 10 seconds from Paddington, virtually ten minutes early, and, in spite of two relaying checks, reached Plymouth a quarter of an hour inside the normal booking. Five days earlier he had run the somewhat easier up train from Exeter to Paddington in a single second over 164 minutes for the 173.4 miles. The honours for the speed side of the 'contest' thus rested with the Great Western, whose drivers undoubtedly had the great advantage of knowing the road better. However, from the coal consumption point of view the smaller 'Castles' were also superior, equally as much on the East Coast Main Line as on the Great Western. As a result, Gresley was persuaded by his staff to make modifications to the valve gear and other details of his 'Pacifics', and this enabled them to realise their full potential, and reduced their fuel consumption. After a quarter of a century, Swindon's locomotive supremacy thus passed to Doncaster, and the LNER was also soon to wrest the non-stop record from the Great Western, running first to Newcastle and then, in 1928, all the way from London to Edinburgh, thanks to the reduced fuel consumption of their locomotives.

The GWR also had to look to its laurels in the 'most powerful' category. The Southern Railway produced its 'Lord Nelson' class in 1926, and their nominal tractive effort out-classed that of the 'Castles', so Collett was given instructions to see how the classic Swindon 4-6-0 could be stretched even further. Utilising the increased weight limits that had resulted from the work carried out by the Chief Engineer's Department over the previous few years – unknown to the other departments – it proved possible to increase the nominal tractive effort of the new design from 31,600 pounds force for the 'Castles' to a figure of no less than 40,300. The new locomotives were known as the 'Kings', after the idea had been toyed with of naming them after cathedrals. They were capable of much greater power outputs, and this was to benefit the GWR very considerably from 1927 onwards.

From our immediate point of view, the arrival of the 'Kings' enabled the Great Western to speed up the 'Cornish Riviera' to reach Plymouth in the level four hours. For the benefit of those who might be worried by the prospect of these higher speeds, the publicity carefully pointed out that the use of the more-powerful locomotives enabled the faster schedules to be maintained without them having to attain such high maxima. To mark the train's Silver Anniversary in 1929, two completely new train-sets were produced for the 'Cornish Riviera Express', and the *Great Western Railway Magazine* provided the very interesting table reproduced here which shows the changes that had taken place in the intervening quarter-century.

Table 4.1.
'CORNISH RIVIERA EXPRESS'
COMPARATIVE DATA – 1904–1929

	1904	1929
LOCOMOTIVE Class	'City'	'King'
No. of Cylinders	2 (18" × 26")	4 (16¼" × 28")
Wheel Arrangement	4-4-0	4-6-0
Tractive Effort (at 85% B.P.)	17,790 lbs	40,300 lbs.
Weight (with tender)	92 tons 1 cwt.	135 tons 14 cwt.
Length do.	56' 4¾"	68' 2"
COACHES Length	54' to 58'	60'
Width (outside)	8' 6¾"	9' 7"
Weight	25 tons	35 tons
No. of coaches on train	7	13
Total weight (behind tender)	182 tons	450 tons
Seating	268	425
Illumination	Gas	Electric
Illumination (natural)	Ordinary window glass	'Vita' glass
Dining Capacity 1st Class	18 ⎫ 50	24 ⎫ 119
3rd Class	32 ⎭	95 ⎭
Heating	Steam pipe	2 radiators per compartment
Roofs	Clerestory	Elliptical (greater air space)
General construction	Wood	Wood framing & steel panelling
Compartments Number	37	57
Length, 1st Class	7' 0"	7' 6"
3rd Class	5' 6"	6' 4½"
Width	5' 9"	6' 8¾"
Corridor doors	Swing	Sliding
TIME OCCUPIED London to Plymouth	4 hrs. 25 mins.	4 hrs.
Penzance	7 hrs	6 hrs. 20 mins.

Source: *Great Western Railway Magazine* (1929).

As is so often the case with statistics quoted by the railways, some of the figures were given a spurious degree of accuracy. Tractive efforts cannot meaningfully be quoted other than to the nearest hundred pounds, and, likewise, a locomotive's length is likely to change by more than a quarter of an inch simply depending on the state of the buffer springs. In the course of the London–Plymouth journey, the amount of coal in the tender would fall by several tons, while the quantity of water in the tender decreased steadily between each lot of troughs, where a new supply of some 2000 gallons, weighing approximately nine tons, was picked up. The inclusion of the odd three-quarters of an inch in the width of the compartments is, however, significant, and it will be seen that the Great Western managed to get the width of the corridor, plus the thickness of the coach sides, down to less than two feet. There is one quite definite error as well, because the 1904 train only consisted of six coaches, as previously mentioned, and authenticated by contemporary photographs.

Particular notice should be taken of the use of the new 'Vita' glass, which transmitted more of the sun's ultra-violet rays than the ordinary type. The accompanying publicity stressed the advantages in these terms:

> An innovation which demonstrates the desire of the Great Western Railway Company to ensure the well-being of its patrons is the glazing of the coaches of the new trains with Vita glass, which admits the health-giving ultra-violet rays from the sun which ordinary window glass excludes.
>
> Sunlight benefits are available in abundance on the sun-drenched beaches of Cornwall and Devon, where so many go year after year for rest and recuperation, and passengers by these new trains will literally commence their sunlight treatment *en route* to the holiday destination.

That was long before today's concern about the adverse effect of too much sun on the human skin, and in 1929 the acquisition of a 'healthy tan' was an important part of the holiday, so the Great Western cleverly cashed in on the new type of glass to publicise its trains. In the light of subsequent technological knowledge, the main change would probably have been to increase the internal temperature of the trains by the 'greenhouse effect'. It has certainly proved economic to provide tinted class in the windows of our more recent InterCity trains to cut down the solar gain, and so reduce the work the air-conditioning units have to do.

The trains' new thirteen-coach formation included just a single slip portion of two coaches for Weymouth. A brake/composite was detached from the rear at Plymouth, and two more similar vehicles for Falmouth and St. Ives were dropped off successively during the stops at Truro and St. Erth. 'Kings' were permitted to take 360 tons unaided over the South Devon Banks, compared with only 315 for a 'Castle' or 'Star', which enabled more of the train to be worked further west. However, because of their great weight, the new 4-6-0s were not allowed across Saltash Bridge, and 'Castles' remained in charge of the train in Cornwall, but, in spite of the greater load west of Plymouth, the train now reached Penzance in the record new time of six hours twenty minutes. The opening of the Westbury and Frome cut-offs in 1933 provided a welcome reduction in running times, even though there was only a very small change in the distance travelled.

Our story of the 'Cornish Riviera' now moves on to 1935, when the Great Western Railway celebrated its Centenary, which was that of its first Act of Parliament rather than the opening. To mark the occasion there were a number of important changes in the train services. As far as the 'Cornish Riviera Limited' was concerned, two new thirteen-coach trains of special 'Centenary Stock' were built, the vehicles having very characteristic recessed doors at each end, mounted at an angle to the main bodyside. Their internal design marked the first use by the Great Western of the compartment arrangements we were to get to know so well with BR Standard stock. The compartments did not have external doors, and large picture windows were provided, in place of the former quarter-lights separated by the drop-light in the door. To begin with the windows could be lowered as a whole for ventilation purposes, but difficulties were caused by the curved bodyside, so sliding ventilators were later substituted. The overall ambience was well received by the travelling public, and similar arrangements were subsequently adopted with other new builds of express stock.

From the operating point of view there was also a big change, with the down train on Mondays to Fridays in the summer being shown as running non-stop to Truro in the public timetable. For those who knew that the 'Kings' were prohibited from crossing Saltash Bridge, it was immediately obvious that there must be a service stop somewhere *en route* to change engines. This took place at Devonport, so the length of GWR's longest daily non-stop run did actually increase, but by little more than a mile. As early as 1923 there had been similar workings on summer Saturdays, but in 1935 the train's first booked Saturday stop was at St. Erth, and the whole train was then worked round to St. Ives, the pair of 45XX 2-6-2 tanks barking their way up the 1 in 60 gradients of the coastal branch with their heavy load. Again there was a stop at Devonport, plus one at Newton Abbot if it was necessary to take a pilot over the South Devon Banks. The up 'Cornish Riviera Limited' was also shown as running non-stop from Truro to Paddington on ordinary week-days, but was no less than twenty-five minutes slower in this direction. With the increasingly limited nature of the 'Cornish Riviera' itself, the second portion gained sufficiently in importance to justify it too acquiring a name, and it was duly christened the 'Cornishman', as described in the section dealing with that particular train.

Until recently this author was under the impression that the 'Limited' retained its 1935 service pattern, like its Centenary stock, unchanged up to the start of World War II in September 1939, and it was only whilst doing the research for this book that it was discovered that this was not the case. Space only permits us to look at some of the changes in its schedules, starting with the summer services in 1936. The down train was now calling at Plymouth again on ordinary weekdays, and then stopped at Par, Truro, Gwinear Road, St. Erth and Penzance, which was reached at 4.55 p.m. On Saturdays the first public stop was at Gwinear Road, rather than St. Erth, and some, at least, of the main train went straight on to Penzance, where its booked arrival time was the same as it was on other days. During the winter of 1937/38, it carried a slip for Taunton, but then called at Exeter before making the rest of the summer stops in Devon and Cornwall, all of which only put an extra five minutes on the overall time to Penzance.

Finally, in the last summer before the war, the public timetable for July showed a somewhat different pattern of calls for the half-past ten group of services out of Paddington. The 'Cornish Riviera Limited' left in its time-honoured slot at 10.30 a.m., but, after calling at Plymouth, made its first passenger stop in Cornwall at Par, where the Newquay portion was detached, the through carriages reaching the resort at 4.40 p.m. By this time the main train, having stopped at Truro to drop the Falmouth portion, was only a minute off making its stop at St. Erth. Here it left the St. Ives portion, the restaurant car continuing with the coaches for Penzance, where the train terminated at 4.55, ten minutes before the St. Ives' coaches finished their journey. On Saturdays the train made its first public stop at Par, taking only five minutes longer to get there compared with an ordinary weekday. It did not convey a Falmouth portion, so cut out the Truro stop, which enabled it to regain its standard timing for the remainder of the journey. The timetable showed three other Saturday-only trains for Cornwall that departed from Paddington between 10.25 and 10.40, but the handling of the summer peaks is not one we have space for in this book.

In the summer of 1939 the up 'Limited' was no longer booked to run non-stop from Truro to Paddington on ordinary weekdays. Leaving Penzance at 10.0, it collected two lots of through coaches – from St. Ives at St. Erth, and Falmouth at Truro. It then called at Par and Plymouth, before running non-stop to Paddington in four hours ten minutes. Overall it took six hours forty minutes from Penzance. On Saturdays it started at the same time, but did not stop at St. Erth, although through carriages from Helston were picked up at Gwinear Road. A twenty-minute stop was made at Plymouth to change engines and pick up passengers, and the booked London arrival was ten minutes later than it was on ordinary weekdays.

So, with the war-clouds on the horizon, we must leave our study of the Great Western's 'flagship' service, but before considering lesser trains, it is worth making a few comparisons with the present day. In early 1989, although the 'InterCity 125' set working the 'Cornish Riviera' leaves Paddington at the somewhat strange time of 10.50, it reaches Exeter in five minutes under two hours, and arrives in Plymouth in just two hours fifty-two minutes from London. After making seven intermediate stops in Cornwall, the set terminates at Penzance at 15.35, which means its overall time is only four and three quarter hours. And lest readers should think that an eight coach HST is much shorter than the steam-hauled 'Riviera' of the late 1930s, it is worth pointing out that, neglecting the dining accommodation, today's train provides nearly fifty seats more than the full thirteen-coach rake of Centenary Stock, of which only ten normally ran as far as Penzance.

'THE PORTS-TO-PORTS EXPRESS'

Before the days of container-ships and super-tankers, it was customary for the crew of a ship to be paid-off immediately after it arrived in a port in its home country. Any subsequent moves necessary within the docks were handled by a skeleton crew of riggers until the ship had acquired a new cargo and was ready to sail once more. For the discharged crew, there could well not be any new berths immediately available in the port concerned, which would necessitate them having to travel to another some distance away. In the middle of the North Yorkshire Moors, half-way between Whitby and Guisborough, is an inn still rejoicing in the name *The Jolly Sailors*. Seamen making their way from Whitby to the Tees, or *vice versa*, to find a new berth were often persuaded to break their journey there and celebrate in appropriate fashion. This explains the rather incongruous name of that particular hostelry, and there are, no doubt, other inns elsewhere in the country with similar origins. By the twentieth century, however, the railways provided a better way for seafarers to travel between ships, and one of the new services put on in the 1900s received the unofficial title of the 'Ports-to-Ports Express'.

This train was introduced in May 1906, and operated in each direction between Newcastle and Barry, serving *en route* the ports on the Tees by means of connections at Darlington. Between here and Sheffield the train followed the East Coast Route to York, before striking off over the North Eastern's and Midland's Swinton & Knottingley Joint Railway (a line which did not actually go to the second of the places mentioned in its title!). At its southern end, this route split at Dearne Junction, with connections being made to both the Midland and Great Central lines into Sheffield. In those days many of the North-East–South-West services, including the 'Ports-to-Ports Express', were routed down the centre of England over the Great Central, and duly took the line from Dearne Junction to Sheffield *Victoria*, where they reversed for the south. After the grouping the LNER developed the scope of this particular train by running a through coach from Hull via Goole to join the main portion here, thus adding a further two to the number of ports served by the train.

The train did not gain Great Western metals until it approached Banbury by the connection off the Great Central at Culworth Junction, used to exchange so much freight traffic between the two railways, each of which had their own extensive yards in the area. To get from Banbury to Cardiff an unusual route was followed, the train swinging right on to the Kingham branch at King's Sutton. This part of the line was also busy with the traffic from the various ironstone mines in the vicinity that were active in those days, while at Chipping Norton the large and conspicuous woollen mill also had its own siding connection with the GWR. The 'Ports-to-Ports Express' was the only regular train to miss calling at Kingham itself, as its journey took it over the Oxford–Evesham line by the bridge on the north side of the triangle there, clear of the main-line platforms. Then came the climb of over 450 feet through the Cotswolds, past Stow-on-the-Wold and Bourton-on-the-Water to the summit at Salperton. Three miles further on was Andoversford, marking the junction with the Midland & South Western Junction Railway, which only made contact with the Midland by utilising running powers over the GWR's steep and twisting tracks for the remainder of the distance into Cheltenham. However, the 'Ports-to-Ports Express' again did not follow the normal route into the Midland's Lansdowne station used by trains off the M & S W Jt, but took the south-to-west curve to continue direct to Gloucester. Cheltenham passengers were served by the call at Cheltenham (South) & Leckhampton, situated before the junction.

From here the train followed the original broad-gauge route to South Wales, switching at Cardiff on to the tracks of the Barry Railway for the concluding few miles of its journey. Subsequently the 'Ports-to-Ports Express' was extended to Swansea, but again followed an unusual route for through trains, as it continued along the Barry's line before rejoining the Great Western once more at Bridgend. In its early days the train consisted of a six-coach set, of North Eastern and Great Western origins on alternate days, complete with restaurant car. With all such workings of GWR stock to the north, care had to be taken to ensure that none of their wider vehicles were used that might foul the less generous loading gauge that existed away from the one-time haunts of the Brunel's 'Great Way West'.

In the summer of 1922 the 'Ports-to-Ports Express' left Newcastle at 9.30 a.m., and only took sixty-five minutes for the forty-six and a half miles from York to Sheffield via the S & K Joint, before reversing in Victoria station between 12.50 and 1.0. While its running on the East Coast Main Line had not been very sparkling, with nothing faster than 48.6 mph for the thirty miles between Northallerton and York, it did better on the Great Central, being booked at an average of fifty-one over the twenty-three and a quarter miles from Nottingham to Leicester. The locomotive change at Banbury took place from 3.26 to 3.31, and the GWR station at Gloucester was reached at 5.4 p.m. This was just sixteen minutes before the through coach for Bristol, that had been dropped off the train at York, was due to roll into the Midland station next door. That had travelled via Sheffield (Midland), Derby and Birmingham, the route used today for our North-East–South-West InterCity services, but the through coach had spent no less than thirty-four minutes in York awaiting the forward connection.

The 'Ports-to-Ports Express' got to Cardiff at 6.40 p.m., and then continued via Penarth on what had been the Taff Vale's coastal route, only joining the Barry Railway's tracks at Cadoxton, two miles before Barry station. Penarth was reached at 7.0, and Barry at 7.19. Today's all-stations diesel multiple units take as little as twenty-four minutes for the direct run from Cardiff to Barry, calling at all six intermediate stations, so the 'Ports-to-Ports Express' was not providing a particularly quick transit between these two Welsh centres. Swansea was reached at 8.45 p.m., eleven and a quarter hours after leaving Newcastle in the morning. The one hour fifty-five minutes required by this train from Cardiff to Swansea should also be compared with the sixty-eight minutes spent between these two cities by the 1.10 p.m. 'South Wales Express' from Paddington earlier in the day. In spite of this far-from-exacting schedule, the train seems to have served a good commercial purpose, as it was running to exactly the same overall times in the summer of 1939, the main difference being the acquisition of the through coach from Hull.

On the northbound direction the train did have its schedule altered between 1922 and 1939, as the run from Swansea to Cardiff was switched to the main line. This enabled the starting time to be put back from 7.30 to 8.15 a.m., but the arrival at Newcastle remained the same at 6.15 p.m. Prior to this change the northbound train had already been the quicker of the two by half an hour, and the rerouting nearly doubled the difference.

In the present BR timetables, thanks to Table 51 and its accompanying route diagram, the progress of the north-east–south-west services can be followed in a way that was not possible in *Bradshaw*. Today's 06.10 'InterCity 125' from Newcastle is into Cardiff well before midday, at 11.24. These units do not work west of here, but a connection into the next HST from Paddington will get the traveller into Swansea at 12.45, which represents a reduction of 41% on the pre-war timing. This should be compared with the 37% reduction in the times of the present-day 'Flying Scotsman's' timing relative to its seven-hour pre-war one between London and Edinburgh. The combination of 'InterCity 125' traction, even when their full speed potential cannot be realised, with route improvements and rationalisations thus gives slightly greater benefits on this cross-country axis than on the East Coast Main Line. Between Newcastle and Cardiff the present-day timing represents only 47% of that of the 'Ports-to-Ports Express' in 1939, and it is now so easy to travel from York to Cardiff and back in a day that, some years ago, the author was able to make a *day-trip* to see the remains of the Pen-y-darren tramroad over which Trevithick had worked his pioneering steam locomotive in 1804.

'TORBAY EXPRESS'

The resorts that ring Tor Bay in South Devon, and now market themselves as 'The English Riviera', have for a long time provided considerable business for the railways, the area having been particularly popular for those able to afford to spend the winter there. In addition, the Royal Naval College at Dartmouth, for so long the means of entry for officers into the Senior Service, situated over the next headland to the south, provided a lot of custom in the days before road transport became widely available. As a result, the Great Western had already given the area a good train service for many years by the beginning of World War I. The 11.45 a.m. for Kingswear then ran non-stop as far as Exeter in three hours, but did drop a slip portion at Taunton, which in the summer was unique in having a restaurant car among its four coaches. Its start was altered to twelve noon just before the war, and this remained the traditional departure time for the down 'Torbay Express' or the 'Torbay Limited', as the train was known at different periods. By 1939 the up train also departed from Torquay at the same time, thus introducing a rare element of symmetry into the schedules of a named train. It retained this un-rushed starting time even after the Great Western's adoption of 'Clock-face' departures in 1924, although for a West of England express the normal time was thirty minutes past the hour.

Like all West of England trains there was always a considerable degree of seasonality with the scheduling of the 'Torbay Express', so much so that the GWR summer timetable in 1923 could refer to the following among the 'principal *new* express trains' (author's italics):

12.0 noon, Torbay express, Paddington to Torquay non-stop (200 miles in 215 minutes). A non-stop train will also run on week-days in the reverse direction.

However, examination of the 1922 timetables shows that the train was running in that form during the previous summer.

By 1939 the schedule of the 'Torbay Express' had been cut to three and a half hours, but this included a five-minute stop at Exeter on ordinary weekdays. This kept it just outside the mile-a-minute mark overall, with an average of 57 mph for the 199½ miles via the Westbury and Frome cut-offs, although its average in the working timetable was as high as 61.6 mph to the Exeter stop. This put it in fourteenth place amongst the twenty-six runs on the GWR that were booked at over 60 mph start-to-stop in the summer of 1938. In the reverse direction the train had the same stopping pattern, but the overall timing on an ordinary weekday was three hours thirty-five minutes. It ran non-stop on a Saturday, but then took no less than three hours fifty minutes to Paddington.

The geography of Torbay made the entrance of the railway into the area somewhat inconvenient for Torquay itself, the town centre being almost equidistant from the stations at Torre and Torquay. The former was shown in the timetable as the station for Babbacombe, situated on the north side of the high ground that runs out to the headland of Hope's Nose. The 'Torbay Express' did not call at Torre, however, but did stop at Paignton and Churston on its way to the terminus at Kingswear, right beside the estuary of the Dart. The connection to Brixham from Churston was booked to leave from the bay, just across the down platform, four minutes after the arrival of the 'Torbay Express', and got to the fishing port seven minutes later, two minutes after the train from London had rolled into Kingswear. The arrival at Dartmouth was at 4.15, after passengers had crossed the river 'By Steamer', which was a slightly grand term for the smallest of the GWR's maritime possessions, the *Mew*, although in the darkest days of the war she did set off in an attempt to play her part in the Dunkirk evacuation.

These days the line from Paignton to Kingswear is operated in the summer by the preserved Torbay & Dartmouth Railway, but is paralleled as far as Goodrington by the BR line leading to the extensive carriage sidings – considerably extended by the Great Western between the wars – situated just inland from the expanse of golden sands. The railway to Kingswear was single beyond Goodrington, and this was probably the only section of single-line track on which the 'Kings' were regularly seen. The steep climbs in both directions to the summit at Churston gave them plenty of hard work to do, while the speeds they attained with their heavy trains were probably little more than those imposed by the light railway orders under which today's preserved railways operate.

Although the operation of the 'Torbay Express' did not present the Great Western motive power with any great challenge, and so largely escaped the detailed scrutiny of the train recorders, it was nevertheless rated highly in list of the railway's prestige services. The author's school in the late 1930s was beside the line just outside Paignton, and he has recollections of the train receiving a new or recently-shopped set of stock at the start of the summer services. On one occasion, at least, they were complete with white roofs, but these did not keep their pristine appearance for very long.

The 'Torbay Express' returned as a named train in the 1980s on an 'InterCity 125' working between Paddington and Paignton. Leaving at 10.10, in 1987 it took two hours fifty-eight minutes to Torquay in the down direction, including ten intermediate stops at stations such as Pewsey, Tiverton Parkway, Dawlish and Teignmouth which its pre-war counterpart would have scorned to notice other than with a passing blast on its whistle. With the introduction of the 'West Country Pullman' in 1988, this took over the role of the 'Torbay Express', the name of which disappeared from the timetable once more. In spite of travelling via Bristol, the schedule of the new service was only two hours fifty minutes to Torquay, thanks to less stops and the benefit of the fastest schedule in the country, over the stretch from Paddington to Bath (103.4 mph).

Back in 1923 the June issue of the *Great Western Railway Magazine* carried the following report, appropriately illustrated:

To make the beauties of Torquay more widely known the Corporation arranged a gala week last month, and entertained a number of journalists, railway officials, and others. The majority of guests travelled in special coaches attached to the 12 noon 'Torbay Limited' express from Paddington to Torquay where the station was tastefully decorated. The week's programme included a mayoral reception and ball, an inspection of the new marine drive, a visit to the medical and electrical baths, a trip by steamer up the River Dart from Kingswear and return by road, a grand water carnival, and an exhibition of classical dancing and Grecian poses on Torre Abbey sands. The Great Western Railway Company entertained the press representatives on the rail journeys between Paddington and Torquay.

It is an interesting comment on the increased pace of life and the improvements in rail travel that have taken place during the intervening sixty-five years that, for the press launch of the 'West Country Pullman' in May 1988, the author made the round trip from York in the day, leaving at 06.51 and arriving back just after midnight. While we were not entertained by any dancing on the sands, nor did we need a visit to the medical baths, on a private visit later in the summer, it was discovered that the parks department had produced a full-sized floral representation of the Stephensons' *Rocket*, which was on display in the Abbey Gardens. On the Pullman press launch, however, we did manage a trip up the Dart and later rode around the street of Totnes in horse buses, as well as travelling by steam special over the Torbay & Dartmouth Railway, packing much into our few hours in the English Riviera.

'CHELTENHAM FLYER'

In 1923 the Great Western decided to accelerate an afternoon train by ten minutes from Swindon, cutting its time for the 77.3 miles to Paddington to seventy-five minutes, thus giving them the fastest non-stop run in Britain. That honour had previously been held by the North Eastern Railway over the racing stretch of 44.1 miles between Darlington to York, their forty-three-minute schedule dating back to 1902, which was for quite a light Alnmouth–York train that conveyed through carriages for the Midland. During World War I it had been discontinued, like all the fastest schedules in the country, but with the resumption of peacetime services the same schedule had been allocated to a heavier Glasgow–Leeds train. That gave them a 61.5 mph average, which was equalled by an even shorter sprint on the Great Central between Leicester and Nottingham Arkwright Street. The Great Western's previous best had been the schedule of a Bath slip coach conveyed on a Paddington–Bristol express, which averaged 61.1 mph, but their new effort put the average up to 61.8 mph. *The Railway Gazette*, even though they initially got the new average speed slightly wrong, welcomed the new development in these words:

> . . . the fact that a new 'fastest train in the British Isles' has made its appearance is a matter of special interest, and we may congratulate the responsible officers upon the spirit of progress which has for so many years now been associated with the Great Western Railway, and of which this constitutes a further example.

The train concerned was the 2.30 p.m. Tea Car Train from Cheltenham, and when the new schedule commenced on 9th July that year, a press party was invited to participate in the inaugural run. At the head of a nine-coach train Driver P. Hopkins and Fireman F. Bailey were in charge of 'Star' 4-6-0, No. 2915 *Saint Bartholomew*, and were accompanied on the footplate by the well-known bearded figure of Chief Locomotive Inspector S. H. Flewellen, resplendent in bowler hat and double-breasted jacket. In spite of a lengthy permanent-way slowing before Swindon, they reached Paddington three minutes early, having averaged 64 mph overall. The correspondent of *The Railway Gazette*, who was one of the large party that thronged the side of the locomotive after its arrival in Platform seven, later commented that

'The running of the train was remarkably steady, even at the highest speeds, and reflected the greatest credit upon the engine crew and incidentally proved the excellence of the track and stock'. The latter was a very varied rake, and included two Dean clerestory vehicles. *Saint Bartholomew* was also only provided with one of the Swindon tapered cast-iron chimneys, which gave the whole train much more of a period look compared with the appearance it was shortly to assume.

The train always appeared in the timetables as the 'Cheltenham Spa Express' but was quickly dubbed the 'Cheltenham Flyer', and these words actually appeared on the wings of the headboard that was carried in later years by the 'Castles'. It is thus open to argument whether the 'Cheltenham Flyer' title was official, but the fact that it was used extensively in the *Great Western Magazine* and even for the title of W. G. Chapman's 1934 publication by the company, argues strongly that it was so.

This seventy-five minute schedule was not an unduly difficult one, and after the inaugural trip it was already being suggested that a further five minutes could be cut from the Swindon–Paddington timing, which duly took place in July 1929, the average speed being raised to 66.2 mph. The train had been withdrawn in the previous autumn, but, after being restored at the faster timing, the Great Western were able to claim that they operated the fastest train in the *world*. By this time the 'Castles' had taken over, and No. 5000 *Launceston Castle* was used for the inaugural working of the accelerated service. The run was completed in exactly two minutes under schedule, which pushed the average up to 68.2 mph. Not long after this O. S. Nock timed a run with No. 5003 *Lulworth Castle*, which cut a further forty-five seconds off the timing in the course of recovering a late departure from Swindon.

Less than two years later the GWR lost their title to the world's fastest train when, in April 1931, the Canadian Pacific booked one of their Montreal–Toronto workings to cover the 124 miles to Smith's Falls in just 108 minutes, at an average of 68.8 mph. The Great Western were quick to counter this move, and in September that year the 'Cheltenham Flyer' was further accelerated, by just three minutes, but this was enough to give them back their pre-eminence in the speed stakes. Although Sir Felix Pole had by this time been lost to industry, the GWR publicity people had a field-day on 14th September, and it is worth quoting much of W. G. Chapman's account that appeared in the next month's edition of the *Great Western Railway Magazine*.

Great public interest was taken in the inaugural run, and when the train arrived at Swindon at 3.44 p.m., hauled by engine No. 5000, *Launceston Castle*, there was a large company of well-wishers present, including railway officials, journalists, press photographers and railway enthusiasts. Mr. C. B. Collett, the Chief Mechanical Engineer of the Great Western Railway, was there, with his assistant, Mr. W. A. Stanier. Inspector H. J. Robinson was on the footplate with Driver J. W. Street and Fireman F. W. Shearer, as was also Mr. John Heygate, who was that evening broadcasting an account of the run for the British Broadcasting Company.

The load behind the tender consisted of six coaches, including a tea car. There were a good number of passengers aboard when the train arrived at Swindon, where many more joined it, including the writer.

At precisely 3.48 p.m. the 'Right-away' was given, and the train started on its run. As soon as we were free of the station, speed began appreciably to accelerate. At Shrivenham we were getting well under way, and soon after were doing a mile a minute, whilst at Uffington the speed was in the neighbourhood of 80 mph. The pace did not drop below 80 mph until we were within a couple of miles or so of Paddington.

It was evident that the news had spread along the line that something exceptional was being undertaken in the way of speeds, for harvesters in the fields and others stopped at their work to see the 'Flyer' pass and to cheer her on her way. This was particularly the case when passing the R.A.F. and R.A.O.D. depots at Didcot, where large numbers congregated along the line, whilst from the lofty roof of the Great Western Railway forage store at Didcot a small party waved encouragement as we flashed by.

Hereabouts, speed increased, and a good 84 mph was maintained through Cholsey and Moulsford, Goring, Pangbourne, and Tilehurst. At Reading, passed at approximately 4.20 p.m., speed had increased to round about 85 mph.

Throughout the trip the pace was much more real than apparent. We were certainly speeding, but there was no sense of very high speed. Passengers passed to and from the tea car and took their meal in perfect comfort. There was an entire absence of jolting or oscillation.

A large crowd had congregated at Reading to see the 'Flyer' pass. From this point onwards there was a further steady acceleration as we passed Twyford and Maidenhead. At Taplow we were doing our best speed so far, which was round about 86 mph. This was well maintained for a considerable distance.

On we flew, through Slough, where we saw the sun for the first time. Here employees at the vast Trading Estate turned out in great numbers to see us flash past. The road overbridge near the station was black with spectators. Soon we were through Langley, Iver, West Drayton and Hayes. At all these places people had turned out to give us a hearty wave, but perhaps the largest concourse of sightseers were those who packed the roadbridge at Southall, which we passed at a speed somewhere approaching 86½ mph.

At all the factories along this length of line workers assembled. Hanwell, the Ealings, and Acton were all passed without any slackening of this speed. It was after passing Westbourne Park that we felt the gradual application of the brakes, and were going quite quietly at Royal Oak. We glided into Paddington station with the hands of the big clock just short of the 4.48 indication, having done the trip start-to-stop, not at the scheduled world record speed of 69.2 miles per hour, but in a portion of a minute under the hour! We had actually knocked a full seven minutes out of the new accelerated schedule.

Then followed a great rush of admirers to the footplate, and the station rang with cheer after cheer for the engine crew. A bouquet of flowers was handed to the driver, whilst passengers and others almost fought for the privilege of grasping the hands of the trustworthy enginemen who had brought us up at record speed, made railway history, and added yet another to the many speed triumphs of the Great Western Railway.

A maximum speed of 89 mph had actually been recorded between mileposts 5 and 3, and the overall time was fifty-nine minutes thirty-six seconds, corresponding to an average of 77.8 mph. On the next two days the same locomotive achieved two even faster runs. The information was published in *The Railway Magazine* for November that year in an article by 'Mercury' (actually C. J. Allen) entitled 'A new *Record of Records*'. The same locomotive was used, but with different crews, although Inspector Robinson accompanied them on each occasion. As the times for the 15th and 16th September were supplied by Collett, they were presumably those recorded by the inspector, and, like those noted by the guards in their journals, were to the whole minute only. They both worked out at fifty-eight minutes, but a detailed examination of the figures indicated that the actual times were probably nearer fifty-eight and a half minutes. There is a further point in this connection worth commenting on, and this is that the clocks at Paddington were operated by a master drive, which only sent pulses to move them forward every half-minute, which meant that the casual observer using the 'big clock' to note the arrival time of a train could be out by that interval. The crew of *Launceston Castle* on 15th September were Driver C. Wasley and Fireman A. Hoyle, while their Old Oak Common colleagues, H. Jones and C. E. Brown, were in charge on the following day. The load on the 16th was similar to that of the inaugural run having six bogies, but an extra coach had been included on the day between.

In the light of the first year's successful operations with the 'Cheltenham Flyer', the train's schedule was cut by a further two minutes in September 1932, which lifted the booked average speed over the 70 mph mark for the first time in the world, to a figure of 71.4. By the way of a preview of their intentions, the Great Western organised an outright speed attempt with the train on 6th June that year, inviting C. J. Allen and Humphrey Baker to time it. Another of the Cornish 'Castles' was used, this one being No. 5006 *Tregenna Castle*, named after the railway's own hotel at St. Ives. Driver Ruddock and Fireman Thorp were in charge of the locomotive, and were accompanied by Inspector Sheldon. The day's fireworks involved three high-speed journeys between Swindon and Paddington, starting with the up 'Flyer'. In the timetables they would only have had five minutes to make the first connection at Paddington with the 5.0 p.m. down express, but we will see later how this actually worked out.

With the usual six-coach load, they reached 70 mph in fractionally over three miles from the Swindon start, and 80 mph just after Shrivenham. Thereafter the acceleration was slower, but the train's maximum of 92 mph was reached at Goring and again at Tilehurst, the latter after slowing to a level 90 mph at Pangbourne. Reading was passed in eleven seconds over the half-hour, by which time they were nearly four minutes in advance of the booked time. A further minute was gained by Slough and another three-quarters between there and Southall. Even over the last nine miles into the terminus time was still being gained, and they finally came to a stand in fifty-six minutes forty-seven seconds, which corresponded to an average of 81.7 mph.

As a result of this magnificent performance, the two recorders had just over a quarter of an hour to make their connection at Paddington, and No. 5005 *Manorbier Castle* with a load of 199 tons on the 5.0 p.m. down only took a second over an hour from the terminus to its special stop at Swindon. The final run up to London was with No. 4091 *Dudley Castle*, and they had a signal check at Didcot and the usual restriction through the platform road at Reading to drop the slip portion. This made the actual time sixty-six and a half minutes, which seemed quite tame after the earlier hectic round-trip, until one realised that the current schedule for the 'Cheltenham Flyer' was only sixty-seven minutes.

Not unnaturally, the performance of the 'Cheltenham Flyer' featured extensively in C. J. Allen's 'Locomotive Practice & Performance' articles in *The Railway Magazine* over the years that were to follow, although the arrival of the LNER streamliners in 1935 was to steal the GWR's thunder somewhat. This was especially so after the scheduling of a booked average of 71.9 mph in 1937 for the 'Coronation' between King's Cross and York put the LNER into first place as far as Britain was concerned. Mr. Allen was fortunate in being able to travel on the 'Flyer' fairly regularly in the course of his business journeys, and in the July 1934 issue summarised the thirty-one runs he had made since the day of *Treganna Castle*'s record. On only seven of these did the actual time exceed the sixty-five minutes scheduled by more than a quarter of a minute. If we apply the 1989 InterCity timekeeping standards, all except one arrived within ten minutes of booked time. This was when No. 5015 *Kingswear Castle* was badly checked by thick fog along the Thames Valley, and took no less than seventy-five minutes forty-five seconds, although the net time was only sixty-three minutes, two less than schedule. The next slowest run was when No. 5011 *Tintagel Castle* took sixty-six minutes twenty-six seconds. On only two trips was the net time more than sixty-five minutes, and then only by a maximum of three-quarters of a minute.

The best run he had timed personally in ordinary service was when No. 5016 worked the train into Paddington in sixty-one minutes, eight seconds, for a net time of fifty-nine minutes. He also included a full log, recorded by one of his correspondents, when Driver Street beat the sectional times of his own 'Record of Records' between Swindon and Goring, and from Maidenhead to Acton, to give a net time of only fifty-six minutes. However that driver was to produce an even more spectacular run in 1937, when, with 223 tons, the train was twenty-three seconds up on the 1932 record at Acton, but then eased right off to give a final arrival in Paddington that was nevertheless all but four minutes early.

The performance of the 'Cheltenham Flyer' has sometimes been criticised because of the relatively-light loads involved. While the records were made with only six coach trains, all except three of the thirty-one runs in Mr. Allen's 1934 table had more than this, with the load being eight bogies on five occasions. In October 1935 he returned to this train for the subject of his monthly article, and gave a further ten logs. On only four runs were there as few as seven coaches on the train, and the others were loaded up to as many as thirteen. No. 5023 *Brecon Castle* was at the head of the train on this occasion, and they dropped only two minutes to Reading. Signal checks before Slough and Westbourne Park caused the overall time to be seventy-one minutes forty-one seconds, but the net time was estimated to be no more than sixty-six and a half minutes. On an earlier occasion No. 5018 *St Mawes Castle* had romped into Paddington in sixty-three minutes four seconds with a load of no less than ten bogies. In later pre-war days the 'Cheltenham Flyer' had to contend with two new slowings *en route* that were imposed on all trains. The first was when taking water from the troughs at Goring, and there was also a general restriction through Reading.

The 2.40 p.m. Tea Car Train from Cheltenham might have been considered an unusual one to be chosen for such outstanding treatment, but it had a number of advantages from the operating point of view. It was primarily a train that attracted the leisure traveller rather than businessmen, which made it less likely to suffer from the peak loading problems, although, as we have seen, it could almost double in length on occasions. From the point of view of the leisure traveller it had the great advantage of reaching Paddington in daylight for virtually the whole year, which enabled passengers to appreciate how fast they were travelling. A five o'clock arrival meant they were running against the evening peak, and also gave tourists, with their cases duly emblazoned with the special luggage labels, the opportunity to get to their hotels in plenty of time to change for a show or similar evening engagement.

During the train's fastest period of running, the 'Castle' only came on when the stock reversed at Gloucester. For the first seven and three quarter miles of its journey from Cheltenham Spa station, the 'World's Fastest Train' could well be hauled by nothing more imposing than a 'Prairie' tank, which might have surprised the occasional passenger who was not aware of the complexities of the Great Western Railway's operations.

By the time war was declared, the development of higher speeds with diesel and electric traction had actually knocked the 'Cheltenham Flyer' out of the 'Top Hundred' of the world's fastest schedules, and the record-breaker never reappeared in the timetables after 1945. However, in recent years the economic growth of Swindon, now even the headquarters of the Western Region, has produced unprecedented loadings on the one-time Great Western main line to London. As a result there are no less than twelve 'InterCity 125' workings in the up direction in the morning between 06.30 and 09.00 – more than one every quarter of an hour. Those that stop at both Didcot Parkway and Reading can take as long as sixty-one minutes for the journey, but the 'Brunel Executive' is booked to cover the 77.3 miles non-stop in just forty-nine minutes. In the list of 'Fastest HST Times' compiled by the Railway Performance Society, the best recorded time, at the time of writing, is only forty-three minutes thirty-eight seconds.

'TORBAY PULLMAN LIMITED'

The 'Torbay Pullman Limited' was a very short-lived named train on the Great Western right at the end of the 1920s, and to get some idea of the reasons behind this it is necessary to go into the workings of the Pullman Car Company in some detail. Although for some years now it has been a wholly-owned subsidiary of British Railways, and is proclaimed as such on a plaque in the foyer of today's BRB headquarters, in the 1920s it was, like the railways themselves, a private company, which did, however, have some links with the Wagons-Lits organisation on the other side of the Channel.

Although I have never seen details of the agreement with the Great Western for the operation of the Pullman cars to Torbay and Plymouth, it was presumably much the same as those with the Southern and LNER, both of which used Pullmans extensively, both before and after World War II. In these cases, the railway hauled the Pullman stock around the country at its own expense, and it kept all the ordinary fares paid by the passengers. Pullman, on the other hand, charged the passenger its own supplementary fare, and also retained the profits of its own on-train catering operations. These arrangements are thus totally different from those of today's PR Pullman services, when there are no supplementary charges, except possibly on the 'Birmingham Pullman' where passengers have to purchase the complete package, which even includes a copy of *The Birmingham Post*. The present-day situation with the Venice–Simplon Orient Express is again different, with passengers buying tickets from the Sea Containers organisation, who have to pay BR for the haulage.

The spring of 1929 marked the appearance of the Pullmans on the Great Western Railway, when they were introduced on the 'Ocean Liner Expresses' that had been operated for some thirty years between Paddington and Millbay Docks in Plymouth, where passengers were transferred to and from the liners in the Sound by one of the railway company's tenders. With the start of the summer services, the cars were also introduced on the new 'Torbay Pullman Limited', their launch being part of the celebrations on 8th July that year, which was the day on which James Milne took over as General Manager with Sir Felix Pole's departure for industry. The main event was, of course, the first successful run of the 'Cheltenham Flyer' on its new seventy-minute booking from Swindon, and the authorities were also marking the 'Silver Anniversary' of the 'Cornish Riviera', which had a new set of stock for the occasion. No. 6000 *King George V* was used on the down 'Limited', the train being seen off by Milne and Collett, the latter ringing the bell on the locomotive's buffer-beam before its departure.

Although these two purely GWR services were undoubtedly given much more publicity than the new 'Torbay Pullman', the latter was certainly referred to at length in the *Great Western Railway Magazine* for that month, as follows:

On Mondays and Fridays a Pullman car train will leave Paddington at 11.00 a.m., for Paignton, and will run non-stop to Newton Abbot, where it will be due at 2.25 p.m., Torquay at 2.40 p.m., and Paignton at 2.50 p.m. In the opposite direction, a similar train, on the same days of the week, will leave Paignton at 4.30 p.m., Torquay 4.40 p.m., Newton Abbot 4.58 p.m., and reach Paddington at 8.30 p.m. These services, which will be known as the 'Torbay Pullman Limited', and convey first and third class cars, are of an experimental nature and constitute an innovation, marking, as they do, the initial introduction of Pullman car facilities on the Great Western Railway. The number of passengers carried will be limited to the seating accommodation available in the cars, which are of the latest and most luxurious type. Supplementary charges of 7/6 (37.5p) first class and 5/- (25p) third class will be made in addition to the ordinary fares. Luncheon, dinner, and other refreshments will be obtainable in the cars in both directions.

Two months later, we find the winter timetable alterations referring to the Pullmans again, as follows:

The provision of Pullman-car facilities, which marked an innovation in Great Western policy from July 8th last, will be continued and extended. The 11 a.m. from Paddington to Paignton and the 4.30 p.m. from Paignton to Paddington, consisting of modern Pullman coaches affording luxurious accommodation for first and third class passengers, will appear in the new time table, and run on Saturdays in addition to Mondays and Fridays.

In spite of this change, the new train, which consisted of a six-car set, including some of the new all-steel vehicles, hauled by a 'King' or a 'Castle', was not a success, and was withdrawn, together with the use of the Pullmans on the Ocean Liner Specials, in 1930. Some authors and Pullman enthusiasts have written scathingly about the poor deal that company got from the Great Western, and, as a staunch supporter of both organisations, the author is perhaps in a reasonably impartial position to comment on the subject. The initiative would appear to have come from the Pullman Car Company, who thus had to show that they could attract more custom than the operating railway had done previously. The latter had additional haulage costs and lost the profits from their own catering operations, their only compensation being the reduced rolling-stock operating costs. From accounts in the literature from time to time, it would appear that the Pullman cars sometimes did not get the servicing required. The introduction of change is one of the hardest managerial tasks, with resentment inevitably being felt at grass-roots level about any new-comer to the scene, particularly one whose advent could be seen as a threat to existing jobs. Even after British Railways had bought up the whole of the ordinary share capital of the Pullman Car Company, they had a strike of catering staff in 1961 when they were trying to introduce a mid-day working from St. Pancras to Nottingham and back with the 'Midland Pullman' set, which was only settled when they also bought up all the preference shares.

In the light of later experience, the popularity of a Pullman service depended on it providing a bonus in overall speed as well as luxury, and the 'Torbay Pullman Limited' was not as fast as the 'Torbay Express'. It also left London an hour earlier, and, as already mentioned, the clientele for the latter train appeared to like a leisurely mid-day start. Furthermore, the running of a train on only two or three days of the week is not easy to market, and today the various FO or SO entries in our timetables are in response to demand rather than attempts to gain custom. The charging of supplementary fares has also traditionally been a source of complaint in this country, in contrast to attitudes on the continent.

The next appearance of Pullmans in Devon was when the 'Devon Belle' was introduced on the Southern Railway at weekends during the last summer before nationalisation. It was initially very popular, but, once seat reservations had become available generally, its loadings fell off, and after trying one or two changes in scheduling, it disappeared in the autumn of 1954. The 'Torbay Pullman's' supplementary fares also seemed high. In 1947, those on the 'Devon Belle' for the longer journey between Waterloo and Ilfracombe were only 8/- (40p) and 4/6 (22$\frac{1}{2}$p).

Finally it must not be forgotten that October 1929 marked the great Wall Street crash, which was to have many serious economic repercussions all round the world, Britain included. It was certainly not a good time to be introducing a new prestige luxury service on the railways. The GWR and LMS ordinary share dividends both dropped by two percentage points between 1929 and 1930, while that of the LNER's preferred stock fell to $\frac{1}{4}$%, before disappearing completely for 5 years. As we have seen with the early years of the Venice–Simplon Orient Express, even in prosperous times it takes a lot of trial and error before a profitable route for such a working can be found, and the Pullman Car Company certainly did not succeed on the GWR with their West Country services. It was up to them to prove their case, and convince the GWR, whose dividend performance was better than those of the other grouping companies, that the change was financially beneficial for them too.

It was not until the introduction of the 'South Wales Pullman' in 1955 that Pullman trains were to reappear on the tracks of the one-time Great Western Railway, and this ran in the morning and evening business-travel peaks, which has always been the best formula for a successful service of this type. In recent years the most popular workings have been up to London in the morning and down in the evening, and the 'West Country Pullman', on its down and up workings to Torbay, already mentioned elsewhere, does not load as heavily as the other Western Region's similar 'InterCity 125' workings.

'CAMBRIAN COAST EXPRESS'

The service over the former Cambrian Railways were revitalised after absorption in 1922, the change of ownership making itself apparent in the alterations to the train services far more quickly than on the lines of the other constituent companies. This was in part due to the fact that the Great Western had already been involved with the operation of many through carriages over the Cambrian, as exemplified by one of the *Bradshaw* entries for January that year:

Through Carriages, London (Paddington) to Aberystwyth and Towyn; also Through Carriages, London (Euston) to Aberystwyth, and Birmingham (New Street) to Aberystwyth and Barmouth. Through Carriage, Manchester (London Road) and Liverpool (Lime Street) to Aberystwyth.

A year earlier, the express from Aberystwyth that was involved in the head-on collision at Abermule contained a GWR coach, and four London & North Western vehicles, with just a solitary example from the Cambrian. The Whitchurch local also contained more LNWR coaches than Cambrian ones, so the cosmopolitan nature of their services can be well appreciated.

The London–Birmingham–Birkenhead axis was one of the few places where the GWR and LMS competed directly after grouping, and it was natural for the new owners of the Cambrian to want to use it more intensively for through services from Paddington. By the summer of 1939, those from Euston had thus disappeared, even although the LMS was still running London–Swansea through coaches via the Central Wales line at the same fares charged by the Great Western for their direct route through the Severn Tunnel. There were, nevertheless, through carriages to and from LMS centres such as Manchester (Victoria and London Road) and Liverpool (Lime Street), the reverse working of the last of these, on certain Saturdays, actually being combined in the same train with the GWR's own portion for Birkenhead on the other side of the Mersey.

The adoption of the name 'Cambrian Coast Express' dates from 1927, but its predecessors can be seen in the earlier timetables back to 1921, when a daily restaurant-car train was introduced in the summer, leaving Paddington at 9.50 a.m. for Aberystwyth, Barmouth and Pwllheli. Throughout their history, these trains saw a lot of changes in their workings, and a year later the through coaches to Aberystwyth were off the 10.40 from Paddington, taking six hours twenty minutes overall, inclusive of twelve minutes spent reversing at Shrewsbury. However, at the height of that summer, they were supplemented by another train for Aberystwyth, Barmouth and Pwllheli. This left Paddington at 10.15 mrn., as *Bradshaw* then referred to the times, including those in the tables headed 'G.W. (late Cambrian)', which appeared somewhat later in the publication than the rest of the Great Western's, whose own still occupied their traditional place right at the front.

The additional peak-summer train had a number of interesting features about its working. Leaving Paddington it took the West of England line at Old Oak, to enable it to call at Ealing

Broadway. It then followed the West Ealing–Greenford Loop to gain the Birmingham line, using the route used by today's single-unit diesel multiple units that operate the half-hourly shuttle from Paddington. In spite of this tour of the western London suburbs, the train only took five minutes over the two hours to reach Snow Hill station in Birmingham. The distance is one and a quarter miles more by this route, but there were the two additional slowings to contend with over the triangular junctions at each end of the loop. At Snow Hill in Birmingham the train stopped for five minutes, except on Saturdays, before taking a further nineteen minutes for the restricted stretch on to Wolverhampton. By taking the Abbey Foregate curve at Shrewsbury the reversal there was avoided, with the next stop being at Welshpool. Machynlleth was reached at 3.23, where the portions split for the coastal resorts of north and central Wales. First away at 3.28 was the Pwllheli section, which made a limited number of stops before reaching the terminus at 5.45 aft. The second section departed from Machynlleth at 3.35, and called at Borth only, before reaching Aberystwyth at 4.20, forty minutes ahead of the later through coaches off the 10.40 from Paddington, so the additional peak-summer train saved a quarter of an hour overall from London.

In the opposite direction the through coaches for Paddington, complete with Luncheon Car, left Aberystwyth at 10.15 mrn. attached to the train for Birkenhead. During their twenty-seven minute stop-over at Shrewsbury they were transferred to the 12.25 *from* Birkenhead, which reached Paddington at 5.0 aft., after calling at Wolverhampton, Birmingham, Leamington Spa and Banbury. In spite of the two stops south of Birmingham, it was only allowed two hours five minutes for this stretch. At the height of the summer, a separate train from Pwllheli also left at 10.15, conveying its own 'Luncheon and Tea Car', and at Dovey Junction picked up a portion that had departed from Aberystwyth at noon, the combination arriving in Paddington at 6.40 aft, except on Saturdays when it got in twenty minutes earlier. Like the corresponding down train, it did not call at Shrewsbury, taking instead the west-to-south curve at Abbey Foregate.

As on so many routes, the down services were appreciably faster than the corresponding ones in the opposite direction. The peak summer additional train took just six hours and five minutes to Aberystwyth, but the up working required thirty-five minutes more on ordinary weekdays, although this, somewhat unusually, was twenty minutes quicker on Saturdays. The overall times for the other through coaches to and from Aberystwyth earlier in the day were six hours twenty minutes down, but six hours forty-five minutes up, thus maintaining the differential.

By 1927, the workings of the new named train had changed again. It ran on Fridays and Saturdays only, leaving Paddington at 10.10 a.m. After calling at High Wycombe and Leamington Spa, it spent ten minutes standing at Snow Hill before continuing at 12.30. During the six-minute stop at Wolverhampton the locomotive would have been changed, as the next stop was at Moat Lane at 2.37 p.m., Shrewsbury having been missed. With further calls at Machynlleth and Borth, Aberystwyth was reached at 4.20 p.m., after a journey lasting six hours ten minutes. In the opposite direction, the train left at 11.25 a.m., and, following the stop at Borth, called at Dovey Junction for eight minutes. Leaving there at 12.10, it ran straight through to Welshpool, and, following a further ten-minute stop there, got to Wellington at 2.53. The locomotives were presumably changed at this point, as the up train missed Wolverhampton, becoming the 4.0 p.m. two-hour express from Snow Hill to Paddington, with the usual stop at Leamington Spa. True to form, the up train took twenty-five minutes longer overall.

At the time of the grouping, the Cambrian could boast nothing larger than a 4-4-0 in the way of express locomotives, but even the Great Western was unable to replace them by any of its favourite 4-6-0s for some time, because of the lightness of the underline bridges. To provide replacement motive power for the Cambrian 4-4-0s that were scrapped the GWR drafted in some of its own 'Duke' class locomotives, until the last three years before World War II saw the arrival of the hybrid 'Dukedogs'. Still with the 4-4-0 wheel arrangement, they were constructed by putting a 'Duke' boiler on the frames of a withdrawn 'Bulldog'. Originally it was intended to reuse the 'Duke' names, but a switch was then made to use those of earls. This only lasted for a short time before one of the noble gentlemen apparently objected at the puny size of the locomotive bearing his name, and the plates were duly transferred to some of the 'Castles'. The 'Dukedogs' then soldiered on in un-named form for the rest of their days. It was only during World War II that the 'Manor' class 4-6-0s were first allocated to Oswestry, but they were to be associated with the 'Cambrian Coast Express' during its post-war revival. The sight of a pair of them double-heading the train during busy periods, with their rake of BR standard coaches painted in chocolate and cream, helped give the illusion that the GWR was still in business.

From May 1986, after a long absence, the 'Cambrian Coast Express' returned to the timetables as the only daily InterCity working on the line, the remainder of the services on the one-time Cambrian Railways now being in the hands of the Provincial sector's 'Sprinters'. To cope with the extra business these new diesel units have generated, a peculiar hybrid has had to be introduced, just for these lines, to handle the business until other stock becomes available. These consist of a single Class 150/2 car marshalled between the two vehicles of the earlier Class 150/1 design, which differ in not having end vestibules to provide access *between*, as distinct from within, units. Prior to 1985 the Saturdays-only workings in the summer from London to Aberystwyth and back had been worked over the Cambrian by pairs of elderly Class 25s, but that year they were replaced by the more powerful Class 37s. In the spring of 1986, following the reopening of Barmouth Bridge to locomotives after the repair work to make good the ravages of the ship worm, *Teredo Norvegica*, the availability of the Class 37/4s, with electric train heating equipment, permitted the introduction of a summer Saturday working from London to Pwllheli and back, to supplement the new year-round 'Cambrian Coast Express', running daily from Aberystwyth with air-conditioned stock, plus full restaurant-car service on ordinary weekdays.

In the Winter 1988/89 timetables the 'Cambrian Coast Express' leaves Aberystwyth at 07.14, and reaches London at 12.33, but its destination is now Euston rather than Paddington. With a reversal at Shrewsbury, and a change to electric traction at Wolverhampton, the train takes its place in the regular sequence of London–Birmingham trains over the very busy West Coast Main Line, which now run at half-hourly intervals. In the return direction the train departs from Euston at 15.40, arriving back on the Cambrian coast at 20.59, so its overall timings in both directions are now identical at five hours nineteen minutes. The forthcoming acceleration of the Euston–Birmingham services will presumably see the timings of the 'Cambrian Coast Express' also being speeded up slightly. The Pwllheli train–the 'Snowdonian'–left Euston at 07.40 on Saturdays in the summer of 1988, and had made a twenty-six-minute turn-round at Pwllheli, arriving back in London at 22.25 after its 553-mile trip out-and-back.

'CORNISHMAN'

Although the name 'Cornishman' only started appearing in the timetables in 1935, the name went back unofficially to the days of the Broad Gauge. Prior to 1887 there were six such West of England expresses in and out of Paddington daily, of which two operated no further west than Plymouth. Two of them were known by names, these being the 'Flying Dutchman' and the 'Zulu', which were, in the down direction, respectively, due out of Paddington at 11.45

a.m. for Penzance, and at 3.0 p.m. for Plymouth. As traffic grew, two more expresses were added, the first, in 1887, known as the 'Jubilee' because of the celebration of Queen Victoria's Golden Jubilee in that year. The second additional train was the 'Cornishman', which first appeared in June 1890, and so was to run for less than two years in its Broad-Gauge form. It left Paddington at 10.15 a.m., and only called at Swindon, Bristol and Exeter, before reaching Plymouth at 3.50. The schedule of the down train to the first stop at Swindon was the same as the other pair of named expresses, but the omission of the stops at Bath, Taunton and Newton Abbot was a new feature. In its short existence it quickly became the most important of the expresses, and on Friday 20th May 1892, with *Great Britain* at its head, it was the last Broad-Gauge train to leave Paddington for Penzance.

During the rise in business that followed the gauge conversion, the 'Cornishman' became a very popular train, its speed and departure time both commending it to the traveller from London. By 1896 it was having to be run in two parts during the summer months, and in the following year the advance portion was booked non-stop to Exeter. This run of 193.9 miles via Bristol was the longest such booked working in the world, and the time of three hours forty-three minutes corresponded to an average speed of 52.2 mph. It was then leaving at 10.30, five minutes ahead of the main train, and finished at Falmouth after making further stops at Plymouth, Lostwithiel, Par, St. Austell and Truro. The overall time was more than an hour quicker than the through coaches off the 'Flying Dutchman'. As recounted in the section on the 'Cornish Riviera Express', the 'Cornishman's' slot was taken over by that new express in 1904, and the use of the unofficial name lapsed.

In the summer of 1935, as part of the GWR's centenary celebrations, it was arranged that the 'Cornish Riviera Limited' would travel all the way from Paddington to Truro on ordinary weekdays without any publicly booked stop. Passengers for the intermediate stations east of Plymouth who had traditionally been conveyed by slip coaches were served by a new express. This left Paddington at 10.35, and was formally given the name 'Cornishman'. It carried the Weymouth slip portion, dropped at Heywood Road Junction, and reached its first booked stop at Plymouth in four hours from Paddington, thus equalling the timing for the 'Limited'. Four intermediate stops were made in Cornwall, at Par, Truro, Gwinear Road and St. Erth, all of them at stations serving branches with important holiday business. Penzance was reached at 5.5 p.m., after a journey lasting six and a half hours.

In the return direction the 'Cornishman' started its journey at St. Erth five minutes after the up 'Riviera'. The latter was shown as running non-stop from Truro to Paddington, so the new named train had to make all the usual stops through Cornwall before running non-stop from Plymouth to Paddington. This last stretch took four hours twenty minutes, which was twenty minutes slower than the down run, but even the 'Limited' took twenty-five minutes longer from Truro to London than it did in the other direction.

In the last summer before World War II, the name 'Cornishman' was absent from *Bradshaw*, and the relief to the 'Cornish Riviera Limited' was leaving Paddington at 11.00 a.m. It was referred to as 'London to Exeter, Plymouth and Penzance Express', with through carriages for Kingsbridge and Newquay, and a restaurant car for Penzance. All this information was printed vertically in the timetable column, as was normal practice in those days, hand-setting of the type being more flexible in this particular respect than today's computer-driven equipment. The train made a lot of intermediate stops, the first at Taunton, and, as a result, took seven hours thirty-five minutes overall. The up weekday workings were very different from what they had been four years earlier, but the 9.0 a.m. from Penzance, which reached Paddington just ten minutes ahead of the 'Limited', was probably the nearest equivalent to the 'Cornishman'. It had through coaches from Newquay, Plymouth, Kingsbridge and Exeter, but the restaurant car was only attached with the Plymouth portion. A coach was slipped at Reading, this being the only intermediate point served after leaving

Exeter, and the 173.3 miles to Paddington were booked to be covered in 185 minutes at an average of 56.2 mph.

After World War II the name 'Cornishman' was revived, but for a totally different service, the 1952 morning Wolverhampton–Penzance through train, running over former Great Western metals via Birmingham Snow Hill, and Stratford-on-Avon. In the years that followed it became partially Midlandised in the route rationalisations of the 1960s, and was also extended at the northern end, to become a through train to and from Bradford, but the name finally lapsed in 1975 after a quarter of a century's use. However, with the coming of the HSTs, the name was readopted, and is currently carried by the HST set that leaves Edinburgh at 07.50. With a considerable amount of 125 mph running over the East Coast Main Line as far south as Doncaster, it then takes the North-East–South-West route to Bristol. Having regained what was once Great Western territory, the old Great Way Round is followed all the way to Penzance, which is reached at 18.09, less than a hour later than the 1935 'Cornishman' arrived after its far shorter journey. The final 300½ miles from Birmingham New Street are covered in five hours twenty-four minutes, which should be compared with the six and a half hour schedule of the 1935 train over the 305¼ miles from Paddington. Today's corresponding train in the opposite direction leaves Penzance at 09.23, and reaches Edinburgh at 20.10, so achieving a somewhat slower time going north.

'BRISTOLIAN'

As part of the events organised by the Great Western to mark their centenary in 1935, a new high-speed service was introduced on 9th September between Paddington and Bristol. This was given the name 'Bristolian', and operated non-stop each way with a timing of 105 minutes. In the down direction, leaving Paddington at 10.0 a.m., the train ran via the old route through Bath, by which the distance is 118.3 miles. For the return working at 4.30 p.m. the new express took the Badminton line, which is three-quarters of a mile shorter and this reduced the average speed from 67.6 to 67.2 mph. From the GWR's point of view, these figures took the two workings into second and third places in their table of average speeds, being beaten only by the 'Cheltenham Flyer'.

The new services were announced at the Centenary Lunch, held in Bristol on 31st August that year, the guests from London being conveyed both ways by a special train. No. 6000 *King George V* was the obvious choice of motive power, but the weight of the special was appreciably higher than the formation used for the normal train, and included four of the latest saloons, two observation saloons and a kitchen car. There had been hopes amongst those invited to take part that there would be a very fast run in no more than ninety minutes, but going down the train operated to the old two-hour timing. Coming back, however, they ran in the path of the future new train, which gave a striking demonstration of the acceleration proposed. Apart from dropping time initially, they kept closely to schedule, and the fastest speed of the day was recorded at Old Oak Common, when Driver Sparrow and Fireman Sims whipped the train up to no less than 88 mph as they were passing their home depot.

Although the Great Western had scheduled two down trains to Bristol in 116 and 118 minutes in 1932/33, the best run in the summer of 1935 took two hours, inclusive of a stop at Bath, so the acceleration was quite appreciable. In regular service the 'Bristolian' had a load of just seven coaches, one of which was the latest type of buffet car, with a full-length counter, complete with pedestal seats on which passengers could perch while they ate. One of these vehicles is preserved as part of the National Collection, and is on loan to the Severn Valley Railway. A load of some 220 tons was not unduly heavy for such a fast working, and, coming up, the new schedule called for a time of only 62 minutes from passing Swindon, which was three minutes less than the booked start-to-stop time for the 'Cheltenham Flyer'. The difference equated closely to the extra time necessary to accelerate the latter train to full speed compared with passing the station at 75 mph, but the 'Flyer' was booked to be hauled by the less powerful 'Castles'.

The new train quickly settled down to its fast schedule, and no special all-out runs were made initially as had been the case with the earlier accelerations of the 'Cheltenham Flyer'. By the time he wrote his November 'Locomotive Practice & Performance' article in *The Railway Magazine*, C. J. Allen was able to tabulate four runs with the train in each direction. All had kept very closely to time, the best being a down trip with *King George V*, when, on a foggy morning, the train was stopped shortly after leaving by signals at Westbourne Park. Speed remained in the range 70–80 mph all the way up the gently rising gradients of the Thames Valley, but through Didcot they accelerated to 79 mph before sustaining 75 mph on the long 1 in 834 approaching Swindon. After 79 mph at Wootton Bassett they eased back slightly, but touched 82 mph down Dauntsey Bank. There was a permanent-way check at Box, following which they reached 70 mph again before the regulation slowing to 25 mph through Bath. A slight signal check spoilt the run in to the Temple Meads stop, but even so they only took 103 minutes 57 seconds, in spite of the three out-of-course slowings, which between them accounted for a full four minutes.

On the journey in general, Mr. Allen had this to say:

It is only just that comment should be made, not only on the comfort and smoothness of running of such journeys at these, on which the long-continued high speed becomes entirely deceptive until reference is made to one's stop-watch, but also on the effortless ease of the locomotive work. Not a sound from the engine is heard in the train except during the few minutes after starting and recovering from slacks. A journey of such a service as this affords an impressive commentary on present-day railway progress.

While the speeds reached on the 'Bristolian' were not quite up to those achieved on the LNER's 'Silver Jubilee', it is worth noting that C. J. Allen admitted that he deliberately dodged a trip on the first down public run of that streamliner after the excitements of its launch on 27th September that year because of its lively riding. His comments on the GWR express are thus a significant indication of the way the coaches rode and the standards of their track.

The 'Kings' were never the best of Great Western locomotives for continuous high-speed running, so it was not altogether surprising that the 'Castles' should take over the working of the 'Bristolian', No. 4082 *Windsor Castle* actually appearing at the head of one of the up runs in the article just mentioned. When Mr. Allen returned to the subject in the summer of 1938 he was able to recount the details of a fine round-trip with No. 5044 *Earl of Dunraven*. Both ways they had the usual seven-coach train of 231 tons tare, and the performance had been recorded by E. W. Maybank. The driver was the noted Old Oak personality, F. W. Street, known to his admirers as 'Quality Street', who has featured in the 'Cheltenham Flyer' section earlier in this chapter. On the down trip, in spite of a slight signal check at Acton, speed was continuously above the 80 mph mark from West Drayton to Steventon, but signals checked them to 60 mph just before Swindon. A maximum of no less than 96 mph was reached on the descent of Dauntsey incline. The usual restrictions to 60 mph at Box and 25 mph through Bath were faithfully observed, after which they were content with a maximum of 58 mph before the Bristol stop. Their overall time was only ninety-nine minutes twenty-six seconds, corresponding to a net time of ninety-eight and a half minutes, and an average of 72.1 mph. On the return journey they reached 91 mph at Little Somerford and passed Swindon almost two minutes early. Speed remained well above 80 mph for over sixty miles beyond Shriven-ham, with a maximum of 88 mph, but as they were nearly five minutes early passing Southall the locomotive was eased and the arrival at Paddington was in 102 minutes 55 seconds from Bristol, just over two minutes early.

The schedule of the 'Bristolian' remained unchanged right up to September 1939, and, like all the fast trains in the country, it was withdrawn at the beginning of World War II. With the post-war austerity over, the old schedule was restored in the mid-1950s, the 'Kings' again being initially rostered for the working. As in the 1930s, the 'Castles' subsequently took over once more, the double-chimney variety giving a very good account of themselves, with speeds of 100 mph being attained on occasions. No. 7018 *Drysllwyn Castle*, which is *not* the locomotive of the same name now preserved by the Great Western Society at Didcot, made the up run in no more than ninety-three minutes fifty seconds at an average of 75.2 mph during steam's final fling before succumbing to the diesel-hydraulics. While there is no 'Bristolian' today, the InterCity 125 set working the 'West Country Pullman' that leaves Paddington at 09.50 is booked to reach Bath in sixty-two minutes, which makes it the fastest train in the country, with a start-to-stop average of 103.4 mph. The next leg of its journey sees it arriving at Bristol in just seventy-seven minutes from Paddington.

'Cornish Riviera'
4-6-0 No. 6015 *King Richard III* at the head of ten coaches of Centenary Stock on the up 'Cornish Riviera' near Witham.

'Torbay Express'
4-6-0 No. 6003 *King George IV* with the down 'Torbay Express' on the Frome Cut-off.

'Ports-to-Ports Express'
The southbound 'Ports-to-Ports Express' in 1929 near Woodhouse, shortly after leaving Sheffield. A former Great Central Atlantic hauls the train of GWR clerestory stock, with a van or horsebox at the rear. By this time the locomotive had become LNER Class C4 No. 5267. *(P. Ransome-Wallis Collection, National Railway Museum, York)*

'Cheltenham Flyer'
4-6-0 No. 5000 *Launceston Castle* hurtles through Tilehurst at 84 mph on the occasion of the record-breaking inaugural run of the 'Cheltenham Flyer' on 14 September 1931. As described in this chapter, its new schedule, its new schedule, which made it the fastest train in the world, was comprehensively beaten with an average of 77.8 mph between Swindon to Paddington. *(M. W. Earley Collection, National Railway Museum, York)*

'Bristolian'
Streamlined 4-6-0 No. 6014 *King Henry VII* on the down 'Bristolian' near Box in May 1936.

'Devonian'
Although the 'Devonian' was a named train on the LMS, only a through portion continued west of Bristol, attached to one of the GWR's unnamed expresses. It has not therefore been included in the text, but this photograph shows 4-6-0 No. 4098 *Kidwelly Castle* at Brean Road with the Bradford–Paignton through coaches.

'Torbay Pullman Limited'
4-6-0 No. 4092 *Dunraven Castle* heads westwards at Ruscombe on the short-lived 'Torbay Pullman' in September 1929.
(M. W. Earley Collection, National Railway Museum, York)

'Cambrian Coast Express'
A 'Duke' class 4-4-0 No. 3258 *The Lizard* with a train of assorted stock at Machynlleth on the former Cambrian Railways line used by the 'Cambrian Coast Express'. When built in 1895 the locomotive was just called *Lizard*, but the name was altered in 1904 to clarify the connection with the Cornish headland, rather than being mistaken for a mere reptile. *(M. D. England Collection, National Railway Museum, York).*

CHAPTER FIVE

BRANCH LINES

The closure of so many of the branch lines in this country in the 1950s and 1960s focused people's attention on their poor economics, but the problem was by no means a new one for the railway companies. We thus need to understand the climate in which they were operated between the two world wars before we can appreciate the changes in the patterns of the train services over the Great Western's branches. At the time of the Grouping, the Great Western had Parliamentary authority for a further eighty miles of line, but no more than a quarter of these were actually under construction. A few years later the grouping companies were suggesting that further construction should be put in hand with government finance to reduce the level of unemployment, one of the GWR proposals being a line from Bridgwater to Watchet, which would have markedly reduced the distance to Minehead from the Bristol direction. In 1923 the Hallatrow–Limpley Stoke loop, south of Bath, was also reopened to passenger traffic after its closure early in World War I. In spite of this enthusiasm for new branch lines, their economic viability was already being called into question in the mid-1920s, and the Limpley Stoke line referred to above was closed again for passengers in 1925, being severed at the west end so it became a freight-only branch running to Camerton. The combination of its scenery and accessibility were subsequently to result in two railway films being made there in the days of the GWR, while that all-time classic, 'The Titfield Thunderbolt' followed after World War II.

In 1925 a comprehensive survey of their branch lines was carried out by the GWR, and a report issued in the following year. The terms of reference were as follows:

1 Are Branch Lines being worked to-day on the most economical lines and is the present system capable of improvement?
2 How far would it meet the case to abolish steam locomotives and our heavy rolling stock and substitute a motor rail coach with a light trailer for goods and luggage: and on which lines would this be possible, for it is realised that not all Branch Lines are alike?
3 Is there any case in which rails could be taken up and the road used as a motor road by the Company, in which case possibly one man in charge of the station would be adequate to attend to tickets and goods?

As far as the second heading was concerned, the technology was not yet available in a form that was satisfactory for the British railway companies of the time, although the GWR was to inaugurate the use of diesel railcars over branch lines before the start of World War II. The answer to the third point was quite simple, as we will see later in this chapter, but the studies necessary to provide the answers to the first heading were very comprehensive.

The report examined the originating revenue on many of the company's branches, and compared it with the expenditure involved in working and maintaining them. The latter figures could be easily and accurately determined, even by the accountancy systems of the time, but the full amount of revenue earned by the branch was much more difficult to determine. While the actual income from ticket sales and originating goods and parcels business was easy to determine, it was only possible to calculate the revenue generated by incoming passengers long after the formation of BR. To do this a purpose-designed ticket issuing system covering the whole country was needed, together with accounting procedures that were backed up by a main-frame electronic computer. And even today the highly sophisticated system used will not take account of the appreciable numbers of overseas visitors with their BritRail Passes, many of whose journeys are over our less heavily-used, scenic routes. On the other hand, in the 1920s the network effect, which was unfortunately largely ignored during the Beeching era, would not have been so great. The low car-ownership in those days would not have prompted many of those whose local branch-line station had been closed to drive all the way to their destination, rather than to the main-line railhead. However they might well not have travelled at all, and this was appreciated by the compilers of the 1926 report, although they could not quantify it.

Of the fifty-three branch lines studied, recommendations were made for savings on thirty-eight of them, and the main recommendations were contained in four slightly-over-lapping tables, under the following headings:

1 Closing of Branch Lines.
2 Branch Services to be confined to eight hours (one set of men).
3 Transfer Passenger Service to Road Motor Service, the Goods, Milk, etc., Traffic being worked by rail within an eight-hours turn of duty.
4 Reduction in Train Service or Hours on Branch Lines.

We will now look at each of these in detail, and in the tables that follow I have included the date when passenger services were actually withdrawn over each of the lines concerned.

The first section of the report suggested that six branches should be closed, which would have produced gross savings of £46,302, although if all the originating business was lost the net total would have dropped to £10,992. The lines concerned are listed in Table 5.1, the receipts and expenditure figures being those for 1925:

Table 5.1. Recommended Branch Closures in 1926

Branch Line	Total receipts (£)	Maintenance, Renewal Charges and Working Expenses (£)	Net savings (£)	Passenger services withdrawn (year)
Yealmpton	11,810	13,881	2,071	1930
Cowbridge and Aberthaw	4,315	4,827	512	1930
Titley and Eardisley	2,512	4,808	2,296	1940
Pontrilas and Hay	7,805	11,631	3,826	1941
Dinas Mawddwy	4,357	4,653	296	1931
Welshpool and Llanfair	4,510	6,502	1,992	1931
TOTALS	35,309	46,302	10,992	

It will be seen that only three of these lines were actually to lose their passenger services within the next five years, while the other pair staggered on into World War II. The actual closure decisions were thus not solely based on the straight-forward accountancy figures, and this is reinforced by the fact that in most cases the goods services continued to function for some years after the passenger trains had ceased. The branch from Cowbridge to Aberthaw Low Level closed completely in 1931, but that area was well served by the nearby coastal line of the Barry Railway, and goods services over the Titley and Eardisley line finished at the same time as the passenger trains were withdrawn. In the other four cases, however, the goods facilities continued for a minimum of another twenty years, those at Yealmpton even outlasting its second passenger closure.

Table 5.2 gives details of the next five branches in the Great Western's 1926 report which recommended that their services should be confined to 8 hours a day, which meant that they could be worked by one set of men.

Table 5.2. Branch lines to be confined to one-shift working

	Estimated savings (£)	Passenger services withdrawn (year)
Welshpool and Llanfair	748	1931
Cleobury Mortimer and Ditton Priors	490	1938
Dinas Mawddwy	867	1931
Vale of Rheidol	1,527	Still open
Clynderwen and Letterston	590	1937
TOTAL	4,222	

It will be seen that there was an element of 'belt and braces' about these suggestions, since two of the lines also appeared in the total closure list. In this case, however, some action was taken much more promptly, and the report included the information that the change on the Clynderwen and Letterston line had already come into effect on 1st December 1925. However before the beginning of World War II conditions had changed drastically on two of these lines. The one from Cleobury Mortimer to Ditton Priors was to be closed to passengers in 1938 and completely in the following year, while the stretch between Clynderwen and Letterston Junction lost its passenger services in 1937.

The third category of economies suggested that five lines should have their passenger traffic transferred to road motor services, and the other traffic worked by rail on a one-shift basis, the details being given in Table 5.3.

Table 5.3. Branches to be closed to passengers

	Estimated savings (£)	Passenger services withdrawn (year)
Pontrilas and Hay	997	1941
Oswestry, Llynclys and Llangynog	1,569	1951
Hemyock Branch	810	1963
Moss and Wrexham	1,823	1931
Albermule and Kerry	474	1931
TOTAL	5,673	

Of these we have already discussed the Golden Valley Line (Pontrilas and Hay), but the last two on the list did lose their passenger services as early as 1931. The remaining pair continued to operate normally until after World War II, passenger services over the Hemyock Branch continuing for fifteen years after nationalisation.

We now come to the last main category of the recommendations, which involved a variety of economies, as detailed in Table 5.4, from which it will be seen that all but one of these recommendations had already been adopted by the time the report was issued, but this did not prevent two of the lines losing their services in 1931.

In addition to the branches singled out for attention in this 1926 report, the Great Western Railway closed a number of others between the two world wars. Some of these moves were connected with the process of tidying up the unnecessarily-complicated network in South Wales which they had inherited from their constituent and subsidiary companies at the Grouping. For example, the Pontyrhyll–Port Talbot Central line of the one-time Port Talbot Railway was closed in two stages in the autumns of 1932 and 1933, while the lines leading to the Riverside and East Dock stations in Swansea similarly lost their passenger services in 1933

Table 5.4. Branches subject to other economies

	Estimated savings (£)	Passenger services withdrawn (year)
Brentford Branch		
Withdrawal of auto service, except mornings and evenings (middle of day on Saturdays) for workmen, commenced February 1st	1,480	1942
Cardigan		
Reduction in Branch hours and train mileage	800	1962
Clevedon		
Withdrawal of Sunday service, commenced January 3rd	210	1966
Lambourne		
Reduction of Branch hours, commenced February 1st	540	1960
Tetbury		
Retiming Goods train to reduce overall hours, commenced November 25th	123	1964
Wrexham, Brymbo and Coed Poeth		
Reduction in rail motor trips, commences April 1st	991	1931
Wrexham and Rhos		
Reduction in rail motor trips, commenced April 1st	352	1931
TOTAL	4,496	

and 1936. The latter was a former GWR line, so the closures were not confined to the newer companies that had been swept up in 1922 and 1923. In England as well there were closures of short-distance duplicate routes, such as between Marlborough and Savernake, where trains were diverted off the GWR line on to the Midland & South Western Junction's tracks between the two places. The business of rationalising the use of stations went on elsewhere too, and the Great Western closed their own at Oswestry in favour of the Cambrian's, while at both Basingstoke and Salisbury they diverted their trains into the Southern Railway's premises in 1932. A number of stations situated close to another larger one were closed, such as Carmarthen Junction, as early as 1926.

The opening of Morebath Junction Halt on the Barnstaple branch has been mentioned in an earlier chapter, and this was only one of the many similar additional facilities provided between the wars. Thirty-four new halts were opened in 1928 alone, but this did not stop others being closed, those at Nightingale Valley and Trumper's Crossing having perhaps the most intriguing names. The first was one that opened during the summer period in the Bristol area, and the latter was on the Brentford branch, on the outskirts of London. Closer still to Paddington, however, Park Royal station, just after Old Oak West Junction on the line to High Wycombe, succumbed in 1937, having been opened earlier in the 1930s when the services on the Ealing–Greenford–Acton triangle had been revamped to serve the new housing estates in the area. There was an interesting truncation of a branch at its end nearest the main-line as well. This was the Dauntsey–Malmesbury line, which had been crossed at Somerford by the South Wales & Bristol Direct after its opening in 1903. Thirty years later, in 1933, a connection was built from Little Somerford on the new line to Kingsmead Crossing on the branch, and the southern portion lifted. It was rather amusing to find that the Dauntsey–Kingsmead stretch still appeared on one of the BR route maps after nationalisation.

Down in the West of England there were a few branch-line casualties in the 1930s. Bridport–West Bay closed in 1930, while passenger services between St. Blazey and Fowey had been withdrawn the previous year, leaving the smoky depths of Pinnock Tunnel to the trains taking china clay for shipment. The facilities for loading ships at the Great Western's port on the banks of the river were considerably improved during the period of our study, and traffic from the various 'drys' in the china clay area around St. Austell was staged through the yards at St. Blazey. This is still the centre of considerable business for the Western Region, but the line through Pinnock Tunnel has now been converted to a one-way private road for English China Clays' own lorries shuttling from Par to the loading gantries on the Fowey. At the other end of the one-time Cornwall Minerals Railway, the branch with its rope-worked incline to Newquay Harbour was closed in 1926. This had crossed the main road immediately outside the terminus there, and the removal of this connection considerably aided the successive extensions to the passenger facilities that were carried out at this time. The similar incline down to the even smaller harbour at Portreath was also abandoned in 1936, together with the branch that had pottered its way northwards for three miles from a junction with the main line just east of Carn Brea station.

Closures of some of the branch lines were not the only economy measures pursued by the Great Western in the years between the two wars, and their success in two particular fields of activity undoubtedly gave other marginal lines a longer existence. One of the major expenses incurred by the railways at the beginning of our period of study had been the parish rates, which could be particularly severe in the case of branch lines. The *Great Western Railway Magazine* gave examples of these back in 1921, when the railway was paying no less than 89% of all the rates for Moreton South. In those days the upkeep of the public roads was the responsibility of the parish councils, and the railway companies could thus find themselves in the position of contributing more than 80% of the costs of these, which were then being knocked to pieces by the lorries used by their competitors. On the Falmouth Branch in 1925 the total rate bill came to £1,056, or more than the passenger receipts at Penmere. This factor made it pointless to consider the third of the 1926 Report's terms of reference, since converting the railway trackbed to a road would have meant they were paying towards the upkeep of both rights of way. However, by the end of the 1920s, as a result of a lot of lobbying by the railway companies generally, this rates burden and that of the government-imposed duty on each passenger ticket had both been reduced or lifted.

Another major source of expense for any railway is the maintenance of the track. At the time of our study this was carried out by length gangs, the members of which lived within walking or cycling distance of the particular stretch of track where they worked. On the main lines the ganger had to walk his length every day, noting the condition of the various track components, as well as the state of the ballast and even the drains. He then organised the work of his gang to carry out any corrective work that might be necessary. The length of line that one man could look after in this way was clearly limited, and was largely determined by the distance he could cover on foot, rather than whether there were two or one tracks to examine. On a normal main line the drill was to examine one line in the outward direction and the other coming back, care always being taken to face on-coming traffic. If there was only one track on a branch line it was not possible to double the length he had to inspect, as the return journey was, of necessity, less productive as there was no second track to inspect. With branches that only had a few trains it was probably not necessary to walk the length every day, but this still did not help the railway to extend the stretch for which the ganger was responsible all that much, simply because of the wasted time getting the rest of the gang to and from the places where work had to be carried out.

There was another cause of lower productivity on branch lines, and this involved the provision of look-out men to protect the gang while they were working on the track. On a normal main line, for much of the time only one needed to be positioned in the direction of on-coming trains over the track receiving maintenance, since everyone was clear of the traffic in the opposite direction. On a single-track branch, however, the next train could appear from either direction, and many of these lines had more than their fair share of curves which frequently minimised the distance the look-out could see, which could well have necessitated the provision of two of them, one for each direction. The job of look-out is a full-time one, and the productivity of the gang could consequently drop on a branch line for this reason. To overcome this problem the Great Western adopted the so-called Economic system of track maintenance, whereby for part of each day there were no trains, and the gang was given possession of the line. This sort of thing is still done today, even on the main lines, when work such as relaying is carried out, but between the wars it became a regular *daily* feature on many branch lines, and there would consequently be gaps in the train services over them.

The system involved a degree of mechanisation, and the ganger had his own inspection trolley which he could put on the rails after withdrawing an Occupation Key from a special single-line instrument where the trolley was kept, which was linked in the normal way with the single-line signalling system. By means of his own propulsive efforts with the trolley, his operating range was considerably extended, while the larger 4-wheeled pump-trolley used by the gang enabled them to get themselves and their equipment to site that much quicker. On arrival, the trolleys could be manually removed from the track and, after this had been done, the key could be inserted into the nearest box, which freed the line for use again.

The Great Western had gone in for this system quite extensively, starting on the Golden Valley Branch as early as 1901, and some fifty single-track branch lines had been converted to the system by the late 1920s. However, there were places where severe gradients or the prevalence of strong cross-winds made it impossible to use, and for these situations they developed the Motor Economic system, with petrol-driven trolleys, the first trial being in 1928 on the Cirencester–Rushey Platt stretch of the one-time Midland & South Western Junction Railway. This was situated conveniently near Swindon for the maintenance of the trolleys to be monitored. At the same time it improved the economics of that line, which had caused the Great Western considerable concern after they had taken it over, the absorption being postponed until July 1923, because of its poor financial performance. Four years later they discovered that the whole of the thirteen and three-quarter miles between Cirencester and Andoversford Junction required relaying, and to reduce the cost they singled it and provided two intermediate crossing loops. The Motor Economic system proved very satisfactory, and before the end of 1928 was extended northwards from Cirencester over the newly-singled stretch. Two years later it was in use on seventy single-line branches, with an aggregate mileage of 330. With the new system a single gang could look after a dozen miles of line, which was twice the length possible with the earlier, manually-operated Economic system.

Earlier in the book it was noted that the Table of Contents for the GWR's 1921 timetables listed just over 200 'Local and Branch Lines'. Some of these so classified carried through services to and from London, and their services have already been discussed in Chapter 3, while others listed the connecting services on what were to become the Southern Railway's lines in the West of England. Even excluding these there is no way in which we can look at more than a handful of the total, but it should, nevertheless, be possible to get a general feeling for the way in which their train services changed during the period between 1922 and 1939.

Having just referred to the Midland & South Western Junction line, we can usefully start our study with this branch, the services over which pottered their way for sixty-eight and a half miles between Lansdown station in Cheltenham to Andover Junction. In 1922 there were four week-day trains in each direction, one of which conveyed a through carriage between Liverpool Lime Street and Southampton Terminus via Andover Town, Fullerton and Romsey. The first southbound train left Cheltenham at 10.48 a.m. and the last at 6.42 p.m. Of these the two morning trains were much the faster, their overall times being two hours nine or thirteen minutes, compared with three hours six and seventeen minutes in the afternoon. The spread in scheduled times was not so great going north, and only varied between two hours five minutes for the through train from Southampton to two hours forty-one minutes for the 2.40 p.m. from Andover. The former managed to get all the way from Southampton Terminus to Cheltenham in a minute under three hours. In 1939, in spite of sixteen years' of Great Western ownership, the largest changes in the timetables were alterations of nineteen and thirty-eight minutes in the departure times of the first and last southbound trains from Cheltenham, although the other two in that direction, and all four northbound ones, still left at times that were within five minutes of what they had been in 1922. The first southbound train of the day, and the last one in the opposite direction had also been extended to and from Southampton. It is of interest to note that in 1937 the total receipts on the southern half of the line were two and three quarter times those from north of Rushey Platt, while the passenger revenue was four times as much, which goes a long way to explain why the GWR was so quick to single the track over the less busy half in the 1920s.

Turning now to a branch of a totally different kind, we move to the three and a half mile one between Kidlington and Blenheim & Woodstock. The terminus was extremely well placed for the town and the Palace, and there was a locomotive shed there too. It is thus worth taking a look at all the different classes of business on the branch, because they illustrate the way in which the importance of such a line changed during the twentieth century. Table 5.5 shows how the receipts from the goods, parcels and passenger traffic varied between 1903 and 1938. Unfortunately the Great Western statistics are only available for certain years prior to the 1930s, so we cannot follow all the changes, but the table nevertheless provides a useful insight into what was happening. The peak year for all categories except parcels was 1923, and business then began to fall off. By 1938 the passenger receipts were just less than half of those fifteen years earlier, but the freight was down to a third. Parcels had made most money back in 1903, but had another good year in 1923, following which that business also fell to a third of its value by 1938.

Table 5.5. Blenheim & Woodstock Branch Annual Receipts, 1903–1938

Year	Passengers	Receipts Parcels	Freight	Total	Livestock Handled
	(£)	(£)	(£)	(£)	(Wagons)
1903	1,576	908	2,902	5,386	128
1913	1,475	781	3,354	5,610	242
1923	2,529	849	5,998	9,376	85
1929	1,520	862	4,493	6,875	112
1932	1,196	789	3,272	5,257	30
1938	1,202	282	2,084	3,568	2

Source: *Great Western Railway: Traffic Dealt with at Stations and Goods Depots*

Traffic in livestock was at its busiest just before World War I, with, roughly speaking, one wagon a day being dealt with on Mondays–Fridays throughout the year. Even with Blenheim Palace and its vast estates, there would not be much call for the inward movement of livestock, and there is thus a very strong presumption that these workings involved the dispatch of animals to market. In those days large towns required a steady flow of live animals for slaughter, since there were few or no facilities for storing meat in refrigerated warehouses. Animals used to be driven on the hoof quite long distances to market, and the eight miles between Woodstock and Oxford would not have been too far for this to be done at one time. However, the superior condition of animals that arrived by rail could well have resulted in them being sent by train even over such a short distance. It was the development of road transport in the 1920s that was to change the railways' position dramatically for the worse with medium-distance transport of livestock, and the author has recollections of the large numbers of animals that used to arrive by lorry at the market in Exeter in the mid-1930s.

From 1934 onwards the annual number of wagon-loads of livestock traffic over the

Blenheim & Woodstock branch was down to single figures, which may have represented the movement of prize animals from the estate to agricultural shows miles away. The GWR regularly handled considerable amounts of this sort of traffic, and in 1931, for instance, when the Royal Agricultural Show was held at Castle Park, Warwick, two platforms 700 × 35 feet were installed in their goods yard, each capable of dealing with twenty-two vehicles a side. Five hundred and ninety wagons of livestock were received in thirty-two special trains, with continuous working going on for forty-eight hours, starting at three in the afternoon of Saturday 3 July. However, while the Great Western still considered that such special operations were worthwhile, the same was not the case on individual branch lines, and the one to Blenheim & Woodstock had come under scrutiny in the Branch Line Report as early as 1926.

One of the recommendations of this study was that the locomotive sub-shed on the branch should be closed, like a number of similar ones on other branches, and the line worked from the parent shed at Oxford, which was done in 1927. It was also pointed out that a worthwhile saving in annual maintenance could be achieved by reducing the amount of track at the terminus. On the other hand, a new intermediate halt was opened at Shipton-on-Cherwell in 1929, situated on the embankment where the line crossed the 'A' road from Oxford to Banbury. Unfortunately the passenger receipts for this were not recorded separately, and we cannot thus determine how busy it was.

With this background we can now look at the way in which the branch was worked. Back in 1922 the first train of the day left at 7.50 a.m. for the junction, to make a connection with an all-stations train from Leamington Spa which reached Oxford at 8.20. With the closure of the sub-shed the pattern altered considerably, and the first train of the day in 1939 left Oxford at 7.10, getting to Blenheim & Woodstock at 7.30, in time for the 8.3 return to Kidlington. The connection there was now with a local train from Banbury, which made the arrival at Oxford only five minutes later than it had been in 1922. Overall the journey time had dropped from thirty minutes to twenty-two, in spite of the opening of the halt at Shipton-on-Cherwell during the interim. In 1922 there were nine down and eight up passenger workings over this branch. Although not shown in the branch-line table, the 1.17 p.m. from Blenheim & Woodstock ran through to Oxford, and the 5.23 p.m. from Oxford similarly worked through to the terminus. This was undoubtedly connected with the need to change-over the branch-line locomotive with another from its parent shed at Oxford, but, as there were other services between these up and down workings, a second locomotive had to be available on the branch for part of the day anyway. In 1939 there were two mid-day through workings to Oxford and back, and no activity on the branch while these main-line journeys were being made. The final evening train at 9.55 p.m. from Blenheim also ran through to Oxford.

Much of our study has been concerned with the summer holiday business in the West of England, so we will now turn our attention to the Great Western's Cornish branch lines. As mentioned earlier in this chapter, the passenger services between St. Blazey and Fowey were withdrawn in 1929, but the other eight lines were all busily at work. Before looking at their services in detail it is worth summarising the overall amount of business they undertook, the details being given in Table 5.6. Most holiday-makers from up-country would have been travelling on monthly return tickets issued at their home stations, so their contribution to the branch lines' activities is excluded from these figures, but the table gives a useful indication of how much the different lines were used for local and outgoing traffic.

From the point of view of the holiday-maker, the St. Ives branch formed a useful way of getting to and from Penzance and the other attractions of Mount's Bay, and that line issued by far the largest number of tickets. Falmouth, on the other hand, produced the most passenger revenue, and its average price of over £1 per ticket indicates that a high proportion of these were for long-distance journeys, many of them, no doubt, being connected with the business of the port and its shipping interests. This average was about two and a half times that for the tickets issued at Plymouth, details of which are also included in the table. Fowey, another port, but of a very different kind, only got roughly the equivalent of ten pence for each of its tickets, a tenth of that on the Falmouth branch. Its passenger revenue was thus the lowest of all the Cornish lines, although the length of the branch was the shortest, bearing in mind that most of the Bodmin trains worked through to Wadebridge.

Table 5.6. Cornish Branch Passenger Revenue, 1937

Branch Line	Ordinary Tickets Issued	Season Tickets Issued	Passenger Revenue
			(£)
Looe	23,398	300	5,051
Bodmin	21,220	165	5,082
Fowey	34,379	257	3,489
Newquay	72,905	4,122	19,025
Falmouth	29,534	2,009	32,162
Chacewater–Newquay	21,308	1,400	3,863
Helston	22,019	224	5,751
St. Ives	86,629	1,588	11,917
	311,392	10,065	86,340
Plymouth (North Road + Millbay)	648,345	9,661	273,334

Source: *Great Western Railway: Traffic Dealt with at Stations and Goods Depots*

It can now be seen how the services on each of these branches changed over the period 1922–1939, working our way westwards from the Tamar. Starting therefore, with the Liskeard–Looe branch, and its peculiar operating arrangements that are a relic of the line's history. Overall there was no change in the number of passenger trains between 1922 and 1939 on ordinary week-days, the timetables in each of these two years showing eight down ones and seven in the up direction. In the former year there were two changes in timings on certain days of the week, one on Fridays and the other on Saturdays, but the summer of 1939 saw five more down and four additional up trains on Saturdays. A Sunday service had also been introduced, with eight trains in each direction. Since the branch-line timings were largely fixed to give main-line connections at Liskeard, there were many detailed differences, but there had been a significant speed-up in the overall times, the fastest trains now taking only twenty-five minutes compared with thirty in 1922. There was a locomotive shed at Moorswater, just beyond the reversal point for passenger trains at Coombe Junction. This was a sub-shed of St. Blazey and in 1938 had an allocation of two locomotives.

The next branch off the main line was that from Bodmin Road (now Parkway) to Bodmin, most of the trains over it running through to and from Wadebridge after reversing in Bodmin, and using Southern metals from Boscarne Junction. There was a steep climb up from Bodmin Road, and ten minutes were allowed for these three and a half miles in 1922, but the time had dropped to eight by 1939. The best overall time to or from Wadebridge in the earlier year was thirty minutes, and that was cut to twenty-eight, but there were considerable variations, depending on the time taken for the reversal at Bodmin, which could last as much as fifteen minutes. In 1922 there were seven through trains to Wadebridge and six back, with two and three more between the junction and Bodmin. Seventeen years later there were two additional through trains in the up direction, and on Saturdays three of the five Bodmin Road–Bodmin workings were extended to Wadebridge, the changes being too complex to go into in detail. In 1938 Bodmin had an allocation of two locomotives as a sub-shed to St. Blazey, and the first morning train over the Bodmin–Bodmin Road stretch was thus in the up direction, but its

141

starting time of 8.30 in 1922 had come forward to 6.55 in 1939. There was no Sunday service in either year under study, but in all probability an extra evening working could be laid on if the last down main-line connection of the day was running late, this being standard practice on most of the Cornish branches.

The branch from Lostwithiel to Fowey was one of the most attractive in Cornwall, keeping to the right bank of the estuary all the way. In the upper reaches the valley was very wide, but as Fowey was approached the wooded hillsides closed in, while the depth of water increased to compensate, enabling large vessels to load china clay at the succession of railway wharves situated between the running line and the water. Passenger trains had a much easier run compared with any of the other Cornish branches, but the unchanged standard timing of fifteen minutes, inclusive of the intermediate stop at Golant, was not very demanding. In 1922 there were seven passenger trains in each direction on an ordinary week-day, but the total had jumped to no less than thirteen in 1939, with an extra one on Saturdays. A Sunday service of nine trains in each direction had been provided by 1939.

From the point of view of the general level of passenger traffic, the Newquay branch was the busiest in Cornwall, with a number of through trains in both directions to and from London and the North of England. Between 1922 and 1939 there was a marked increase in the number of trains, from eight to twelve in each direction on ordinary week-days. There was an additional late evening up train which did not run on 7th and 8th August, the significance of which will become apparent later in our study. At the start of our period there were two extra down trains on a Saturday and one on Fridays, all of them third-class only. In the up direction the additional workings only ran on Fridays and there were two of them. St Blazey was open in 1922 and all trains called there, including the 11.00 a.m. from Paddington, although it missed the Luxulyan, Bugle and Quintrel Downs Platform. This service and the Fridays-only 2.40 from Par did the journey in fifty-three minutes, but in the somewhat easier up direction the 7.23 on a Friday evening managed to get through in forty-nine minutes. In 1922 there was no Sunday service, but seventeen years later there were seven down trains and eight going the opposite way. Three of these down ones and five of those in the up direction ran non-stop in forty-five minutes. On Saturdays the number of through trains off the branch increased from three to five, both the extras being for London, one of them leaving Newquay at 9.55 p.m. The time allowed over the branch for the normal daily through trains to London was extended on Saturdays, the first at 9.40 starting ten minutes earlier, while the 11.45 left five minutes later, but cut out the four intermediate stops made during the rest of the week.

The Falmouth branch was, it will be recalled, the end of the original broad-gauge route from London before the gauge of the West Cornwall Railway's track had been mixed. As befitted this ancestry it had a Sunday service in 1922 and, like the Newquay line, had year-round through carriages to and from London. In spite of this, however, speeds over the line were not very fast, the standard timing from Truro being thirty-seven minutes for the eleven and three quarter miles in 1922, although the last down train on Saturday evenings in 1939 only took twenty-nine minutes. The latter left at 10.12, but on other weekdays it was replaced by a Road Motor service, which departed at 10.30 and took no less than an hour to Falmouth Moor, with the ominous footnote 'Heavy luggage not conveyed'. There had been twelve down and thirteen up services on ordinary week-days in 1922, and three trains in each direction on Sundays. By 1939 the total each way had gone up to nineteen, with an aggregate of two more on Saturdays, and ten on Sundays. There was again a change in the evening service on this branch on 7th and 8th August 1939 (the Bank Holiday Monday and the day following), but unlike the Newquay line, which lost a train, Falmouth was one of the places that gained a late working that left at 10.10 p.m. for Truro.

The Chacewater–Newquay branch was an unusual one in Cornwall because it faced the wrong direction, turning north-eastwards from the junction and wandering between the coast and the higher ground all the way back to Newquay. From the passenger point of view, its main purpose was to serve the resort of Perranporth with its splendid sands, which had been reached by rail when the line from the triangular junction at Blackwater, on the Penzance side of Chacewater, was opened thus far in July 1903. Two years later it had been extended to join the Treamble branch at Shepherds, so completing a through route to Newquay, with trains being able to run direct from Penzance and Truro. By 1922 the west-to-north curve at Blackwater had been removed, but there was one afternoon through train from Newquay to Penzance, leaving at 2.28, which had to reverse at Chacewater. It called at all stations and halts (there were six of these on the branch) and reached Penzance at 3.53. This, like all the eight workings in each direction over the branch, was in the hands of motor trains offering one-class accommodation, seven of them running through from Truro, and six continuing to that city in the up direction. In 1939, however, the importance of Perranporth as a resort was sufficient for it to have through coaches to and from London on Saturdays. In the down direction these left Paddington at 9.30 a.m. and arrived at 4.10 p.m., while the return working departed half an hour earlier in the morning, and was five minutes slower overall. Most of the ordinary workings now involved a change at Chacewater, but on Sundays there was a round-trip from Penzance among the six down and five up branch workings. Back in 1922 there had been only four Sunday trains each way, all running to or from Truro.

Moving ten miles further west along the Great Western Railway from Chacewater used to bring one to Gwinear Road station, the junction for the most southerly branch in Britain. This ran for nine miles to Helston, which had been the terminus for the GWR's pioneering road passenger transport service to the Lizard when it was introduced in 1903. In 1922 the branch-line service consisted of eight trains in each direction, the first of the day being from the Helston end as there was a sub-shed there which housed two locomotives from the Penzance allocation. Some of the trains missed out Truthall Platform, the last normal calling point before the terminus, but the best overall timing was twenty-five minutes, regardless of whether the trains stopped there or not. By 1939 the service had been augmented to ten trains each way on ordinary week-days, with an extra up working on Saturdays, while there was an additional non-stop, late evening up train on 7th and 8th August that year which got to Gwinear Road in seventeen minutes. This service and the special Falmouth train connected with the 10.0 p.m. from Penzance, which also only ran on those two nights, and conveyed only sleeping-car passengers for Paddington, where it arrived at 6.35 the following morning. In 1938 these services had only run on the Bank Holiday itself, but had evidently proved popular enough to justify being extended. The cancellation of the up service from Newquay on those two nights was presumably to free the main-line locomotive and/or path for the working from Penzance.

The last Great Western branch in our survey is the one between St. Erth and St. Ives, which was the final broad-gauge branch to be built. In 1922 the train service was a fairly simple one, with thirteen trains in each direction on week-days only. All of them called intermediately at Lelant and Carbis Bay, and took between fifteen and twenty minutes for four and a half mile journey, the stretch round the cliffs beyond Lelant including sections of 1 in 60. In the 1930s when the 'Cornish Riviera Limited' was worked through to St. Ives on certain days of the week, the services of a pair of Prairie tanks were needed on the branch, and they had to work hard up the banks. By 1939 there were eighteen branch-line trains in each direction, but there was additionally one working from St. Ives by bus that was shown in *Bradshaw*. There was also one through train to and from Penzance, while there were two such workings among the eight Sunday trains, with again one additional service by bus being shown in the railway timetable. (There was, incidentally, a frequent bus service between Penzance and St. Ives, worked by the Western National, which was one of the Great Western's associated road transport companies.) In the up direction there was also an evening working at 9.50 from St. Ives on 7th and 8th August, which connected with the extra sleeping-car train to London on those two evenings. Although only just over ten miles from Penzance, a sub-shed was provided right by the station at St. Ives, which had an allocation of a single 2-6-2 tank, so the first working on the branch on a week-day morning was in the up direction, departing in both 1922 and 1939 at 6.55.

It is nice to be able to record that half of the Great Western's Cornish branches are still with us, in spite of the holocaust of the Beeching era, while a fifth—the line from Bodmin Parkway to Bodmin—is well set to become the county's first working preserved railway. The Perran-porth and Helston branches have disappeared, but the Fowey one remains open for clay traffic, while the Looe, Newquay, Falmouth and St. Ives lines are all operating busily under the BR Provincial flag. All the 'Holidaymaker Express' services to Newquay on summer Saturdays are even worked by 'InterCity 125' sets. At Looe and St. Ives the ends of the lines were cut back many years ago to provide extra car-parking spaces, but both branches are now used for 'Park & Ride' schemes. That at St. Ives is the most elaborate, with a new station having been opened at Lelant Saltings, complete with several acres of car-parking space. In 1988 the financial loss on this part of our social railway was only equal to the equivalent of two leading railmen's salaries, thanks to the careful planning of rosters and the re-introduction of through services to and from Penzance. The Falmouth branch is worked as a straight-forward shuttle from Truro.

Our study of the Great Western's passenger services is now complete, but before consider-ing some aspects of their practice and performance in the 1920s and 1930s, we will take a cursory glance at their newspaper, parcels and freight trains.

Branch-line 'B Sets' were not solely hauled by Prairie tanks. In April 1938 Dean Goods No. 2412 was in charge of a Frome–Bristol working, here seen approaching Mells Road. These sets were branded on their ends with the name of the station where they were based, this one being allocated to Taunton.

0-4-2T No. 544 on a 2-coach auto train leaves the tunnel near Wood End with a Birmingham–Bearley working.

Many auto trains were hauled by Pannier tanks, such as this down working, seen near Witham in August 1937, behind No. 5403.

4-6-0 No. 2931 *Arlington Court* on a local for Salisbury near Limpley Stoke, with the Camerton branch on the left. The train, formed of LSWR non-corridor stock, is probably a through working to Southampton.

In September 1935 a northbound train for Cheltenham enters Withington on the former Midland & South Western Junction Railway, not far south of Andoversford. The locomotive is not one of the Collett 0-6-0s, but No. 1011, formerly MSWJR No. 27. Ten of these had been built in 1899 and 1902 to handle the increased goods traffic over the line following the development of Southampton and the military base at Ludgershall. They were all reboilered by the GWR, and No. 1011 was withdrawn in 1937.

A southbound local passenger train on the Midland & South Western Junction line approaching Foss Cross behind 'Bulldog' 4-4-0 No. 3425 in September 1935.

The terminus of the Malmesbury branch in May 1922. Milk churns clutter the platform, while the gas tanks on the right-hand vehicle will have brought a supply from the GWR's nearest gas-making plant for the station lamps and any gas-lit coaches still at work on the branch. Note the flat-bottom track through the platform.

Steam railcar No. 85 on a Reading–Didcot working near Pangbourne. An ordinary clerestory trailer is being hauled, which would have necessitated the railcar running round at the end of the outward journey. This car was withdrawn as a self-propelled unit in December 1927, but continued in use as push-pull trailer No. 154.

CHAPTER SIX

NEWSPAPERS, PARCELS AND FREIGHT

During the period between the two world wars, passenger receipts only accounted for about a third of the revenue of the main-line railways of this country, so it is appropriate for us to take a quick look at the way in which the Great Western Railway developed its newspaper, parcels and freight services during this time. Right at the outset, however, we must accustom ourselves to a totally-different type of working compared with today's Railfreight operations. While we are now used to 2000-ton stone trains rolling along the Berks & Hants at speeds of 60 mph, the average mineral train in the 1920s and 1930s was a very different proposition, with no continuous brakes and most of its wagons consisting of wooden-bodied vehicles, the majority of them privately-owned, and with axleboxes only lubricated by grease.

At the beginning of the 1920s there were over 100,000 of these ten-tonners in circulation in the Welsh coal-mining area. The nature of the coal-exporting business meant that large tonnages had to be accumulated in close proximity to the docks, ready to be loaded as soon as the agents for a particular colliery had secured the business. There was standage for no less than 12,000 wagons at Newport alone, and, while the vehicles were privately owned, the railway company had to provide the siding capacity. Means were required to tip the loads into the ships, each wagon having to be weighed full and empty in the process, and blending of different types of coal sometimes having to take place as the ship was filled.

In 1923 the Great Western proposed a new type of coal wagon as a means of improving productivity. These vehicles were of all-steel construction and held twenty tons, double that which could be got into most of the old wooden ones, and the first of them was brought into use within twelve months. From the railway's point of view a big advantage was the fact that a train of the new wagons was only 60% of the length of the older type, and they very actively promoted their use over the years that followed, spending more than £2,000,000 on modifications to the tipping equipment on the dock-sides to take them. Nowadays the size of the coal carried in vast amounts by British Rail in their trains of Merry-Go-Round wagons is very small, as it will only be pulverised to flour-sized dust for burning in the power stations, but between the two world wars coal was expected to come in large lumps. These were friable too, and special efforts had to be made to prevent it being broken during the loading operations.

Coal was also the universal home fuel, and lumps that had 'fallen off a wagon, Dai' were regularly traded in the back streets. Indeed there were stories of rails being greased so the locomotive hauling a train would slip to a stand to enable coal to be spirited out of the wagons by waiting hands. One could not help recalling such happenings in 1981 when we took the National Railway Museum's reproduction *Rocket* to Cannes in the south of France. Throughout the week's operations our coal supply was kept in a couple of dustbins on the footpath outside the *Palais des Festivals* alongside *La Croissette*, and no one walked off with any of it (even as a souvenir), which would have not been the case beside the Bristol Channel, at Barry Island, for example, fifty years earlier!

The movement of the coal traffic in South Wales benefited considerably from the geography of the area, as most of the loaded trains could use gravity on the way down the valleys to the docks, and the locomotives had to toil uphill only with the empties. Many of the constituent companies had adopted 0-6-2 tank locomotives for this sort of traffic, operated with their smokeboxes facing the collieries, which enabled them to benefit from the guidance of the pony truck under the bunker on the faster downhill stretches. As well as rebuilding many of these locomotives with standard boilers and cabs, the Great Western also produced 200 of their own version of the classic South Wales 0-6-2T in the 1920s, numbered in the 56XX and 66XX series.

In the light of the comments so far in this chapter it will be appreciated that the pace of movement of the average coal wagon in the 1920s and 1930s was not unduly fast. Indeed in 1924 the *Great Western Railway Magazine* was boasting that the standard of freight train working generally had been maintained, but the speed only averaged between 6 and 7 mph over the whole system throughout the previous twelve months. There was, however, a growing number of vacuum-brake express freight trains, running overnight between important centres, whose schedules were very much better than this. As we will see in the next chapter, some of these were booked to run for more than 100 miles between stops and average well over 30 mph in the process. Several schemes were introduced to increase the use of such services, and the GPO's Cash On Delivery service was extended to the railways and would even cover a wagon-load of coal. Larger vans were introduced to match the higher-capacity coal wagons, and containers also came into operation.

Well-produced, illustrated booklets were issued by the Great Western giving details of their goods services, one of them even including the quotation from Lord Bacon:

There be three things which make a nation great and prosperous: a fertile soil, busy workshops and easy conveyance of men and commodities from place to place.

There were also more direct appeals to the traders' pockets, one such being the following bit of information:

Messrs. Burton & Sons, by the combined storage and delivery arrangements created by the Great Western Railway, have effected a substantial saving over their previous arrangements. Does this appeal to you?

Each edition gave details of the latest times when consignments could be received to catch the overnight trains, and the expected time of arrival at the goods stations at a whole range of destinations. The latest time for receipt of consignments at Paddington on week-day evenings went back from 5.0 to 5.30 between 1929 and 1936, and traders could benefit from extra time on Saturdays too, the close-off moving from noon to 12.30. There were various incentives for firms to send goods by rail, traders being issued with season tickets if the amount of their business reached a certain value. In 1929 the limit was lowered to £300 *per annum* and it was possible to transfer them to another named person for periods of seven days on up to twelve occasions in the year.

In 1929 a scheme for the registered transit of merchandise by goods train was started, the details given in the booklet being as follows:

The Great Western Railway announces the introduction of a system of registered transits. Under this scheme, traders will be informed the time at which a registered consignment will be delivered, and the transit of such consignments by the ordinary services will be specially controlled from point to point, to ensure delivery by the time quoted, subject to fog or other unavoidable risks. Proof of delivery will be afforded to the sender where desired.

For this service a Registration Fee of 2/6 (12½p) per consignment will be charged.

Until otherwise arranged, registered transits will apply only to consignments between places on the Great Western system shown on pages (which were then specified in the booklet).

In the days when the railways were common carriers, there were occasions when the unscrupulous used them as a scape-goat for non-supply or non-acknowledgement of goods ordered, and this registration scheme would clearly assist in such cases. The railway could also get incorrectly blamed in public for the non-acceptance of consignments, particularly during short-term gluts, an example of this being quoted in the *Great Western Railway Magazine*, when fish at one Cornish port were thrown back into the sea at a time when the local merchants were not able to find any buyers.

The Great Western's booklets have been used to prepare Table 6.1, which shows the way in which transit times improved between 1929 and 1936 for goods being dispatched from Paddington and Birmingham. The biggest increase in each case was with the number of transits available with delivery next morning. The punctuality of goods trains received a lot of attention, and an All-Line Goods Train Working Competition was launched in 1927, the results being reported monthly in the *Great Western Railway Magazine*. Unfortunately these do not give us any indication of the actual speeds achieved, and the comparison was made on a complicated points basis.

Table 6.1. Speed of GWR Freight Services from Paddington and Birmingham

| | Number of transits in category shown | |
	1929	1936
From Paddington		
With delivery:		
Next morning	106	139
Noon next day	11	10
Next afternoon	10	3
Next day	–	1
Second morning	1	–
	128	153
From Birmingham		
With delivery:		
Next morning	71	108
Noon next day	16	5
Next afternoon	7	13
Second morning	20	22
Second day	–	4
	114	152

Sources: *GWR booklet How to Send and How to Save (1929)*
GWR booklet GWR Guide to Economical Transport (1936)

Many of the regular fast freight services acquired names, given in Table 6.2. on page 152, which is derived from the GWR booklets. As will be seen, they had a mixed origin, some being derived from the nature of the traffic or from the destination, while the basis of others is obscure. It will be seen that the number of such workings was quite considerable, and totalled far more than could be coped with by the nine 47XX 2-8-0s. In their large-boiler form these had appeared in the early 1920s, the prototype (No. 4700) having been built first with a modified Standard No. 1 boiler in 1919. Then they worked almost exclusively on vacuum-fitted express freights from London to Wolverhampton and the West of England, and *vice versa*, but their shed allocations changed with the arrival of the mixed-traffic 'Halls' at the end of the 1920s to join them on these overnight duties. In the earlier days some of the lighter workings had been entrusted to the Churchward Moguls, but even the 'Castles' were not

Table 6.2. Named freight trains on GWR in late 1920s

Time	From	To	Name
1. 5 a.m.	Acton	Bristol	The High Flyer.
7.40 p.m.	Acton	Cardiff	The Early Bird.
9.25 p.m.	Acton	Llanelly	The Leek.
3.40 a.m.	Banbury Jc.	Bristol	The Competitor.
2.10 a.m.	Basingstoke	Wolverhampton	The Cherbourg.
9.35 p.m.	Basingstoke	Wolverhampton	The B.B.C. (Basingstoke, Birmingham, Crewe)
3.55 p.m.	Birkenhead	Smithfield	The Meat.
6. 5 p.m.	Birkenhead	Pontypool Road	The Feeder.
8.20 p.m.	Birkenhead	Paddington	The General.
9. 5 p.m.	Birkenhead	Cardiff	The Mersey.
10.50 p.m.	Birkenhead	Bordesley Jc.	The Birmingham Market
11.35 p.m.	Birkenhead	Oswestry	The Cambrian Pioneer.
11. 0 p.m.	Birmingham	Paddington	The Pedlar.
9.10 p.m.	Bordesley Jc.	Birkenhead	The Shipper.
10.10 p.m.	Bordesley Jc.	Swansea	The Hardware.
6.50 p.m.	Bristol	Birkenhead	The Farmer's Boy.
7.40 p.m.	Bristol	Paddington	The "Bacca."
9.20 p.m.	Bristol	Wolverhampton	The Western Docker.
10. 5 p.m.	Bristol	Paddington	The Cocoa.
10.55 p.m.	Bristol	Laira	The Drake.
12.25 a.m.	Bristol	Carmarthen Jc.	The Bristolian.
3.50 p.m.	Cardiff	Hanwell Br. Sdgs.	The Stock.
9.45 p.m.	Cardiff	Saltney	The Spud.
11.10 p.m.	Cardiff	Paddington	The Ironmonger.
12.55 a.m.	Cardiff	Swansea	Port to Port.
7.30 p.m.	Carmarthen	Paddington	The Up Welshman.
8.35 p.m.	Carmarthen	Bristol	The Open.
11. 0 a.m.	Exeter	Pontypool Road	The Ponty.
4. 0 p.m.	Exeter	Old Oak Common	The Flying Pig.
12. 5 a.m.	Gloucester	Cardiff	The Bacon.
7.50 p.m.	Gloucester	Paddington	The Cotswold.
11. 0 p.m.	Handsworth	Acton	The Queen's Head.
8.20 p.m.	Kidderminster	Paddington	The Carpet.
7.45 p.m.	Manchester	Bristol	The "Mon."
8.42 p.m.	Manchester	Wolverhampton	The Early Riser.
4.58 p.m.	Marazion	Bristol	The Tre Pol and Pen Flier.
10.25 p.m.	Margam	Bordesley	The Tinman.
5.30 p.m.	Newton Abbot	Paddington	The Hackney.
9.32 p.m.	Old Oak Common	Penzance	The Cornishman.
8. 5 p.m.	Paddington	Bristol	The Shopper.
9.10 p.m.	Paddington	Birkenhead	Northern Flash.
9.35 p.m.	Paddington	Carmarthen Jc.	The Welshman.
10.10 p.m.	Paddington	Laira	The Tamar.
10.30 p.m.	Paddington	Cardiff	South Wales Borderer
10.50 p.m.	Paddington	Weymouth	The Jersey.
11. 5 p.m.	Paddington	Wolverhampton	The Hampton
11.15 p.m.	Paddington	Bristol	The Western General.
11.35 p.m.	Paddington	Newton Abbot	The Devonshireman.
12. 5 a.m.	Paddington	Worcester	The Sauce.
12.15 a.m.	Paddington	Fishguard	Irishman.
12.30 a.m.	Paddington	Bristol	The Mopper Up
12.10 a.m.	Park Royal	Stourbridge Jc.	The Stour.
2.50 p.m.	Penzance	Paddington	The Searchlight.
7.20 p.m.	Penzance	Plymouth	The Pasty.
5.40 a.m.	Pontypool Road	Newton Abbot	The Laira.
10.30 p.m.	Reading	Laira	The Biscuit
11.40 a.m.	Southall	Crewe	The Grocer.
3.50 p.m.	Swindon	Tavistock Jc.	The Rasher.
7.10 p.m.	Victoria Basin	Basingstoke	The Cargo.
4.20 a.m.	Westbury	Wolverhampton	The Moonraker.
7.35 p.m.	Westbury	Manchester	The Lancashire Lad.
9.55 p.m.	Westbury	Penzance	Western Flash.
10.50 p.m.	Westbury	Pontypool Road	The Northern.
7.22 p.m.	West Drayton	Wolverhampton	The Drayton.
6.35 p.m.	Weymouth	Paddington	The Up Jersey.
1.30 a.m.	Wolverhampton	Basingstoke	The Southern Docker.
2.10 a.m.	Wolverhampton	Basingstoke	The Southerner.
2.45 a.m.	Wolverhampton	Birkenhead	The Northern Docker.
4. 0 a.m.	Wolverhampton	Crewe	The Northern Exchange.
8.15 p.m.	Wolverhampton	Paddington	The Racer.
10.15 p.m.	Wolverhampton	Westbury	The Crosser.
12.45 a.m.	Wolverhampton	Birkenhead	The Flying Skipper.
6.45 p.m.	Worcester	Cardiff	The Worcester Fruit.
8.35 p.m.	Worcester	Crewe	The "Sparagras."

A 'Saint' Class 4-6-0 No. 2907 *Lady Disdain*, on an up Ocean Liner Special passes West Drayton, with two mail vans behind the tender.

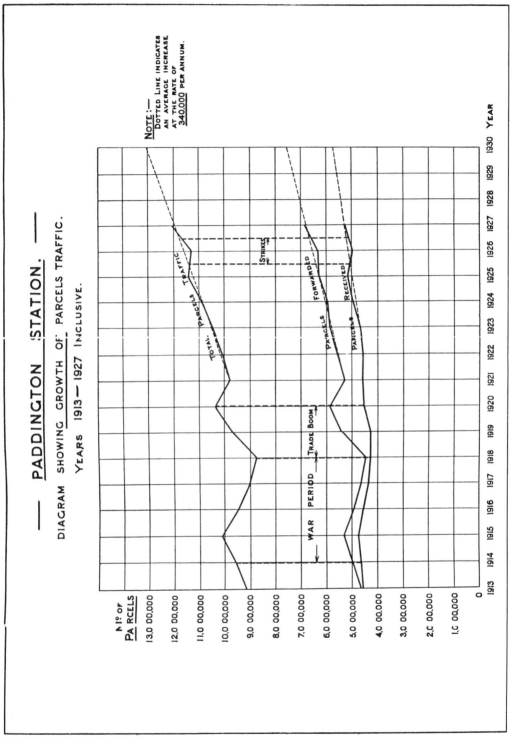

The growth of parcels traffic at Paddington, as shown in the 1928 report from the Chief Engineer's Office.

exempt from such duties, the 9.32 p.m. from Old Oak Common to Plymouth being rostered to be hauled by one of them in 1934, and allowed a maximum load of forty-five wagons plus brake-van.

The development of reliable heavy road vehicles in the early 1920s was utilised by the railways as well as causing them a growing amount of competition. Although their ordinary collection and delivery services were not particularly profitable, it became increasingly economic to use motor vehicles over quite long distances from a number of carefully chosen railway stations, where they could also offer traders storage facilities at the rate of 5/3 (26^1/$_2$p) per square yard per year, as long as they took twenty square yards or more. Among the valleys of South Wales the Great Western found this to be particularly so, and by the end of the 1920s they had developed an extensive 'railhead' distribution system based at Cardiff for small consignments. They published a map of the area covered by this on which the lines represented roads rather than railways. This only formed part of the story, as the 156 stations lying to the north and west of Cardiff that had handled goods traffic prior to 1927 were reduced to forty-six, each of these having its own local area for collection and delivery services, operated by road motor vehicles.

Moving from freight and goods services to the newspaper and parcel business, we once more return to the fully-braked train whose stock was capable of running at speeds comparable to those achieved by express trains. We have already seen how the 5.30 a.m. from Paddington to the West of England was known as the 'Newspaper Train' in broad-gauge days, but by the 1920s that was far too late in the day to start moving papers out of the capital city. The Great Western devoted considerable attention to this class of traffic during the 1920s and 1930s. In 1934 they were twice able to claim that they were operating the fastest newspaper train in the world. The first of these to be introduced was the 12.50 a.m. from Paddington, which ran non-stop to Plymouth in the same timings as the 'Cornish Riviera'. The loadings were, however, a lot less demanding on the 'King' rostered for the working, as the train consisted of just three 'Syphons' and the same number of newspaper vans. A special entry in the working timetables instructed all concerned that 'A clear Road must be kept for this Train'. Later in the same year the faster average of 58.5 mph was scheduled for the 1.20 a.m. Paddington–Newport newspaper train, which was usually worked by a 'Star', and loaded to 9 vehicles, one of them being a 6-wheeled van.

The new 'Fastest Newspaper Train in the World' was followed by the 1.40 a.m., for Plymouth, which additionally conveyed passengers, and so appears in Chapter 3 as the 1.35, having been retimed slightly during the intervening five years. This train was somewhat heavier, and could be hauled by a 'King' or a 'Castle'. The shorter the distance over which the newspapers had to be carried, the later they could leave London, and those for Bristol thus did not depart until 2.30. That train's first stop was at Swindon, and a 'Castle' would appear at the head of its five vans of newsprint. Finally at 3.50 came the last of these overnight workings, heading for Banbury via Oxford, and having the fastest booking of the day to Reading in thirty-eight minutes. It only loaded to three vehicles, and any class of 4-6-0 was used, bar the 'Kings', which were not allowed to Oxford because of the bridge at Appleford.

Parcels traffic was also booming on the Great Western between the two world wars. To illustrate the situation, the diagram on page 154 shows how the quantity being handled at Paddington was increasing in 1927. The rate of increase was nearly 3%, which explains why alterations were necessary to the parcels platforms when the station was rebuilt. From 1937 onwards the diesel-powered parcels railcar No. 17 was at work in the London area, its design being based on that of the earlier streamlined passenger-carrying units, with access being provided by three sets of glazed sliding doors on each side. It was used extensively for produce from Joe Lyons' cake and confectionery factory at Cadby Hall, which was loaded at Kensington Olympia, the car running to Reading and Oxford every day. Space unfortunately does not permit any more detailed examination of the Great Western's parcels trains, nor for the many others run for the General Post Office nor those laid on to convey vast quantities of seasonal agricultural and horticultural produce, be it potatoes or tomatoes from the Channel Islands, strawberries from Brittany via Plymouth or broccoli and spring flowers from Cornwall.

In the previous chapter we looked at the receipts from passenger fares on the Great Western Railway's Cornish branch lines, and it is illuminating to compare these figures with the revenue just from freight. These are given in Table 6.3, which shows each of the line's total receipts, plus the amount and proportion of it which arose from the freight activities. There is a difference between the 'passenger' figures in this table and those in Table 5.6, as the latter were just the fares, and excluded the income received from parcels and miscellaneous sources at the passenger stations, as distinct from the goods depots. It will be seen that overall the revenue from freight came to no less than 84%.

Table 6.3. Freight Receipts on Cornish Branches in 1937

| | Receipts | | Freight as |
Branch	Total	Freight	Percentage of Total
	(£)	(£)	(%)
Looe	15,429	6,889	45
Bodmin	16,540	10,817	65
Fowey	165,498	161,637	98
Newquay	123,761	99,305	80
Drinnick Mill and Meledor Mill	176,267	176,267	100
Falmouth	117,794	78,320	66
Newham	12,654	12,654	100
Chacewater–Newquay	13,444	8,761	65
Helston	46,684	32,559	70
St. Ives	26,687	12,503	47
TOTALS	714,758	599,712	84

Source: *Great Western Railway, Traffic Dealt with at Stations and Goods Depots*

There are some lines which did not feature in the Branch Lines chapter, as there were no passenger services on the Newham, Drinnick Mill or Meledor Mill branches. The last two of these lines handled china clay from the 'drys', which were themselves fired by coal brought in by train, although the revenue from this would have appeared elsewhere in the system. The Newham branch served the wharves on the Truro River, half a mile downstream from the city centre, and was worked from Penwithers Junction, which was also where the Falmouth branch left the main line. Access to the Newham branch was only possible from the Falmouth line itself, but this peculiar operating arrangement was an improvement from the one-time layout here, when the tracks of this eastern end of the West Cornwall Railway had crossed those of the broad-gauge Cornwall Railway on the level. On the Bodmin, Falmouth and Helston branches the passenger:freight revenue was roughly in the usual one-third:two-thirds ratio that characterised the system as a whole, but the Looe and St. Ives lines got just over half their total revenue from passengers, parcels and miscellaneous sources. On all the others the ratio of the freight business was far higher than the average, and in several cases it represented the whole business of the line. Another point of interest in Table 6.3 is the very high revenue from freight on the Lostwithiel–Fowey branch, which did not actually put much onto rail, although it loaded vast tonnages of clay into ships that had arrived by rail from sources inland. The revenue in this case was presumably due to the charges raised for the use of the docks and loading facilities.

Our study of the GWR's non-passenger traffic will conclude with an examination of their arrangements for taking cars by rail. We tend to think that Motorail services were a development of the last three decades, but in the 1920s the motorist was being very actively encouraged by the Great Western to put his car on the railway. Although their timetables pointed out that 'Horses, Carriages and Motor Cars are not conveyed by Express Trains', potential users were invited to inquire for details of those services that could be used. This continued the tradition established in the early days of the railways when those who could afford to do so took their own carriages on the back of the train on which they were travelling.

By 1927 the arrangements were subject to a number of constraints. Not less than twenty-four hours' notice was required, which was not unreasonable, since it could well have been necessary to move the wagon to the forwarding station. The timetable stated that Covered Carriage Trucks for this purpose were kept at Paddington, but one must assume that they were, in practice, spread round the system, and their movements only co-ordinated from that point. When the necessary arrangements had been made, the load had to be at the station '. . . at least half-an-hour before the Train by which they are being sent is due to start'. It was also pointed out that 'Horses and Live Stock are not accepted for transit from Paddington between 10.0 a.m. and 5.0 p.m. on Saturdays throughout the year'. Nowadays it is certain categories of tickets that debar their holders from travelling out of some of the London termini at peak times.

The mileage rates in the 1920s for cars and carriages look remarkably modest by today's standards. A single vehicle weighing not more than two and a half tons would be conveyed for 9d/mile (3.75p) at Owner's Risk, although the rate quadrupled if you wanted it to go at Company's Risk. The contemporary single fares per mile were $2^1/_4$d/mile (0.94p) for first-class travel, and $1^1/_2$d/mile (0.63p), third class. If one belonged to a two-car family and wanted to take them both by train together, the rates came down by a sixth at Owner's Risk, but only by an eighth if the railway company were liable for any damage. There was a similar differential between the two rates if three carriages or motor cars were being sent in the one carriage truck, which perhaps implies that damage was more likely to occur when more than one vehicle was sent together. There were minimum charges corresponding to a journey of fifteen miles, which seems to have been a remarkably short distance, bearing in mind what we would now refer to as the terminal costs, since such transits would have, even in those days, involved a considerable amount of special shunting.

At the present time Eurotunnel's activities on both sides of the Channel are focusing our attention on the transport of cars by rail through an underwater tunnel. More than sixty years ago, however, such operations were commonplace for the Great Western Railway, whose Severn Tunnel presented them with an opportunity to move people and their cars across the watery gap between England and Wales. There was, however, one important difference between that and the Channel Tunnel, which was that it was possible to outflank the Severn crossing by driving to the first bridgehead and back along the other side of the estuary. This 'long road detour via Gloucester' did however involve driving some fifty-five miles extra, which was an appreciable distance for early motorists and their cars. So the GWR instituted a car-carrying service through the tunnel, between Severn Tunnel Junction on the Welsh side, and the two railheads of Patchway and Pilning on the other, in competition to the ferry service.

They were thus repeating with this new market the tactics they had adopted with the ordinary foot passengers back in 1886, when the tunnel was first opened. In December that year a service of ten local trains was introduced in each direction between Bristol and Cardiff. The previous rail/ferry/rail fares increased by roughly 50% for first- and second-class travellers, but the third-class fares only rose by 40% for a single and 20% return, the *Railway Times* pointing out that:

'The railway company feel that this increased charge is warranted by the superior arrangements made for the conveyance of passengers, as the journey is made in much less time, and the disagreeable crossing of the New Passage is avoided'.

The new fares were only about two-thirds of those permitted by the Act of Parliament, which gave the railway company power to levy charges that were increased by an extra mileage, over and above that actually travelled, to compensate for the huge cost of the new undertaking. This has always been a common arrangement with many railways that have been built at greater-than-usual-cost, the most recent examples being the French *Lignes à Grande Vitesse* and the West German *Neubaustrecke*, all of which still charge for the old number of kilometres travelled before the construction of the new shorter cut-offs.

One of the advantages of such charging freedom is that the railway company can subsequently cut its fares to stimulate traffic or to compete with an alternative means of transport. This in fact took place with the car traffic through the Severn Tunnel in the period between the two world wars. In 1927 both the English railheads were still in use, but by 1939 the service was only being operated over the shorter stretch of just under five miles between Severn Tunnel Junction and Pilning (High Level), as the latter station was now known. Cars were loaded on to open wagons at either end for conveyance at Owner's Risk, although in 1927, by giving twenty-four hours' notice, it was possible to order a covered carriage truck, which enabled the car to be sent at Company's Risk.

However, if one did so, the charge for the single journey went up from eleven shillings and three pence (56p) to fifteen shillings (75p), but by 1939 the only option mentioned in the timetable was Owner's Risk, and the price of a single journey was now determined by the rating of the car. There were just two charging brackets, depending on whether the car was under or over 8 hp. This 'RAC' power rating was based on the engine's stroke and capacity measurements, and was also the means used at that time to fix the amount paid for the Road Fund licence. For cars not exceeding 8 hp, the cost of a single had dropped to five shillings and three pence (26p), while anything larger than this was charged six shillings and four pence (31$\frac{1}{2}$p). There was also a reduction in the time that had to be allowed to load the car, the gap before the booked departure of the train dropping from thirty to ten minutes over the same period. This clearly indicated that the saving of time was also perceived to be a factor when the motorist made a choice on how to travel, although the changed regulations about fuel supplies on the cars, to be referred to later, undoubtedly helped. By the end of the Great Western era, however, the loading time had gone up to twenty minutes in the October 1947 timetable.

Motor cycles travelled in the guard's van, and were charged on weight. In 1927 they could go at Company's or Owner's risk, the latter being 6d (2$\frac{1}{2}$p) cheaper at two shillings and eight pence (13$\frac{1}{2}$p) for the smallest weight bracket of not more than two hundredweight (224 pounds). Machines weighing more than half a ton, if such a thing existed, were rated as cars, as were those that had a non-detachable sidecar. By 1939 the weight brackets had altered slightly, but the rate for a machine weighing in the range 120–200 pounds had dropped to one shilling and seven pence (8p), and only a Company's Risk rate was being quoted. Again a lapse of twelve years had seen much lower rates being offered to the passenger.

It is not entirely clear from the table whether the rates quoted included the driver's fare. The timetable stated that the motor bicycles had to be accompanied, but by 1939 the passenger fares were specifically quoted. Since one could choose to travel first class at three shillings and four pence (16$\frac{1}{2}$p) or third class at two shillings (10p), it would appear most likely that the passenger fare was *not* included in the cost for the car or motor cycle.

Although most of the later transits were at Owner's Risk, the driver was able to take steps to protect his vehicle if required. A waterproof sheet could be hired in 1939 for one shilling (5p), which would ensure that no sooty drips that might come from the roof of the tunnel landed on the car, but also protected it from any sparks the locomotive might emit on its way up the steep incline from the smoky depths below the deepest part of the estuary. In 1924 the ventilation system for the tunnel was altered, with a new induction fan being installed in place of the previous suction one. This meant that fresh air was blown into the centre of the tunnel down the Sudbrook shaft, a mile-and-a-half from the Welsh end, which made conditions for everyone in the tunnel a lot better. It particularly benefited the crews of the double-headed, heavily-loaded eastbound freight trains as they struggled up the 1 in 100 gradient, but the improvement was also an advantage for passengers. Those taking their cars across travelled in ordinary coaches, and not in their own vehicles as will be the case with the Eurotunnel Shuttles between Kent and the Pas de Calais.

The railway was understandably concerned about the fire hazards of petrol in the confined bore of the four-mile tunnel, and, in the course of the period in which we are interested, various changes were made in the regulations, to match the technological improvements taking place with motor vehicles. Back in 1920s the instructions read as follows:

Motorists are permitted to retain a maximum of two gallons of petrol under certain conditions. An additional supply is kept on hand at Severn Tunnel Junction, Pilning and Patchway Stations, and the Railway Company provide from these stocks (without additional charge) to the owners of cars or cycles which have passed through the Tunnel, an amount of motor spirit equivalent to any taken from the car or cycle before entraining, on presentation of a voucher from the forwarding Station.

Motorists can also purchase up to a maximum quantity of 6 gallons at the Stations.

By 1939 things had been eased somewhat, the instructions being changed to:

There is no restriction as to the quantity of petrol that may be left in the tanks of Motor Cars provided that –
The flow of petrol to the carburettor has been stopped, all pressure released from the tank, and the car is free from leakage of petrol. Note:- Where the flow of petrol to the carburettor is stopped by means of a shut-off cock, the engine must be run by the person in charge of the car until the petrol in the carburettor is exhausted and the engine stops automatically.

As a result of further changes, by the end of the GWR's days in 1947 the instructions had altered still further, as follows:

A quantity of petrol (not exceeding one quart in the case of motor cycles) may be left in the tanks, provided that –
(a) In the case of vehicles with gravity or autovac feed, the flow of petrol to the carburettor has been stopped by means of the shut-off cock provided.
(b) In the case of vehicles with electric petrol pump, the flow of petrol to the carburettor be interrupted by switching off the electric pump (switch key, if fitted, must be removed).
(c) With cars fitted with mechanical petrol pumps, it is sufficient to stop the engine and remove the ignition key.
(d) The motor is free from the leakage of petrol.

By this time there was no mention of petrol being available for purchase at either end, possibly because of rationing. While motor cycles were at that time fairly thrifty when it came to their petrol consumption, it might nevertheless have been difficult to find a garage at which to fill up with only a quarter of a gallon left in the tank when one left the railway premises.

The section of the timetable in 1927 does not give details of the train services between the various railheads, but this information is included in the 1939 version. Then there were six westbound weekday services from Pilning, between 9.43 a.m. and 9.28 p.m. One more service was provided in the opposite direction, and they ran somewhat earlier at each end of the day, the first leaving Severn Tunnel Junction at 6.24 a.m., and the last at 6.30 p.m. There could be an extra eastbound trip on Fridays, if required, operating just eight minutes before the 4.28 p.m. working. On Sundays there were two trips in each direction, those from Pilning leaving exactly twelve hours apart at 9.50, while those in the opposite direction departed at 9.16 a.m. and 8.55 p.m. During the era of austerity and petrol rationing in this country after World War II, there were only three weekday workings in 1947, two of them only running on Mondays and Fridays. There was a single Sunday evening round-trip from Severn Tunnel Junction during the winter period, except on the two Sundays either side of Christmas, when there was an additional morning working in each direction, being booked to depart exactly twelve hours earlier in each case. Journey times overall varied in a somewhat random fashion between eleven and eighteen minutes.

Throughout the inter-war years, the typical GWR main-line goods train anywhere in the system consisted of upwards of fifty hand-braked vans or wagons behind one of the Churchward 2-8-0s. During the Interchange trials after Nationalisation in 1948, one of these locomotives on Welsh coal achieved the best specific fuel consumption of all the locomotives tested. Here No. 2802 passes Kings Sutton, just south of Banbury, with an up train, the first twenty vehicles of which are all wooden-bodied open wagons.

Another Churchward 2-8-0 No. 2851 hauls a down goods near Chippenham in March 1935.

The GWR purchased some of the Robinson 2-8-0s of Great Central design built for overseas service in World War I. They appeared on many parts of the system, and were known as the 'ROD' (Railway Operating Division) class. Here No. 3046 is in charge of an up goods train near Bathford in April 1935.

Perishable traffic was usually handled by locomotives with larger diameter wheels than the ordinary 2-8-0s. Here one of the Churchward 2-6-0s, No. 7305, works an up Channel Islands potato train from Weymouth past Witham.

Branch-line freight. Pannier tank No. 3736 trundles its short train along the Limpley Stoke–Camerton branch near Combe Hay in March 1938, long before the line was used for the filming of the *Titfield Thunderbolt*.

A down train of milk empties near West Drayton behind 'Castle' class 4-6-0 No. 111 *Viscount Churchill*. This locomotive was the nominal rebuild of the only Great Western Pacific, *Great Bear*.

Less than four months before the beginning of World War II, 4-6-0 No. 5039 *Rhuddlan Castle* worked this up Ocean Liner special from Plymouth, seen here passing Dawlish with a windowless bullion van immediately behind the tender, followed by a mail van.

In the 1930s, 4-6-0 No. 5003 *Lulworth Castle* was photographed near Frome on a down West of England train. There are two restaurant cars next to the tender, which were probably being worked to the West of England for up Saturdays-only trains, such as the one which featured in D.S.M. Barries journey described in Chapter Seven.

CHAPTER SEVEN

PRACTICE AND PERFORMANCE

Having now looked at many different facets of the Great Western Railway's train services between the two world wars, it is appropriate to consider one or two of the operating practices that were characteristic of the company's ways of operating, and how well their performance matched the aspirations of the timetables.

The large-scale use of slip coaches by the GWR will already have been noted, and this particular feature is worth describing in some detail. They were not alone in the adoption of such a practice, but were to persist with their widespread use for far longer than any other railway in this country. In 1922 there were thirty-six such operations daily on the Great Western out of a total of seventy-nine throughout the British Isles, but by the beginning of World War II they virtually had the field to themselves in this respect, and were the only company to re-introduce the practice after it had been withdrawn during the period of hostilities. Something like three decades have now passed since the Western Region of British Railways dropped their last slip portion, and for those readers who never experienced this somewhat unusual type of operation, here is the way in which they worked on the GWR, whose designs and techniques had been developed to a high pitch over the years.

Each slip coach had three windows on the end of the vehicle, and immediately inside the central one was the slip lever. This looked remarkably like one from a signal box, and was connected mechanically to the coupling hook and the vacuum brake system. When not in use it was padlocked in the forward position, known as 'Main Train', and this is how it was kept when the train travelled normally along the line. After the padlock had been removed, lifting the catch would enable the lever to be pulled backwards to the third position, which was 'Slip and Brake On'. This action withdrew a flat bar which normally prevented the special pivoted coupling hook from moving. Freed from this restraint, the point of the hook rotated forward, dropping the rear end of screw coupling on the coach ahead, and so releasing the slip coach from the main train.

As implied by its name, in the 'Slip and Brake On' position the lever also made a partial application of the vacuum brake on the slip coach, by admitting air into the train pipe through a special valve, which caused the slip portion to fall away immediately from the main train. The hose connections between the two sections of the train were also disconnected by being pulled apart. Normally, if a train becomes divided, the automatic vacuum brake would immediately apply the brakes on both sections, so special arrangements had to be made to ensure this did not occur when a coach was slipped. Instead of the two flexible brake hoses just being joined together in the normal way, a special Slip Hose Connection was fixed between them. Hidden inside the two halves of this were two small flap valves which kept each other open when the pipe was connected to ensure continuity, but, as soon as they were pulled apart, the sprung flaps turned to seal both the open ends, which prevented the inflow of air which would otherwise have applied the brakes on the main train.

On the slip coach, the movement of the slip lever from the 'Main Train' position had additionally sealed off the front vacuum brake connection from its train pipe, so, even if its half of the Slip Hose Connection failed to seat properly, no air could get into its braking

165

system in that way. However, with the lever fully back, a port in the valve was opened, providing an alternative entry for the air, and this was how the brake was applied after the coach had separated from the main train. Chains slung from the end of the vehicle were used to prevent the two halves of the heavy Slip Hose Connection from swinging down after the pipes had been separated. In the winter, when the steam heating system was in operation, special cocks on the ends of the two flexible pipes between the slip coach and the main train could be shut by the guard pulling a chain to prevent any loss of steam after these pipes had pulled apart.

Once his portion was on its own, the slip guard's constant duty was to keep looking ahead. As soon as he judged that he had opened up sufficiently large a gap from the end of the main train, he could move the control level back to the central notch of the three, which was known as the 'Release' position. This enabled the vacuum in the large reservoirs on the underframe of the vehicle to be used to release the brakes so that the slip portion ran freely. As soon as the coach had been slipped, the guard had to remember to let go the catch on the lever, which ensured that it could then only be used in the 'Slip and Brake On' and 'Release' positions, since moving it right forward would activate the train pipe again, and, if the Slip Hose Conection had not sealed properly, the slip would grind immediately to a halt. Moving the lever between the two rear positions enabled him to control the braking of the slip portion, finally bringing it to a stand at the right place. It was possible to apply and release the brake in this way a number of times, thanks to the reservoirs. They were exhausted by the driver's controls on the locomotive via the train pipe in the usual way, but a one-way valve was installed in the connecting line, which maintained the vacuum in the reservoirs even if the driver made a normal brake application.

Compared with the other grouping companies, the Great Western used a higher degree of vacuum in its braking systems, the customary figure corresponding to twenty-five inches of mercury. Their brake cylinders were also arranged so that several inches of vacuum had to be destroyed before the brakes actually came on, and the successive release operation on the slip portion all had to be accommodated within this range. It was thus important that the vacuum in the brake system was virtually at its full working level at the time the slip coach was released, and the guard had to check that he had at least twenty-three inches of vacuum when he first pulled the lever. In turn, this meant that, up at the front of the train, the driver had to operate his brake controls on the locomotive to achieve this. When a down train was slipping a portion at Bath, for example, it was necessary for the speed to be reduced well in advance for the restriction round the curve through the station, and the brake then 'blown off' in plenty of time so that the system had been fully exhausted again by the point at which the slip guard would be letting go.

Another place where slipping could be difficult was with up West of England expresses at Reading. After making the usual slow passage round the curve from Reading West, these trains had to take the turn-out into one of the platform roads, which slowed them still further. It was also possible for the main train's onward progress towards London to be checked by signals at the far end of the platform, and, in order to give the slip guard advance warning of this, special 'slip distant' signal arms were installed on brackets below the main signals concerned. If for any reason the driver had to apply the brake on the main train after the slip had been released, he had to alert the guard immediately by sounding the deeper-toned brake whistle with which all GWR locomotives were additionally fitted. If it was foggy or snowing the local stationmaster had to take the decision whether to stop the train rather than risk the dangers of carrying out the slip operation in conditions of poor visibility.

Slip portions were not always brought to a stand actually in a station platform. In real life, the sort of operating practice that took place in Buster Keyton's *The General* was strictly forbidden, and the points could not be moved between the passage of the main train and the slip portion until the latter had come to a stand. As an example of this, after the completion of the Westbury Cut-Off in 1932, the non-stop 'Cornish Riviera' took the new line from Heywood Road to save the time previously spent negotiating the curves through the station. The slip portion for Weymouth was thus released before this point, and brought to a stand clear of the junction, to permit a locomotive to come out and collect it. A similar sort of operation used to take place at certain stations where the main train would run through the centre road at speed and the slip needed to use the platform loop. In the summer of 1950, on the last occasion when the author slipped, we stopped at Princes Risborough as per the regulations at the facing-point home signal on the double-track section before the start of the platform loop. We stood there for just two and three quarter minutes before the 0-4-2T and its auto-trailer had come out from the platform road, coupled up and restarted back into the loop, where the passengers alighted on to the platform a minute and a half later. That particular slip portion continued in a slow train to Banbury, the tank locomotive propelling its auto trailer and hauling the two-coach slip portion.

As just indicated, it was quite possible for more ordinary coaches to be marshalled behind a slip coach and released with it. This is why reference was sometimes made to slip *portions* rather than slip coaches. The number of vehicles was limited by the special draw-hook with which slip coaches were fitted, and care also had to be taken not to over-tighten the screw coupling so it interfered with the release action. The maximum load that could be put on to the slip coupling at the time of operation was equivalent to six 4- or 6-wheeled vehicles, or four bogie ones, the 1936 General Appendix making it clear that in this sense seventy-feet bogie vehicles counted the same as the ordinary variety, rather than being equivalent to five axles as was reckoned when certain other calculations about train loads were being made.

The length of a slip portion also had an effect on the number of times the brake could be released by the guard after slipping had taken place. The greater the length of train pipe and the more brake cylinders that had to be re-exhausted each time the guard moved his lever to the 'Release' position, the fewer times this operation could be carried out before the capacity of the vacuum reservoirs on the slip coach was used up, and the brakes were irretrievably applied. With a single slip carriage, as many as six or seven releases were possible, but this came down to 'probably only three' when the maximum number of vehicles was being slipped.

Amongst the nine pages of instructions on slip-carriage operations in the GWR General Appendix for 1936, were the following that laid down how the free-running slip portion could provide the necessary warning of approach required by the railway inspectorate:

In order that Slip Guards may be able to give warning of the approach of Slip Carriages after they have been slipped, bells have been provided on the Slip Carriages worked by a foot lever placed in such a position that it can be readily operated while at the same time leaving the Slip Guard's hands quite free to manipulate the slipping lever.

Whenever, after slipping, Slip Guards find it necessary to give warning of the approach of slip vehicles, they must sound the bell vigorously several times. This should, in any case, always be done before passing Level Crossings or entering stations.

These bells were similar to those used on the auto trailers, but were mounted lower on the body-end. The word 'SLIP' was also painted in large white letters on the end of the vehicle, and both these features provided a quick means of recognising such a coach, most of which were double-ended to simplify their use in up and down trains without having to be turned.

In those days when ordinary block signalling was in use over virtually the whole of the Great Western's system, the observation of every train's tail-lamp was a vital operation as it passed each signalman in his box. For trains with slip coaches it was thus important for him to be able to determine that it had not accidentally been dropped off too early, and so was still standing in his section. To achieve this, special tail-lamps were provided for all trains carrying slip coaches, and a complicated set of additional signalling regulations laid down. We cannot go into them all in detail, but the visible indications given by the tail-lamps are of sufficient interest to be included. With those conveying a single slip, the main train carried two tail lamps, arranged one above the other on a special bracket. The fitting was put into place at the station where the slip coupling was set up (usually the previous calling station), and it had to be removed at the next booked stop and sent back to the 'station to which it belongs, as indicated on the brass label affixed to it, by the first available train'. The slip portion carried the usual single tail lamp, but a white head-lamp also had to be used if the slip operation took place after dark.

When there were two slip portions, the rear of the main train carried the usual slip tail-signal, but the inner slip portion had its own version, with the twin lamps this time mounted horizontally rather than vertically. A third variant was required for the 'Cornish Riviera' when it had the three slip portions, and the second one then carried a unique triangle of three red lamps. So, between Paddington and Westbury the signalmen would be looking for the normal single tail-lamp, and would not give 'Train out of Section' if more than one were seen on the rear of the train. From there to Taunton the train would be known to be complete if it was displaying the triangle of three lamps on the back, while over the next thirty miles to Exeter the signalmen were looking for a pair of lamps arranged horizontally. Finally, after the Exeter portion had been dropped off, the train would continue to Plymouth with the two vertical tail-lamps displayed after the slip had been detached.

As will be seen from this description, to achieve the necessary safety standards the system had to be a remarkably complicated one, and the manpower needed was considerable. We have already referred to the guard required on each slip, but the services of one of the Carriage Department staff were required to fit and adjust the vacuum hose adaptors (and those on the steam heating system if it was in use) at the station where the slipping arrangements were set up. Afterwards people from the Traffic Department had to remove the two halves at the stations where the separate portions next stopped, put them carefully into the special boxes provided, and send them back to the station where they belonged by the next available train. Not only was the system labour-intensive, but an extremely high level of discipline had to be achieved with all the different aspects of the workings. In the days between the world wars the system nevertheless worked well on the Great Western, and, as already mentioned, a limited number of slip services were reintroduced after 1945, continuing into British Railways days.

As we have seen, the number of trains running over the GWR on a summer Saturday was enormous, and it became increasingly difficult for signalmen at junctions to know which particular train was approaching. Down trains, for example, could easily arrive in Taunton out of course because of delays north or east of Cogload Junction, and they were likely to continue in the same order from there to Newton Abbot, as there were effectively only two running lines as far as the expresses were concerned. Just beyond Newton, the signalman at Aller Junction had to be certain that the trains for Paignton and Kingswear were correctly routed down the branch, with those for Kingsbridge, Plymouth and Cornwall being signalled so they could continue along the main line.

To provide a better means of identification, the GWR introduced a system of reporting numbers in 1934, and on summer Saturdays and other very busy days the locomotive of each express carried a three-digit number on its smokebox door. In the words of the *Great Western Railway Magazine* in 1934:

In order to facilitate train working during the summer holiday period, the Great Western Railway Company have introduced a system of numbering express passenger trains to and from the West of England on Saturdays.

The new system will make it possible to tell at a glance the starting time and place of an express train, its destination, and also whether it is the second, third, fourth or fifth part when divided. This immediate recognition will be of great value to signalmen and will also enable station staffs to deal more speedily with trains on their arrival.

The numbers were displayed on a frame that was fixed to the front of the smokebox door, and three plates carrying white-painted figures on a black background could be slotted in to give the required identification number. These were coded so that the first digit indicated the area where the train originated, as shown in Table 7.1.

Table 7.1. GWR Train Identification Numbers in 1934

Numbers	Originating area
100–199	Paddington
200–299	Shrewsbury & LMS
300–399	Wolverhampton & Birmingham
400–499	Bristol & LMS
500–599	Exeter & Torbay
600–699	Plymouth & Penzance
700–799	South Wales

All timetabled trains had numbers that ended in '0' or '5', and if they were being run in more than one portion, the number would step up by one for each subsequent train. Thus the third part of the down 'Cornish Riviera' would carry the number '128', since that of the first portion was '125'. The up train's basic number was '615', while the up and down identifications for the 'Torbay Express' were '515' and '150'.

A couple of years later the system was extended to cover other routes, and the significance of the first digits was changed, so that in 1939 they were allocated as given in Table 7.2, but there were minor variations from this standard system, which are not listed.

Table 7.2. GWR Train Identification Numbers in 1939

Numbers	Originating area
100–199	Paddington
200–299	Shrewsbury & LMS: also for some trains from the north to London
300–399	Weymouth (for London & north)
400–499	Bristol & LMS
500–599	Exeter & Torbay
600–699	Plymouth & Penzance
700–799	Birmingham & Wolverhampton (for the West & for the SR via Reading)
800–899	South Wales (for Paddington and for the West of England)
900–999	Southern Railway via Reading

The number allocation system was a complex one, and varied from week to week, so their use as a means of 100 per cent accurate identification of photographs of GWR summer expresses also requires information on the date of the picture, as well as access to the appropriate list for that particular day, if available.

Let us now turn our attention to a few of the aspects of the Great Western Railway's train performance, and the first point to be made concerns their safety record. Railways in this country have always paid a lot of attention to safety, and the Great Western particularly so. Throughout the period under study they pressed ahead with the installation of their Automatic Train Control (ATC) which gave audible indications in the cab in advance of each distant signal, and applied the brake if it was displaying a caution, unless the driver cancelled the warning. The last actuating ramp between London and Penzance was installed just before the World War II. Another peculiar Great Western practice was for the signalman to put a collar over the distant signal lever whenever there was a permanent-way slowing in the section ahead, so the driver was reminded of it by the signal remaining at caution.

These were the two most obvious examples of the company's safety procedures, but the drive to avoid accidents of all sorts was going on continuously and with great effect. A driving school was started, while other members of the road transport staff were encouraged to enter safe driving competitions. From the point of view of train accidents the results of this policy were remarkable. The bad collision at Shrivenham in January 1936, when the signalman failed to realise a goods train had divided in section, resulted in the death of only one passenger, although the 'King' involved had to be scrapped and replaced with another. This fatality, however, was only the second involving a passenger during a period of twenty years.

Looking at the performance of individual trains, the progress of the many outstanding schedules operated by the Great Western during the period under study are charted both from the point of view of their average speeds and the distances travelled non-stop. This information is based on the articles that were regularly contributed to *The Railway Magazine* by C. J. Allen under one of his pseudonyms 'Voyageur' or 'Mercury'. The form of presentation varied slightly from time to time, but the comparisons are as consistent as possible.

Since the Great Western's pioneering scheduling in the 1900s was more concerned with distance than speed, the listing in Table 7.3 shows the number of daily non-stop runs of more than 100 miles. In the details for 1922 there were two by slip-coach to Bath, but although the speed shown for these, because theirs was the fastest booking to that city, the trains themselves appear under the Paddington–Bristol entry. It will be seen that the number involved increased from twenty-six to thirty between 1922 and 1937, but the latter year includes several runs with newspaper and freight trains, which had not been introduced in 1922. The only Paddington–Plymouth schedule shown in 1937 was, in fact, that of the

Table 7.3. Daily non-stop runs of 100 miles or more on GWR, including fastest average speeds (Summer services)

Between	1922				1937			
	Miles	No of runs	Mins.	Speed (mph)	Miles	No of runs	Mins.	Speed (mph)
Paddington–Plymouth	225.7	1	247	54.8	225.2	‡1	240	56.3
Paddington–Torquay	199.7	2	215	55.7	–	–	–	–
Paddington–Newton Abbot	–	–	–	–	193.7	2	193	60.2
Paddington–Exeter	173.7	2	179	58.2	173.5	4	193	60.2
Greenford–Coton Hill (Shrewbury)	–	–	–	–	145.3	‡1	225	38.8
Paddington–Taunton	142.9	2	150	57.2	142.7	3	139	61.6
Newbury Racecourse–Newton Abbot	–	–	–	–	141.3	‡1	207	38.8
Exeter–Reading	137.7	1	145	57.0	–	–	–	–
Paddington–Newport	133.4	5	153	52.3	133.4	§7	137	58.4
Oxley Sidings–Old Oak West	–	–	–	–	121.3	‡1	205	35.5
Paddington–Worcester	120.5	1	130	55.6	–	–	–	–
Paddington–Bristol (via Bath)	118.3	2	120	59.2	118.3	2	105	67.6
Bristol–Paddington (via Badminton)	117.6	2	120	58.8	117.6	3	105	67.2
Paddington–Birmingham	110.6	2	120	55.3	–	–	–	–
Paddington–Bath	106.9	3	105†	61.1†	106.9	3	102	62.9
Reading–Taunton	106.9	1	115	55.8	–	–	–	–
Ealing (Broadway)–Birmingham	106.3	2	114	56.0	–	–	–	–
Park Royal–Bordesley Junction					104.2	‡2	172	36.3
TOTALS		26				30		

† The fastest times to Bath were by slip coaches off trains included in the Paddington–Bristol entry.
‡ *Non-passenger (parcels, newspaper, fish, meat, mail or other fast freight trains).*
§ Includes one or more non-passenger services.
Source: *The Railway Magazine, October 1922 and March 1938*

overnight newspaper train, as the 'Cornish Riviera' that summer was being booked to stop at Newton Abbot to attach a pilot for the South Devon banks, and so comes lower down the table. All these services ran on Mondays–Fridays at least, but in both years there were additional services that operated over 100 miles non-stop on Fridays or Saturdays only. Back in 1922 C. J. Allen's table included fourteen of these, including one that ran the somewhat-unusual 102.3 miles from Newton Abbot to Trowbridge. The number of Saturdays-only specials that would have qualified for inclusion in the late 1930s was very large indeed.

We have already referred to many of the Great Western's mile-a-minute schedules, but in Table 7.4 these are listed for a number of different years during the period of our study.

Table 7.4. Number of daily British runs at 60 mph or over

Year	Number of runs	
	On GWR	On other railways
1922	2	2
1932	13	11
1934	14	14
1936	21	44
1938	26	83
1939	24	92

In all cases the GWR total includes at least one slip-coach working.

It will be seen that the number of GWR runs increased from two to twenty-six over the first sixteen years, before falling back by two in 1939. This was less than the increase in the rest of the country, but, proportionately to the route mileage of the different systems, the 1939 figure is still higher than that for the other railways, since their lines extended, *in toto*, for almost exactly four times the length of the Great Western's. To complete this particular picture, Table 7.5 on page 172 lists all the Great Western 60+mph schedules in 1938, which is the nearest to the end of the period of our study for which such information is available in C. J. Allen's summaries.

In that year the GWR and LNER were the only two railways to have schedules in the 67+ and 70+mph brackets, the latter holding the record for the fastest individual train (the 'Coronation's' 71.9-mph dash from King's Cross to York), and having more such schedules, covering greater distances. The best the LMS could achieve was 65.1 mph from Rugby to Watford, but their total of sixty-three runs at 60 mph or over, and their aggregate mileage in this bracket, was more than those of the other railways put together. It should, perhaps, be remarked in passing that a very high proportion of the LMS motive power involved in their mile-a-minute runs was based on Churchward's ideas, albeit with Stanier/Crewe implants.

Before moving on to the punctuality achievements of the Great Western between the two world wars, an idea of the numbers of trains that were operated by that railway is given. The annual totals are given in the booklets of *General Statistics* produced by them at intervals for internal use. From these Table 7.6 on page 173 has been prepared which shows how the numbers of different classes of train varied from year to year. Up to 1927 all their own expresses were grouped together, but after that were divided into the three main geographical routes, with the Boat Trains being included separately. 'Cross Country' trains were those that ran to or from a 'Foreign' Line, while the 'General Through' classification applied to trains that ran through two or more different divisions. The other classes are self-explanatory. The compilation of statistics for 1939 was upset by the start of World War II, but then restarted, and for interest are included the figures for 1940, although it lies outside our main period of study.

Table 7.5. Daily GWR trains scheduled at 60 mph or over in summer of 1938

From	To	Departure time	Distance (miles)	Time (mins)	Speed (mph)
Swindon	Paddington	3.55 p.m.	77.3	65	71.4
Paddington	Bristol (via Bath)	10.00 a.m.	118.3	105	67.6
Bristol	Padington (via Badminton)	4.30 p.m.	117.6	105	67.2
Oxford	Paddington	10.10 a.m.	63.5	60	63.5
		5.35 p.m.	63.5	60	63.5
Swindon	Reading	5.40 p.m.	41.3	39	63.5
Chippenham	Paddington	8.28 a.m.	94.0	89	63.4
Kemble	Paddington	9.03½a.m.	91.0	86½	63.1
Paddington	Bath	1.15 a.m.	106.9	102	62.9
		1.15 p.m.	106.9	102	62.9
		5.05 p.m.	106.9	103	62.3
Westbury	Paddington	10.18 a.m.	95.6	92	62.3
High Wycombe	Leamington Spa†	9.44 a.m.	60.8	59	61.8
Paddington	Exeter	12.00 noon	173.5	169	61.6
		11.10 a.m.	173.5	170	61.2
Swindon	Paddington	1.14 p.m.	77.3	76	61.0
Paddington	Kemble	5.00 p.m.	91.0	90	60.7
Westbury	Reading	5.09 p.m.	59.6	59	60.6
Moreton-in-Marsh	Oxford	9.35 a.m.	28.3	28	60.6
Oxford	Paddington	3.17 p.m.	63.5	63	60.5
Paddington	Westbury	3.30 p.m.	95.6	95	60.4
Paddington	Taunton	11.35 a.m.	142.7	142	60.3
Paddington	Newton Abbot	10.30 a.m.	193.7	193	60.2
Swindon	Paddington	4.18 p.m.	77.3	77	60.2
Didcot	Paddington	9.24 a.m.	53.1	53	60.1
Westbury	Taunton	5.09 p.m.	47.1	47	60.1

†By slip coach

Looking at the table generally, there are two separate periods of growth, with a dip coming in 1932/1933 as a result of the Great Depression. 1939 represented the high-water of all types of train service on the GWR, except for 'Perishable' and 'Excursions'. The former peaked in 1936, and their subsequent decline ws almost certainly due to road competition. The excursion story is not quite so straight-forward, and the best year for these was back in 1929. There were, however, changes in the basis of train classifications over the years, and many of the services which rated 'Excursion' status were transferred to other categories, including expresses, since some of the latter which ran on Fridays and Saturdays at peak periods used to be referred to as 'Weekend Excursions'.

To gain an idea of the summer holiday business, a similar set of figures for certain classes of trains as recorded in the GWR's four-weekly reporting periods in 1938/39 is used. The latest set was always printed on the second page of the *Great Western Railway Magazine* every month, but as there were only twelve issues of that a year, and thirteen reporting periods, one of the latter always got lost. Therefore, some of the missing figures from the *General Statistics* book, which unfortunately do not split the Class 'D', 'E' and 'F' workings, which explains the small number of blank entries at the end of Table 7.7 are used. Boat Trains were excluded from these four-weekly presentations.

As far as the expresses are concerned, given the absence of a holiday period, it is remarkable how constant was the number operated in a four-week period – 1164 to and from the West of England, 504 on the South Wales line and 860 to and from the North. The normal four-week total of 2,528 did however rocket upwards in the summer, reaching 2,824 during the period that included the 1939 August Bank Holiday. This was an increase of 12%, but the services to the West of England jumped by 20%, and there were no less than 25% more Cross-Country trains a week to or from other railways. The numbers of none of the other categories of trains

Table 7.6. Annual numbers of passenger trains operated on GWR
1923–1940

Type of train	1923	1924	1925	1927	1928	1929	1930	1931	1932	1933	1934	1935	1936	1937	1938	1940
Class 'A' Through Expresses to and from London																
West of England	Not avail.			13,757	13,677	13,833	14,042	12,996	12,553	12,848	13,499	14,578	15,857	15,702	15,722	10,496
South Wales				5,673	5,922	5,848	6,293	6,506	4,977	6,822	7,044	7,330	7,100	6,754	6,962	4,786
Northern				10,091	10,281	10,504	10,578	10,222	10,155	10,175	10,151	10,427	10,770	10,762	10,913	8,610
Boat Trains				1,084	1,136	1,133	1,032	1,133	1,133	1,134	1,134	1,133	1,132	1,133	1,140	363
TOTAL	31,971	30,240	30,573	30,605	31,016	31,318	31,945	30,857	28,818	30,979	31,828	33,467	34,859	34,351	34,737	24,255
CLASS 'B' Cross Country	11,535	12,060	12,270	12,301	12,161	13,698	13,802	13,672	13,973	14,133	14,303	14,658	15,123	14,792	14,700	8,578
CLASS 'C' General/Through	94,728	104,418	101,750	104,821	106,910	105,410	106,095	105,547	103,172	104,833	107,232	109,660	111,121	114,657	114,852	83,838
CLASSES 'D' 'E' AND 'F' Local, Branch and Workmen	1,431,126	1,409,251	1,448,359	1,445,192	1,467,391	1,480,029	1,477,801	1,426,356	1,428,686	1,443,065	1,457,153	1,477,789	1,504,170	1,501,427	1,511,873	1,175,699
CLASS 'G' Perishable	27,152	28,545	31,537	34,586	37,021	36,501	37,513	35,717	34,960	33,048	34,188	36,553	38,233	37,333	35,504	30,004
CLASSES 'H' AND 'J' Excursion and Other Revenue Earning	15,787	17,908	19,848	18,935	21,010	21,929	20,768	18,091	18,524	17,805	16,845	18,078	18,319	17,603	16,226	13,957
TOTAL	1,617,669	1,607,181	1,649,146	1,650,844	1,677,598	1,692,423	1,691,075	1,623,704	1,633,427	1,647,475	1,665,277	1,693,507	1,725,488	1,723,769	1,731,394	1,342,435

All Revenue Earning Trains (including Duplicates and Reliefs)
Source: Great Western Railway, General Statistics, issue No. 23, October 1941

173

remained quite so constant, but the 'General Through' ones increased by nearly 6% between March and August 1939. As one goes down the table the increase is less, and a comparison between September 1938 and March 1939 shows the summer services resulted in the running of an extra 3% trains a month during the holiday season.

Table 7.7. Numbers of GWR trains operated in 4-weekly periods September 1938–August 1939
Four Weeks ending on:

| Type of train | 1938 | | | | 1939 | | | | | | | | |
	17 Sept	15 Oct	12 Nov	10 Dec	7 Jan	4 Feb	4 Mar	1 April	29 April	27 May	24 June	22 July	19 Aug
Class 'A' Through Expresses to and from London West of England	1,379	1,210	1,164	1,164	1,149	1,164	1,164	1,164	1,112	1,172	1,201	1,357	1,399
South Wales	564	517	504	504	506	504	504	504	478	505	498	547	562
Northern	866	860	860	860	836	860	860	860	813	860	850	865	863
TOTAL	2,809	2,587	2,528	2,528	2,491	2,528	2,528	2,528	2,403	2,537	2,549	2,769	2,824
CLASS 'B' Cross Country	1,303	1,092	1,052	11,052	1,039	1,052	1,052	1,052	1,001	1,052	1,073	1,239	1,318
CLASS 'C' General Through	9,168	8,783	8,704	8,694	8,582	8,739	8,740	8,756	8,307	8,783	8,770	9,124	9,235
CLASS 'D' Local	44,404	43,484	43,134	42,790	41,803	43,078	43,155	42,243	40,596	43,258	42,809	–	–
CLASS 'E' Branch	70,885	69,014	68,561	67,274	67,439	68,624	68,748	68,741	65,777	68,937	69,129	–	–
TOTAL	128,569	124,960	123,979	122,338	121,354	124,021	124,233	124,320	118,084	124,567	124,330	–	–

Source: *Great Western Railway Magazine*
Great Western Railway, General Statistics, Issue No. 23, October 1940

It is one thing to plan trains in a timetable and another to operate them out on the tracks. From one point of view the constant four-weekly totals in Table 7.7 would indicate there were few, if any, cancellations, but another of the traditional yardsticks of a railway's efficiency is its punctuality performance. Tables 7.8 and 7.9 (opposite and on p 176) show these figures on annual and four-weekly bases, corresponding to the train total figures in Tables 7.6 and 7.7 already described. These are all presented in the form of 'Average Minutes Late', and cannot thus be readily related to the present-day BR figures, which are now in the form of percentages arriving 'On Time or early', and 'Not more than x Minutes Late', x varying between sectors. In the case of InterCity, they revised the value of this from five to ten minutes late a few years ago, and their target is currently to get 90% of trains to their destination within this time. If a group of GWR trains averaged five and a half minutes late, that does not necessarily imply that, using the current method of presentation, 100% would have reached their destinations more than five minutes late.

However it still comes somewhat as a surprise to discover that from 1922 to 1938 the Great Western's *average* lateness for its expresses was never less than 4.7 minutes overall. This was achieved in 1935, which seems to have been a good year all round, although the previous twelve months were the best for the Boat Trains, which, as always, were at the mercy of storms in the English or St. George's Channels. Cross-Country trains were not such good timekeepers as the GWR's own captive expresses, which is another perennial problem even today. Lower down the table the 'inferior' categories of passenger trains were, in the main, much better timekeepers, and it was their vast numbers that were responsible for the overall figure of just two minutes average lateness in 1935. The inclusion of the 1940 figures shows how far the standards of timekeeping deteriorated at the beginning of the war, which, it must be noted, was over and above the major decelerations which were included in the timetables.

Table 7.8. Punctuality of GWR passenger trains, 1923–1940
(Average lateness in minutes)

Type of train								Year								
	1923	1924	1925	1927	1928	1929	1930	1931	1932	1933	1934	1935	1936	1937	1938	1940
CLASS 'A' Through Expresses to and from London																
West of England	–	–	–	7.3	6.1	7.2	5.1	8.2	6.7	7.0	5.8	4.7	6.7	5.0	5.2	41.5
South Wales	–	–	–	6.9	5.2	7.1	4.8	5.3	4.9	7.5	5.3	5.2	7.3	6.7	4.7	38.8
Northern	–	–	–	7.3	6.5	6.9	4.8	5.6	5.8	7.2	5.4	4.4	6.8	5.2	4.3	35.0
OVERALL	5.4*	7.4*	7.0*	7.2	6.0	7.1	4.9	6.7	6.7	7.2	5.6	4.7	6.9	5.4	4.8	38.6
Boat Trains	–	–	–	21.3	19.2	14.4	10.4	12.6	9.9	12.7	9.2	11.4	15.7	16.0	11.1	51.5
CLASS 'B'	7.9	9.4	8.9	8.7	8.0	8.60	7.1	9.6	8.3	9.3	8.9	7.1	9.1	8.5	7.0	40.3
CLASS 'C' Cross Country	5.8	9.4	5.6	4.8	4.2	4.5	3.4	4.0	3.6	4.2	3.7	3.2	4.5	3.9	3.1	16.0
CLASSES 'D' 'E' AND 'F' General Through	2.8	2.9	2.6	2.4	2.9	2.1	1.6	1.8	1.6	1.9	1.8	1.5	2.0	1.9	1.5	6.8
CLASS 'G' Local, Branch and Workmen	10.7	13.3	15.5	17.3	14.0	15.5	11.3	11.3	7.8	8.0	8.3	8.2	11.15	10.5	8.3	51.1
CLASSES 'H' AND 'J' Perishable Excursion and Other Revenue Earning	10.4	10.5	9.9	9.3	9.0	9.2	7.7	8.9	8.3	8.9	7.8	7.4	8.1	8.5	7.0	18.2
OVERALL	3.3	3.6	3.3	3.1	2.6	2.8	2.1	2.4	2.1	2.4	2.2	2.0	2.6	2.4	2.0	9.4

All Revenue Earning Trains (including Duplicates and Reliefs)
*These figures include the Boat Trains
Source: *Great Western Railway General Statistics, Issue No. 23, October 1941*

Turning now to the four-weekly punctuality figures, we find that there were considerable variations during the course of the year. One would expect the punctuality to fall off during the summer peaks, in spite of the Saturdays-only trains frequently being more easily timed compared with their ordinary week-day counterparts. All 1,399 of those to and from the West of England averaged ten minutes late over the peak summer period that included the August Bank Holiday. However, that lot of four weeks was nothing like as bad as the one that included Christmas, when the entire system averaged six minutes late and the expresses no less than 23.8. The reasons for this were complex.

Fog, for which December was particularly noted in the days of the 'Pea Souper' prior to the Clean Air Acts, could be a big obstacle to good punctuality. The Great Western's widespread use of Automatic Train Control did give them an advantage, as it enabled their trains to run at virtually full speed in such conditions, but only as long as the tracks ahead were clear. First of all, therefore, we must look at the weather, but there were no fogs worth speaking about in the period concerned, although the weather got quite cold just before Christmas. On 21st there was widespread snow over the whole country, so much so that *The Times* had a page of pictures the following day, although the falls appeared to be more picturesque than disruptive. The snow lingered after Christmas, and the classic shot of Ivatt Atlantic No.4446 on the up 'Silver Jubilee', taken on the 28th, shows a thin covering. There was a much worse period of snow in late January 1939, as the *Great Western Railway Magazine* subsequently published a photograph of a pannier tank at Dowlais on 26th January, with only the extreme top of its chimney, dome and cab just visible above the snow-drift.

Another perennial source of delay at this time of the year was the Christmas post. The author has clear recollections of returning home from school in Paignton one year at about this time, and kicking his heels for an inordinate time on St. David's station in Exeter, awaiting his Southern Railway connection for North Devon. Not only was it extremely cold, but his portion of the train from Waterloo was delayed even further by postal activities going on with the Plymouth section ahead of it. The driver of the 'T9' on that did, however, invite

Table 7.9. Punctuality of GWR trains in 4-weekly periods September 1938–August 1939
(Average lateness in minutes)
Four Weeks ending on:

| Type of train | 1938 | | | | 1939 | | | | | | | | |
	17 Sept	15 Oct	12 Nov	10 Dec	7 Jan	4 Feb	1 Mar	29 April	27 April	24 May	22 June	19 July	Aug
Class 'A'	4.9	5.4	3.4	5.7	22.2	8.4	2.9	2.5	4.9	3.0	4.6	4.4	10.0
Through Expresses to and from London West of England													
South Wales	3.4	4.1	3.0	5.1	25.4	104	3.1	2.6	6.1	3.6	4.7	4.7	8.7
Northern	3.7	4.2	4.6	7.5	24.8	11.1	5.7	5.5	7.3	5.0	6.1	6.2	9.6
OVERALL	4.2	4.7	3.7	6.2	23.8	9.7	3.9	3.5	6.0	3.8	5.2	5.0	9.6
CLASS 'B'	7.2	5.0	4.7	5.0	23.2	7.9	4.6	4.0	7.5	4.3	6.6	7.6	18.8
Cross Country													
CLASS 'C'	2.7	2.8	2.4	3.3	1.0.2	4.2	2.5	2.4	3.4	2.4	3.2	3.2	6.6
General Through													
CLASS 'D'	2.0	2.1	1.9	2.5	7.3	3.3	1.9	1.8	2.3	1.8	2.2	–	–
Local													
CLASS 'E'	1.1	1.1	1.1	1.3	3.8	1.6	1.0	0.9	1.3	1.0	1.3	–	–
Branch													
OVERALL	1.6	1.6	1.5	2.0	6.0	2.6	1.4	1.4	1.9	1.4	1.9	–	–

Source: *Great Western Railway Magazine*
Great Western Railway General Statistics, Issue No. 23, October 1940

him to get warm in front of the firehole-door during his train's protracted station stop. On 23rd December 1938 *The Times* reported that Euston and St. Pancras had dealt with no less than 112 parcels trains. That day also marked the start of the peak of the Christmas passenger travel, and Paddington expected to dispatch a combined total of some 30,000 people to South Wales on the 23rd and 24th. On the first of these two days the Southern reported that its delays did not average more than fifteen minutes, but the lines serving Scotland and the North of England did not do as well. Arrivals at King's Cross were about twenty minutes late while, on the LMS, the delays into Euston were given as being twenty to thirty minutes.

On the other hand, the *departure* of the Great Western's trains out of London on 23rd December averaged about forty-five minutes late, but there was a particular reason for this. Mention had been made earlier of the electrical fires in the signal boxes at the approach to Paddington, and the second of these actually occurred on 23rd December. As these undoubtedly added to the GWR's operating difficulties at this particular time, it is worth going into the events in some detail. The first fire occurred in the Arrival Side box at Paddington on 25th November, putting it completely out of action. Within twenty-four hours teams of district relief signalmen had been assembled from all over the system, and were at work in the 'throat' area in shifts of twenty moving points individually by working the motor switches themselves and giving the necessary hand-signals to the trains, their operations being controlled by loud-speaker from the temporary block post. This phase of the operation lasted from 25th November to 18th December, and there was not a single mishap or error during the whole period. It should be noted that these arrangements were in operation for more than half of the four-week period ending on 10th December, when the arrivals of all the GWR's expresses averaged only 6.2 minutes late.

On 11th and 18th December temporary signal frames were brought into use on the Hammersmith & City and main arrival lines, and the railway thought all would be well for the Christmas rush. However, on 23rd December it was the turn of Westbourne Bridge box to catch fire, although the damage caused on this occasion was fortunately less severe. Some of the hand-signalmen had been retained in the area just in case there were any problems with the operation of the temporary frames on the Arrival Side, and they were immediately mobilised to deal with the new emergency. A block post was established very quickly indeed, but, on the actual day of the fire, all the incoming locomotives had to be sent all the way out to Old Oak Common to be turned and serviced, which no doubt caused some of the delay referred to in *The Times*. Once the temporary block instruments had been installed in the ganger's hut, it was possible to use Ranelagh Bridge depot to turn round twenty-six of the sixty locomotives normally handled there every day. All was finally restored to normal when the replacement Arrival Side box was brought into service at the beginning of July, and, at the same time, the operation of the through trains to and from Liverpool Street recommenced after a gap of seven and a half months.

Great credit was due to all those who planned and operated the emergency arrangements, and, while these events undoubtedly did not help the punctuality performance, the aftermath of the fires was clearly not the only reason behind the poor figures for the four-week period ending on 7th January 1939. It will be noted that the cross-country trains were also equally as late over the Christmas period, and these were unlikely to have been held up to make connections with the late-running trains to and from Paddington. The figures for the corresponding period the year before showed that the expresses in and out of Paddington averaged 11.3 minutes late, while the delays with the cross-country ones were worse at 17.2 minutes. In the light of all the surviving information, the author's inclination is to blame a very high proportion of the delays in December 1938 on the parcels and other peak Christmas traffic, with the signalbox fires adding to the problems, rather than being the main cause.

From this examination of the Great Western Railway's punctuality performance from the past, it is clearly evident that steam trains frequently ran late, and their overall timekeeping was not all that wonderful. Then, as now, the operation of a tight-knit, real-time operation does not give much scope for recovery when there has been some sort of hiccup out on the line.

To end our study of the performance of the Great Western Railway's trains in the years between the two world wars, let us look at one particular holiday working as recorded at first hand by the author's old friend and fellow writer, the late Derek Barrie, who finished his railway career as General Manager of the Eastern Region. As a young railwayman on the LMS, his interest in train performance resulted in his becoming one of their official recorders on high-speed test runs, and, from our point of view, the benefits of first-hand information from such a source are considerable. Those who log train performance are not only used to recording large amounts of information quickly in the course of each journey, but they write it down at the time, which provides a permanent record that is available afterwards, long after details may have faded from the unprompted memory.

As a railwayman, Derek had an entitlement to certain free travel facilities on other company's lines, but, as at present, there were restrictions on their use at busy times, which, in the 1930s, meant summer Saturdays. However, travel was permitted on the overnight trains out of Paddington, and he consequently took advantage of this in 1933 and 1934 to travel to Cornwall on the 1.40 am newspaper and passenger working from Paddington, already described in Chapter 6. The 'King' had to work loads of 275–333 tons as far as Plymouth, with a 'Castle' taking over at that point, but even with the limited passenger accommodation provided, he had a compartment to himself, and could time the train through the night. In the first of these years, with No.6001 *King Edward VII* in charge, they were up to even time by Twyford. Although the Westbury and Frome cut-offs had been opened for freight services the previous March, they took the original route through the stations, encountering four additional slowings because of the engineering work at the sites of the junctions the ends of the cut-offs. In spite of this they trimmed the 148–minute schedule for the 142.9 miles to Taunton to $145^{1}/_{2}$ minutes, giving an average of 59 mph start-to-stop. In the following year his locomotive was the next of the 'Kings' to be built, No.6002 *King William IV*, and the train was delayed as far as Southall. They were now able to use the Westbury and Frome cut-offs, but only at reduced speed, and there was a further permanent-way slowing after Brewham. In spite of a final scamper at 80 mph near Langport they reached Taunton two and a half minutes down on the faster 139-minute schedule, but had still covered the slightly shorter distance in $141^{1}/_{2}$ minutes, which meant they had done it in under even time.

His next journey on this train followed his marriage during the intervening period, so it was with his wife Myrra, who had formerly worked in the LMS Chief Mechanical Engineers Department at Derby, that Derek Barrie decided to make the same journey in the summer of 1937 at the start of two weeks' holiday in Newquay. Unfortunately, as soon as they reached Paddington they realised that the popularity of a nocturnal trip to the West had caught on amongst the travelling public (or maybe it was just railwaymen) during the interim, and, even at this hour the Lawn was crowded with people. As a result they did not get the expected compartment to themselves, and, with the lights dimmed in deference to the other occupants, he was unable to do any consistent timing.

The interest on this occasion, however, shifts to the return journey a fortnight later, when they caught the 12.32 pm Saturdays-only train from Newquay through to Paddington. They had taken the precaution of booking seats on this on the morning of their arrival in Newquay fourteen days earlier, and, as soon as the barrier was opened, they had been able to get two reservations for the first sitting for lunch from the conductor, who was out on the platform as the passengers joined the train. It was a combined kitchen and dining car, and its seating capacity was consequently rather limited, but they both thoroughly enjoyed their meal. At

An example of the reporting numbers that were fixed to the locomotives' smokeboxes on summer Saturdays and other occasions. This is an up working for Swindon, seen behind 4-6-0 No. 4089 *Donnington Castle* near Bathampton.

The two steamlined locomotives presented problems when it came to displaying the reporting numbers. In August 1938 4-6-0 No. 6014 *King Henry VII* works the up 'Limited', consisting of 13 coaches. The ordinary set of Centenary Stock has been strengthened with an extra three vehicles.

this distance in time, they could not remember the exact menu, but typically a GWR lunch would comprise Brown Windsor soup, followed by roast beef or lamb, with potatoes and somewhat hard peas. A favourite sweet was Castle pudding, and the cost of this for the pair of them, inclusive of a drink, coffee and the tip, still produced some change from a £1 note.

The train consisted of eleven coaches, weighing 347 tons with all the compartments filled four-aside with passengers, which necessitated the services of a couple of 2-6-2 tanks as far as Par, although on other trains 4-6-0s worked through. Allowing for the 1 in 66 climb, and the slowings for the crossing loops, they took no less than forty-eight minutes to reach St. Blazey, 20.3 miles from the start, so their average was only 25.3 mph, but even then had to wait time before being allowed round the curve on to the main line at Par. Not long after the 'Castle' had taken over for the main-line stretch to Plymouth, my friends returned to their compartment. Throughout the long afternoon they read, watched the scenery or dozed as the train made its way towards London, slotted into its allotted place in the procession of returning holiday expresses. Filtering into the open windows came the exhaust beat from the 'King' at the front of the train, its intensity varying as the driver opened up when he spotted a clear distant or eased back again if one of them was somewhat slow in clearing, implying that they were closing up on the next train ahead.

Somewhere about Charlton Mackerell or Keinton Mandeville, or perhaps it was nearer London still, came a tired voice along the corridor, as the dining-car steward, napkin over shoulder, made his way the length of the train intoning the message, 'Take yer seats please, tickets only for the sixth (or was it the seventh?), and (*crescendo*) POSITIVELY THE LAST SITTING FOR LUNCH. Hurry along to the dining car please'. Surely there cannot be a better way of concluding this book than with this story, which sums up, at the personal level, just what travel was like during the Heyday of the Great Western Railway's train services.

INDEX

Page numbers in *italics* denote illustrations

Locations on the GWR's main lines appear too frequently in the text to be included in this index. For ease of reference, however, some relatively major routes have been listed under the **Branch Line** heading.